Saint Thomas More

VINTAGE SPIRITUAL CLASSICS

General Editors
John F. Thornton
Susan B. Varenne

ALSO AVAILABLE

Saint Thomas More

SELECTED WRITINGS

TOGETHER WITH

The Life *of* Sir Thomas More

BY WILLIAM ROPER

EDITED BY

John F. Thornton and *Susan B. Varenne*

PREFACE BY

Joseph W. Koterski, S.J.

VINTAGE SPIRITUAL CLASSICS

VINTAGE BOOKS
A DIVISION OF RANDOM HOUSE, INC.
NEW YORK

A VINTAGE SPIRITUAL CLASSICS ORIGINAL, APRIL 2003
FIRST EDITION

Editing and arrangement of the texts,
About the Vintage Spiritual Classics, Preface to the Vintage Spiritual
Classics Edition, Chronology of the Life of Saint Thomas More,
and Suggestions for Further Reading
Copyright © 2003 by Random House, Inc.

Grateful acknowledgment is made to Yale University Press for permission to reprint an
excerpt from *Selected Letters* by Saint Sir Thomas More, edited by Elizabeth Frances
Rogers, copyright © 1961, copyright renewed 1989 by Yale University and excerpts from
The Tower Works: Devotional Writings by Saint Thomas More, edited by Garry E. Haupt,
copyright © 1980 by Yale University. Reprinted by permission of Yale University Press.

Library of Congress Cataloging-in-Publication Data
More, Thomas, Sir, Saint, 1478–1535.
 [Selections. 2003]
 Selected writings / Saint Thomas More. Together with, The life of Sir Thomas More /
by William Roper ; edited by John F. Thornton and Susan B. Varenne ; preface by
Joseph Koterski.—1st ed.
 p. cm.—(Vintage spiritual classics)
 Includes bibliographical references.
 ISBN 978-0-375-72572-2
 1. More, Thomas, Sir, Saint, 1478–1535. 2. Great Britain—History—Henry VIII,
1509–1547—Biography. 3. Christian martyrs—England—Biography. 4. Christian
saints—England—Biography. 5. Statesmen—Great Britain—Biography. I. Thornton,
John F., 1942– II. Varenne, Susan B. III. Roper, William, 1496–1578. Life of Sir
Thomas More. IV. Title: Life of Sir Thomas More. V. Title. VI. Series.
DA334.M8 A25 2003
942.05'2'092—dc21   2002028062

Book design by Fritz Metsch

www.vintagebooks.com

CONTENTS

A turn or shift of sorts is becoming evident in the reflections of men and women today on their life experiences. Not quite as adamantly secular and, perhaps, a little less insistent on material satisfactions, the reading public has recently developed a certain attraction to testimonies that human life is leavened by a Presence that blesses and sanctifies. Recovery, whether from addictions or personal traumas, illness, or even painful misalignments in human affairs, is evolving from the standard therapeutic goal of enhanced self-esteem. Many now seek a deeper healing that embraces the whole person, including the soul. Contemporary books provide accounts of the invisible assistance of angels. The laying on of hands in prayer has made an appearance at the hospital bedside. Guides for the spiritually perplexed have risen to the tops of bestseller lists. The darkest shadows of skepticism and unbelief, which have eclipsed the presence of the Divine in our materialistic age, are beginning to lighten and part.

If the power and presence of God are real and effective, what do they mean for human experience? What does He offer to men and women, and what does He ask in return? How do we recognize Him? Know Him? Respond to Him? God has a reputation for being both benevolent and wrathful. Which will He be for me and when? Can these aspects of the Divine somehow be reconciled? Where is God when I suffer? Can I lose Him? Is God truthful, and are His promises to be trusted?

Are we really as precious to God as we are to ourselves and our loved ones? Do His providence and amazing grace guide our faltering steps toward Him, even in spite of ourselves? Will God abandon us if the sin is serious enough, or if we have episodes of resistance and forgetfulness? These are fundamental questions any person might address to God during a lifetime. They are pressing and difficult, often becoming wounds in the soul of the person who yearns for the power and courage of hope, especially in stressful times.

The Vintage Spiritual Classics present the testimony of writers across the centuries who have considered all these difficulties and who have pondered the mysterious ways, unfathomable mercies, and deep consolations afforded by God to those who call upon Him from out of the depths of their lives. These writers, then, are our companions, even our champions, in a common effort to discern the meaning of God in personal experience. For God is personal to us. To whom does He speak if not to us, provided we have the desire to hear Him deep within our hearts?

Each volume opens with a specially commissioned essay by a well-known contemporary writer that offers the reader an appreciation of its intrinsic value. A chronology of the general historical context of each author and his work is provided, as are suggestions for further reading.

We offer a final word about the act of reading these spiritual classics. From the very earliest accounts of monastic practice—dating back to the fourth century—it is evident that a form of reading called *lectio divina* ("divine" or "spiritual reading") was essential to any deliberate spiritual life. This kind of reading is quite different from that of scanning a text for useful facts and bits of information, or advancing along an exciting plot line to a climax in the action. It is, rather, a meditative approach by which the reader seeks to savor and taste the beauty and truth of every phrase and passage. This process of contemplative reading has the effect of enkindling in the reader compunction for past behavior that has been less than beautiful and true. At the same time, it increases the desire to seek a realm where all that is lovely and unspoiled may be found. There are four steps in *lectio divina:* first to read, next to meditate, then to rest in the sense of God's nearness, and, ultimately, to resolve to govern one's actions in the light of new understanding. This kind of reading is itself an act of prayer. And, indeed, it is in prayer that God manifests His Presence to us.

PREFACE TO THE
VINTAGE SPIRITUAL CLASSICS
EDITION

by Joseph W. Koterski, S.J.

To many people, the life of Saint Thomas More is known largely from *A Man for All Seasons,* a memorable play by Robert Bolt that vividly captures the dramatic conflict between More and King Henry VIII. It deftly portrays More's silence as a decision to keep his own conscience while facing almost unimaginable pressures to assent to the intended royal marriage to Anne Boleyn, or else to impale himself in the very effort to explain his position.

A reservation one might have, however, comes from the play's suggestion that More was a martyr for conscience in the modern sense of that word. Ever suspicious about authorities ready to force their claims upon the individual, Bolt chose the theme of individual conscience for this play in order to stress the importance of personal integrity.[1] At one crucial juncture he has More say, "But what matters to me is not whether it's true or not but that I believe it to be true, or rather, not that I *believe* it, but that *I* believe it. I trust I make myself obscure?"[2] This is to take conscience as a matter of fidelity to one's chosen moral principles— and so high-minded a view seems irreproachable. But sadly, this

1. See Adrian Turner, *Robert Bolt: Scenes from Two Lives* (London: Hutchinson, 1998), esp. pp. 161–70.
2. Robert Bolt, *A Man for All Seasons: A Play in Two Acts* (New York: Vintage Books, 1990; first published in 1960), p. 91. Turner (p. 162) documents Bolt's deliberate allusion here to Bertold Brecht's *Galileo*.

is actually to twist beyond recognition the position for which More died. Now, to stress "fidelity to ... moral principles" is clearly essential to a sound notion of conscience. The problem arises with holding that conscience is a matter of one's "chosen" principles. The modern understanding of conscience presumes that one must select one's principles. Being conscientious, then, means remaining consistent with whatever principles one has chosen, as if there were something self-sufficient about an individual's choice of principles and as if any subsequent judgments faithful to those principles must be respected independently of any objective morality. In certain ways this modern position on conscience may be historically rooted in the emphasis given to the supremacy of individual judgment by some Protestant denominations. But under no circumstances should it be mistaken for More's notion of conscience.

In his speech at the conclusion of his trial on July 1, 1535,[3] there is a stubborn fact that resists any such interpretation. More had been imprisoned precisely because he could not, in good conscience, swear allegiance to the oath King Henry demanded, and yet until this moment he refused to explain his stance one way or the other. He simply kept silent, and Henry seems all the more to have craved his approval. But in his final speech, once the verdict had been rendered and the death sentence imposed, there no longer remained any reason to reserve his opinion. Only then did he make clear what it was that required him in conscience to refuse the oath: the superiority of the authority of the Church to that of the king:

> Seeing that I see ye are determined to condemn me (God knoweth how) I will now in discharge of my conscience speak my mind plainly and freely touching my Indictment and your Statute, withal.

3. Reflected in Act II of Bolt's play.

And forasmuch as this Indictment is grounded upon an Act of Parliament directly repugnant to the laws of God and his Holy Church, the supreme Government of which, or of any part whereof, may no temporal Prince presume by any law to take upon him, as rightfully belonging to the See of Rome, a spiritual pre-eminence by the mouth of our Saviour himself, personally present upon earth, only to St. Peter and his successors, Bishops of the same See, by special prerogative granted; it is therefore in law, amongst Christian men, insufficient to charge any Christian man.[4]

His refusal to swear the oath, he insists, was not an attack on the king. In fact, it was precisely to avoid any attack on the king that he had long clung to silence, however much this silence might be misinterpreted. Rather, his silence on the king's "great matter" was a choice made in light of something that More recognized in his conscience as truly independent of any choices on his part. Where Henry tried to replace the "higher law of God and Christ's Church" with his own law, More felt the need to witness to that higher law, even if so witnessing required the sacrifice of his life.

Besides the important legal points at issue—about the marriage, about the very nature of law, about the exact wording of the oath—we also find here a telling piece of evidence about More's own understanding of conscience. It is a very traditional Catholic understanding of conscience[5] as the faculty by which an individual can pass moral judgments about the choices one intends to make as well as about choices already made. A well-formed con-

---

4. Thomas More, in Nicholas Harpsfield, *The Life and Death of Sir Thomas More*, in *Lives of Saint Thomas More* (William Roper and Nicholas Harpsfield), ed. E. E. Reynolds, Everyman's Library, no. 19 (London: J. M. Dent and Sons, 1963), p. 161.
5. For a modern statement of the Catholic understanding of conscience, see *Catechism of the Catholic Church* (Washington, D.C.: U.S. Catholic Conference, 1994) nos. 1776–1802. One of the classic statements of this position can be found in Thomas Aquinas's *Summa theologiae* I, q. 79, aa. 12–13; he provides a more expansive treatment of this topic in qq. 16–17 of his *Quaestiones disputate de veritate*.

science will evaluate these choices on the basis of moral truths that are entirely antecedent to the will of the moral agent. In accord with the scholastic tradition that More knew from his days at Oxford,[6] he took the formation of conscience to be the effect of a lengthy process of *discovering* the moral order and not a matter of *deciding* on what such an order was to be, for himself or for his age. For this long tradition in ethics, having a well-formed conscience depends on coming to know and appreciate what the truths of morality are; it is never a matter of choosing a morality, however stern or rigorous. To use a metaphor that reflects More's own profession, individual conscience is the courtroom in which a trial must be held, but the trial must be conducted by abiding principles of law, not by any principles specially created for the occasion.

The traditional Catholic position on conscience focuses on the judgments an individual makes in applying the objective norms of morality in order to determine the rightness or wrongness of an action. According to this position, the entire body of ethical principles depends upon a first principle that is naturally known to all human minds[7] without need for any special investigation (namely, that good is to be pursued and evil avoided); while a given person might never think about stating this principle in so many words, it is nevertheless present as a principle by which

6. In this period Oxford University was a stronghold of medieval scholasticism; see Hastings Rashdall, *The Universities of Europe in the Middle Ages,* rev. ed., ed. F. M. Powricke and A. B. Emdem (Oxford: Oxford Univ. Press, 1936), vol. 3, pp. 140–68.

7. The technical name for the faculty by which a person has this infallible knowledge of the first practical principle is *synderesis.* The term *conscience* is then reserved for the disposition that is built up in an individual (however well-formed or ill-formed this disposition may be) to make judgments of moral evaluation in practical cases. For a sense of the range of positions taken on these matters in medieval scholasticism, see Timothy C. Potts, *Conscience in Medieval Philosophy* (Cambridge: Cambridge Univ. Press, 1980).

everyone operates.[8] And yet this first practical principle is far too general by itself to decide on all the practical matters one faces in life—somehow one still has to determine just what is good and what is not for specific situations. Some of the more specific principles that are needed for good judgment can be obtained through reasoning about the natural law, which can articulate secondary and even tertiary precepts in order to concretize the primary practical principle. But some of the more detailed principles needed to form conscience aright will be known only through revelation and the decisions of divinely commissioned authorities. In fact, for most people, the acquisition of moral beliefs comes about unreflectively through the guidance of parents, school, church, and public opinion. Despite the external nature of these sources of moral guidance, there always remains the inner seat of reasoning and judgment about moral matters. From both sources, proper authority and reason's discovery of the natural law, one can form one's conscience.

Aquinas notes that judgments of conscience are evident in a variety of experiences, including (1) the recognition that we have done or have not done something (in this regard, conscience is said to be a *witness*); (2) the judgment that something should be done or should not be done (here conscience *binds* and *incites* us to some action); and (3) the judgment that something is well done or ill done (thus conscience is said to *excuse, accuse,* or *torment* us).[9] As individuals mature, they may well find reason through experience to affirm the more specific moral principles they have acquired or to correct them in light of the first principle (prejudice, for instance, may have encouraged some evil practice under the appearance of good, or some long-standing rationalization

8. Aquinas traces this position back to Aristotle's *Nicomachean Ethics,* VI. 6.
9. Aquinas, *Summa theologiae,* I, q. 79, a. 12.

may have caused a kind of moral blindness about some good that ought to be pursued or respected).

The proper formation of conscience is crucial for the development of a disposition to pass sound judgments upon practical matters in light of moral principles. Since the correctness of the principles used in one's reasoning is indispensable for arriving at correct moral judgments, there is need for individuals and for societies to examine their moral principles in the process of building up a body of moral truths, and this process is called the formation of conscience. A judgment of conscience based on false principles or on a faulty application of genuine principles renders the judgment of conscience erroneous. There are also subjective factors, such as the certainty or uncertainty one might have about the relevant principle or about how to apply moral principles. Accordingly, there has developed a sophisticated casuistry for handling such problems as what to do in cases when one is unsure about what the right course of action is, or what to do when even the learned are divided in their opinions on a moral question. The respect that this opinion accords to the subjective factor in measuring personal culpability and in acknowledging the diminution of moral responsibility in no way denigrates or imperils the intellectual orientation of this understanding of conscience.

From the beginning of his career to its end, More held a traditional view of conscience and recognized the need for its proper formation. This is already evident long before the moment of his trial. In a letter to his children's teacher, for instance, he writes: "The whole fruit of their endeavors should consist in the testimony of God and a good conscience. Thus they will be inwardly calm and at peace and neither stirred by praise of flatterers nor stung by the follies of unlearned mockers of learning."[10] Truth can easily become a casualty when sycophants exaggerate in hope of gain and when cowards weasel their way out of danger by

10. Letter to Gonell, in *Selected Letters*, p. 105.

deception. But for More, acknowledging within oneself the truth about any given situation will generate the inward calm and peace of a good conscience.

In order to appreciate More's sense of the demands of conscience in the matter of Henry's desire to obtain a divorce from Catherine of Aragon in order to marry Anne Boleyn—involving a question of a truth based on revelation and the determination of authority (rather than in any direct way a question of natural law)—one would have to attend not only to the range of questions about the facts of the case. Was, for instance, the dispensation by which Henry had been allowed by the Church to marry Catherine (his deceased brother's wife) valid? One would also need to consider Henry's actual disposition at any given time—a complicated question because of the changing demands of political intrigue and the pressing dynamics of international relations, not to mention the vacillations in Henry's own mind by reason of such factors as his poorly restrained lusts, his desires for an heir, his anger at Catherine's resistance, and his general frustration at not getting what he wanted. There are also difficult questions on the subjective side about such things as exactly when Thomas More knew what. His biographers have tried to recount the likely stages of More's acquaintance with Henry's growing desire for the divorce.[11] The process of gathering data appropriate for making sound moral judgments about one's own course of action is a crucial part of the formation of conscience. The record shows a picture of More working vigorously for his king on this matter in precisely the ways that lawyers are trained to explore all sides of a question at law, and yet he was careful never to yield to expediency on a matter of principle, no matter how hard the king

11. See, for example, Peter Ackroyd, *The Life of Thomas More* (New York: Doubleday, 1998), pp. 263–75; R. W. Chambers, *Thomas More* (Ann Arbor: Univ. of Michigan Press, 1958), pp. 223–30; James Monti, *The King's Good Servant but God's First: The Life and Writings of Saint Thomas More* (San Francisco: Ignatius Press, 1997), pp. 301–12.

pressed him for support. One may surmise that More held for Henry's obligation to continue to recognize his wedding vows to Queen Catherine until such time as they were proven not to be binding, and in this respect he was like the official called the defender of the bond in any annulment proceedings. The burden of proof rests with the party trying to prove that a presumptive bond does not exist.

But in order to appreciate More's understanding of conscience, we should broaden our consideration beyond this famous case. Years earlier More had agonized about whether to enter public service at all, and from what we know about the details of his early years, as well as about his early writing, one can already detect the same careful dedication to forming his conscience properly in order to work out a decision. Although his father, John More, had early on staked out a career in public service for his son, More did not actually join Henry's staff until 1517 when, at nearly forty years of age, he was made a member of the Privy Council. In the two years prior to that decision he was hard at work on the *Utopia,* in Book I of which one can almost see More trying to think out the foreseeable problems of possible coopera- tion with evil when More has his characters weigh the good one can do in public service against the risk of compromising on moral principles that is attendant on any voyage upon the seas of political life.

The path that John More laid out for his young son included two years of service (beginning about age twelve) in the house- hold of John Morton, the archbishop of Canterbury.[12] After receiving two years (1492–94) of spiritual and intellectual forma- tion in traditional scholastic learning at Oxford and tasting the new humanist scholarship through his acquaintance with the likes

12. In the long tradition of ecclesial appointments to the post of Lord Chancellor, Archbishop (later Cardinal) John Morton served in that capacity under Henry VII from 1487 to 1500. In 1529 More (succeeding Cardinal Wolsey) became the first layman to hold that post.

of John Colet and Desiderius Erasmus,[13] More longed to continue
with literary and theological studies. But his father's ambitions for
his son brought about his transfer to the New Inn, a London institution that trained young men for a career in law. By February
1496 More was sufficiently prepared for admission to the presti-
gious Lincoln's Inn, which possessed the unique privilege of recommending candidates for admission to the London bar.

During the four years of his legal studies, More was engaged in
vocational discernment. Under the care of John Colet's spiritual
direction,[14] he sought clarity about the state of life to which God
was calling him. His spiritual reading during this period is
known to have included *The Imitation of Christ* by Thomas à
Kempis and *Scale of Perfection* by Walter Hilton.[15] Each morning
and each evening he prayed with the Carthusians of London's
Charterhouse. Eighteen members of this order were eventually to
die as martyrs for their fidelity to the papacy.[16] He was testing the
possibility that he had a vocation to the priesthood and in particular to their ascetic form of religious life.[17] Toward the end of his
legal education, once it became clear to him that marriage and not
religious life was to be his vocation, he relatively quickly sought

13. John Colet (1466–1519) brought back to England a passionate interest in biblical, patristic, and Greek subjects developed during his studies with Italian
humanists. Although it is not possible to establish the precise date when More
came into contact with Colet, we do know that Colet lectured on the epistles of
Saint Paul at Oxford in 1499, became More's spiritual director in 1504, and was
appointed the dean of Saint Paul's Cathedral, London, in 1505.

From Erasmus's own letters of 1499 (see Nichols, *Epistles,* vol. 1, pp. 200, 226)
we learn of the already well-established scholar's delight at meeting a young man
like More.

14. See More's letter to Colet of 1504, 23 October, in *The Correspondence of Sir
Thomas More,* ed. Elizabeth Rogers (Princeton: Princeton Univ. Press, 1947), pp. 5–9.

15. Monti (p. 65) notes that in *The Confutation of Tyndale's Answer,* More believes
the author of *Imitation of Christ* to be the French spiritual writer Jean Gerson.

16. See Dom Bede Camm, O.S.B., ed., *Lives of the English Martyrs,* vol. 1: *Martyrs
under Henry VIII* (London: Longman, Green, & Co., 1914).

17. There is a letter from More to his daughter Meg written shortly after he was
dismissed from the chancellorship about how he can now at last live a form of life
like that of the Carthusians, something he has never ceased to desire.

marriage to Jane Colt, a young country girl from a virtuous family of his acquaintance. Before her untimely death at age twenty-two in 1511, they had four children, for whom More then provided a new mother by his marriage to Alice Middleton, a widow some eight years his senior.

One can also see something of More's understanding of conscience in his literary activity from this period, especially in his *Life of John Picus* (that is, Giovanni Pico della Mirandola, 1463–1494). This work is a close translation from the Latin text of the biography that was penned by Pico's nephew. To it More added his own preface, a translation of some of Pico's letters on Christian spiritual formation, and a set of his own poems on "Spiritual Warfare" that were inspired by Pico's ideas. There can be no mistaking that Pico was a heroic model for More—a layman whose conversion from hedonism had entailed committing himself to an intensely spiritual life of penance and asceticism (he was admitted to the Order of Preachers just before his death). More admired this humanist scholar who had devoted no small portion of his energies to the public good of his city of Florence. More's own academic interests and ascetic practices resembled those of Pico, and one can see something of More's own care for the ongoing formation of his conscience in the "Twelve Rules for Spiritual Warfare," which recurrently counsel us to overcome temptations by imitating one or another of the traits of the Heart of Christ as he undergoes the Passion. As advice for keeping the judgments of one's conscience sharp, More set down a dozen "rules" for spiritual warfare and a matching dozen "weapons." In this he employs a hallowed notion within the tradition of Christian spirituality, the need to act directly against an enticing temptation. When inclined, for instance, to take undue pride in one's own good actions, the remedy is a cultivation of humility. When aroused by the likely pleasure of a sinful act, one should recall that these short-lived pleasures will invariably be succeeded by sorrow and loss.

Near the end of More's life, in his writings from the Tower, we find More still recommending the practice of a careful and daily examination of conscience in which he had steeled himself since his youth. For this purpose some sort of solitude is crucial, and we may well suspect that the remarks in his *Dialogue of Comfort against Tribulation* about reserving a time and place for the examination of conscience reflect his long practice of retiring for a certain time each day (and for longer periods on Fridays) to the oratory he built on his estate at Chelsea:

> Let him also choose himself some secret solitary place in his own house as far from noise and company as he conveniently can. And thither let him some time secretly resort alone, imagining himself as one going out of the world even straight unto the giving up his reckoning unto God of his sinful living. Then let him there before an altar or some pitiful image of Christ's bitter passion, the beholding whereof may put him in remembrance of the thing and move him to devout compassion, kneel down or fall prostrate as at the feet of almighty God, verily believing him to be there invisibly present as without any doubt he is. There let him open his heart to God and confess his faults such as he can call to mind and pray God of forgiveness. Let him call to remembrance the benefits that God hath given him, either in general among other men, or privately to himself, and give him humble hearty thanks therefore. There let him declare unto God, the temptations of the devil, the suggestions of the flesh, the occasions of the world, and of his worldly friends much worse many time in drawing a man from God than are his most mortal enemies. . . .[18]

*   *   *

18. *A Dialogue of Comfort against Tribulation,* bk. II, ch. 16, ed. Louis Martz and Frank Manley, in *Complete Works of St. Thomas More* (New Haven: Yale Univ. Press, 1976), vol. 12, pp. 164–65.

As here described, the examination of conscience is envisioned as taking place not just as a mental exercise but in prayer before Christ. The stress is on honesty before God, both about one's faults and weaknesses and about one's talents and accomplishments, with great effort to be truthful about the precise nature of one's inclinations and temptations, lest rationalization take over and carry off the soul. By emphasizing not only sorrow for sin but gratitude for blessings, More is portraying conscience as a prayerful place of intimate dialogue with God and thus an indispensable aid in the quest for holiness and virtue.

Among all More's writings, *Utopia* rightly holds a special place. That work is a fascinating humanist exercise of the imagination that has been legitimately interpreted in diverse ways—as a political program, for instance, as an ironic satire, and even as an anticipation of Marx's communism. But the book, especially the first of its two parts, may also be understood as an exercise in the formation of conscience undertaken by More just two years before he entered Henry's service. In contrast to Raphael Hythloday, the intellectual world-traveler who cannot bring himself to consent to public service for fear that his conscience would be compromised by the insatiable quest of this world's princes for territory, wealth, and glory in war or by the pressures of the sycophants at royal courts, the character More argues that politics is the art of the possible. It is a matter of remembering one's nonnegotiable principles and then determining what is negotiable, and how far one may go without compromising those principles. In the give-and-take between the characters More and Hythloday, one need not look too far to see More, in the humanist tradition of concern for morality and politics, readying his conscience for the inevitable tests that lie ahead.

What gives More confidence is a deeply Augustinian sense of the genuine possibility, if one stays mindful of the hierarchy required by the proper order of one's loves, for reconciling the City of God and the City of Man. The actual configuration of the

Utopia described in the second part of More's volume may seem on the surface to be devoid of reference to institutions historically prevalent in Christendom. Yet the dramatic setting for Hythloday's opportunity to recount what he saw in Utopia is a conversation that takes place just after More has come from mass at Notre Dame, "the most beautiful and most popular church in Antwerp." In the preliminary part of their conversation the figure of More's old patron, Cardinal Morton, looms large as the very embodiment of prudence, both on such policy questions as capital punishment and the proper penalties for thieves and on the way to redirect a dinner conversation that has become inflamed by stubborn passions.

What is more, the long discussion of political philosophy and its political embodiment in *Utopia* turns out to have deep roots in the Augustinian distinction between the two cities in *City of God*. As Gerard Wegemer has shown,[19] there is reason to think that the utopian proposals of the second book of *Utopia* are not just straightforwardly intended in the fashion, say, of Cicero's *Republic;* instead, they are carefully ironic in the satirical vein of Horace, Lucan, and other classical authors so dear to the humanist renaissance. The freedom of imagination that marks this work uses as a literary conceit the contrast between the dingy, stale Old World and the charming vistas of the New World, then just recently discovered (1492). The delight that the characters take in wondering whether the incredible reports of a new continent could possibly be accurate provides an engaging literary strategy for discussing political philosophy. One need only think of Pico della Mirandola or of More's contemporary Machiavelli[20] to

19. Gerard Wegemer, *Thomas More and Statesmanship* (Washington, D.C.: Catholic Univ. of America Press, 1996).
20. No formal connection between More and Machiavelli (1469–1521) is known, and yet there are many ways in which More's position stands directly contrary to that of Machiavelli. *The Prince* was already written (1513) but not yet published when More published his *Utopia* (1518).

remember how fascinated the humanists were with rethinking the purpose of government and the proper relationship of virtue and power in society. Wegemer has shown that the Utopia proposed in the second book systematically violates all the principles of Augustinian political philosophy, principles with which More must be presumed to have been familiar—not just on the basis of the allusions to *City of God* that lace *Utopia* but from the fact that he had lectured with great success on historical and philosophical aspects of this book at the parish of Saint Lawrence Jewry in London, at the invitation of the learned cleric William Grocyn.

So considered, the first book of *Utopia* shows us Thomas More carefully thinking through the struggles that public life will involve, not as if he somehow already knew what we know by the hindsight of history, but with an Augustinian optimism about the ways in which the Earthly City can be reconciled to the Heavenly City, an optimism clearly tempered by a realistic sense that politics is the art of the possible. The earnest debate between More and Hythloday about whether one's commitment to moral principle will necessarily have to suffer unacceptable compromise in the battles of politics adds an important dimension to the interpretation of *Utopia,* for the author has already had a decade and a half of prior experience in law and public office. His religious faith has generated and grounded a commitment to moral principles. This humanist essay provides a rhetorical vehicle in the first book for exploring certain issues relevant to the decision about entering public life, and in the second book, a way to explore the nonnegotiable principles of politics as part of the necessary formation of conscience.

One could well make a case that many of More's writings during his chancellorship were in part the efforts of a Catholic humanist to form King Henry's conscience. In some of them More makes a direct argument in his own name, as, for instance, in his openly apologetic work *The Confutation of Tyndale's Answer*.[21] At other times, More works by indirect persuasion with all the cleverness available to an author using a pseudonym, as in *The Debellation of Salem and Bizance*.[22] What is at stake for More is the struggle for the Christian order of England, an order threatened both by the religious reformers then trying to enter England from Germany with various forms of Protestant ideas and by political opportunists who played on Henry's weakness with flattery and pretension in a manner much like that More had anticipated in the worries Hythloday expresses in the first book of *Utopia*. Perhaps the direct argumentation of works like *Confutation* (1532–33) or *Dialogue Concerning Heresies* (1529) are more readily intelligible as appeals to Henry to make his decisions upon clearly argued principles. But why, we might ask, write such an elaborate and curious tour de force as a fictional account of the Turkish attack upon Hungary? Not far beneath the figures and symbols one finds direct applications to the situation of England, ready for the king's eyes to recognize and to choose as his policy, without being backed into the corner in a way that more direct writing might have done. In short, More realized that there were various ways in which he could try to form his king's conscience.

In More's last letters from his imprisonment in the Tower there is also compelling evidence about his notion of the place of reasons of conscience. Besides producing such works as *A Dialogue of Comfort against Tribulation* and the shorter (unfinished) *The Sadness of Christ,* More wrote numerous letters during the fourteen months of his captivity. Among his twenty-four surviving letters from the period there are four to Thomas Cromwell (in one of

21. *The Confutation of Tyndale's Answer,* ed. L. Schuster, R. Marius, J. Lusardi, and R. J. Schoeck. Volume 8 of the Yale Edition of the *Complete Works of St. Thomas More* (New Haven and London: Yale Univ. Press, 1973), 3 parts.
22. *The Debellation of Salem and Bizance,* ed. J. Guy, R. Keen, C. Miller, and R. McGugan. Volume 10 of the Yale Edition (1987).

which he writes: "upon that I should perceive mine own conscience should serve me"), one to Henry VIII, eight to Meg, two
to fellow prisoners: the theologian Nicholas Wilson and the priest
Leder, one to his friend Antonio Bonvisi, and the longest, composed by More but addressed from Margaret Roper to Alice
Alington. These letters have recently been gathered together in
an attractive volume by Father Alvaro de Silva (see Suggestions
for Further Reading, p. 251), whose introduction points out that
the word *conscience* is extremely common throughout these final
letters. It appears more than a hundred times, and some forty
times in a single text, the letter from Margaret to Alice. This letter
is in Meg's hand but is widely regarded by scholars as the product
of More's mind, with all the careful distinctions he was cultivat-
ing in the long Tower months. It is presumed that a real conversation between More and Meg in the Tower was the source for the
imaginary dialogue presented in the letter, for Meg was trying to
win over her father to swear the oath in order to regain his liberty,
urging that his reservations were simply a "scruple of conscience." More returns to the literary license of his humanist education to portray Meg as a kind of temptress like Eve tempting
Adam, but happily a temptress who gains reassurance and even
joy at her father's ultimate insistence upon having "a respect for
his own soul."

In this clever letter, More tells Meg the story of a certain man
named Company, "an honest man from another quarter" who is
unable to join in on a questionable verdict delivered by his fellow
eleven jurors. The reader might here think of the film *12 Angry
Men* (1957), or perhaps a work already a classic in More's day,
Piers Plowman, by William Langland. Enraged that Company is
delaying the verdict by his stubborn resistance, the eleven try to
prevail on him to be "Good Company" and sign on to their opinion. That Company is but one against eleven does not bear on the
truth of his position. The fact that many important people in
More's England took the oath without a crisis of conscience was

for More no evidence that he was wrong. He speaks with the greatest respect for his opponents in these late letters, but he also suggests that they should have known or did know better. In this letter More has Company make an important disclaimer: he is open to the possibility of being corrected, but he explains that he has already weighed the matter, so now he asks the eleven "to talk upon the matter and tell him . . . *reasons*" why he should change his stance. His fellow jurymen refuse his offer, and so Company decides to keep his own company, lest "the passage of [his] poor soul would passeth all good company." More reminds Margaret that he himself "never intended (God being my good lord) to pin my soul to another man's back . . . for I know not whether he may hap to carry it."

In letter after letter More talks of his reasons of conscience, and his insistence on the point makes clear that for him conscientious resistance is grounded in something other than personal integrity or sheer voluntarism. De Silva notes a range of meanings for the word *conscience* in these final letters.[23] It refers, first, to one's "mind" or "inmost thought" as the understanding by which one has built up personal conviction of a reasonable sort about a matter. Although accompanied by feelings of various sorts, it is not just a feeling of contentment, or self-satisfaction, or emotional tranquillity, but the tranquillity that comes from purity of heart. Second, de Silva argues that conscience refers to a person's specifically "moral" sense, one's consciousness of right and wrong in the matters for which one bears responsibility, and thus one's awareness of good and evil. Third, the term *conscience,* by its etymological origins in *cum* and *scire,* denotes a certain kind of "knowledge" that we have "with" another. One sees this especially in More's sense that, for all the solitude of his captivity, he found himself alone with his God. Christian teaching on con-

---

23. *The Last Letters of Thomas More,* edited and with an introduction by Alvaro de Silva (Grand Rapids, Mich.: William B. Eerdmans Publishing Co., 2000), pp. 9–11.

science has regularly championed a strong sense of the intimate relation between conscience and God. This is evident both when it makes the cornerstone of Christian anthropology the conviction that the human being is made in the image of God and when writers on morality speak about the voice of conscience as the voice of the divine lawmaker.[24] Now, to become a proper image of God, the Christian must look at himself in Christ as in a mirror, so that the image reflected there may become more and more Christ's own image. Coming to accept and share the wisdom of Christ by better knowledge of oneself and by increasingly conforming to the model of Christ is clearly at the heart of More's understanding of conscience in these late letters.

More believed firmly that Christ had entrusted to the Church the mission to hand on in her teaching the truth about God and about human freedom. For More, this freedom was to be found in the obedience we render according to the same spirit that marks the famous line from Saint John: "You will know the truth, and the truth will make you free." The problem, of course, is how one is to use one's freedom, how one is to handle the formation of conscience. He constantly urges those to whom he writes that it is to be formed through study and reflection. For the Christian believer, the proper formation comes about through the authority of the Church as she teaches the truth—even if this ultimately means giving up one's life, as More did, for the spiritual primacy of the Roman pontiff.

In the letter from Meg to Alice, one sees More struggling for his own spiritual integrity—it is a merry story, to entertain his daughter as well as to enlighten her. Unlike the vision of conscience in Bolt's *A Man for All Seasons,* this is not the notion of conscience that philosophical individualism champions but the

24. This is the understanding of conscience preferred by Cardinal Newman in *A Grammar of Assent*. See John Henry Cardinal Newman, *An Essay in Aid of a Grammar of Assent* [1898], ed. with an introd. and notes by Ian T. Kerr (Oxford: Clarendon Press, 1985).

idea of conscience found in Christian tradition—a conscience that knows most truly when it knows what it knows *along with* Christ. Even the play on words about "Company" and "good company" may well be an allusion to the importance of ecclesial unity in the face of so much "bad company" that More opposed so vigorously during the period of his chancellorship. For reasons of his own, Bolt has More end in moralizing: "Finally, it is not a matter of reason but of love"—but, like the passage cited earlier from that play, this line also fails to do Thomas More full justice. For him it was *always* a matter of reason: a matter of careful discernment about principles he did not choose or create himself but which he honored as the groundwork for a reasonable decision.

In that touching letter, More is thus telling Meg that she may not just change her mind about something for the sake of pleasing others or for personal convenience. But this is not stubbornness—the character Company is reasonably ready to change his mind, but only if a set of good reasons can be presented, and not just reasons of political expediency. Otherwise, he would not be changing his mind but simply saying what he does not mean. His action would actually be a betrayal of his own self, a lying to his own mind. By swearing the oath in the way that many of England's clergy and nobles had decided to do, More would have lost himself and lost the place of solitude with his God. He preferred to accept prison and even death in order to be truly free. As he writes to Meg, "I have of pure necessity for respect unto mine own soul."

Thomas More, knighted by Henry VIII and named lord chancellor of England as the king's most trusted advisor, was beheaded for treason on order of this same authority. Who is the betrayer in this tragic drama, Henry or his good servant? How did Sir Thomas rise in his career to be given the keys to sovereign authority in the English realm, only to find himself under sentence of death in the Tower of London so shortly thereafter?

A brilliant lawyer, loyal servant to the king, devoted family man, and Renaissance humanist, Thomas More was, before all else, deeply religious and a profoundly spiritual Roman Catholic. Friend to Desiderius Erasmus, the Dutch humanist; John Fisher, bishop of Rochester; and John Colet, Greek scholar at Oxford and then dean of St. Paul's, London, More aligned himself with fellow Catholic intellectuals who campaigned against the Protestant reforms that flowed into England from the Continent. Henry VIII earned himself the title "Defender of the Faith" in 1521 when he wrote his *Defense of the Seven Sacraments* against Luther's *The Babylonian Captivity of the Church,* in which he had reduced the seven to three. But then Henry determined to put away his wife, Catherine, to marry Anne Boleyn in the hope of securing a male heir for the throne, and he appealed to Pope Clement VII to annul his first marriage. Obsessed with Anne and furious at the resistance of papal authority to his petition, Henry forced the hand of the Church by having Parliament declare him to be supreme power in Church and State. He was henceforth excommunicated by Rome, and the English schism began. Soon all citizens were required to take an oath by which they recognized the succession of Elizabeth, daughter of Anne and Henry, thereby repudiating papal authority, and to accept the king as sole head of the Church in England. For their refusal to do so, John Fisher and Thomas More earned the wrath of Henry and were executed—good servants of the king but loyal above all else to God and His Church.

The chronology that follows traces the development of this fatal conflict by highlighting the Protestant influences that, on the one hand, strengthened Thomas More's resolve to defend the Church of Rome while, on the other, worked to destroy Henry's commitment to papal sovereignty. The life spans of Thomas More, his colleagues, and Henry VIII straddle the era that saw the shrinking of the medieval worldview together with the expansion of new boundaries heralded by the theological, artistic, and geographical explorations of the times. Former metaphysical, aesthetic, and navigational limits to human reason and imagination were transformed by new information and revolutionary ways of thinking. It was the difficult work of conscience and consciousness to discern anew the final, irrefutable verities of life.

Early Life

1478 Thomas More is born on February 7 to John More, barrister and later judge, and Agnes, daughter of Thomas Granger. The family lives on Milk Street in London and is prosperous.

1483 Martin Luther is born in Eisleben, Germany (d. 1546).

Charles VIII succeeds Louis XI to rule in France.

Richard of Gloucester (1452–85) murders his nephews Edward V and Richard of York. He becomes King Richard III of England.

Raphael Santi, Italian painter, is born (d. 1520).

1484 More attends St. Anthony's school in London, a Latin grammar school where the students are required to converse in Latin.

Ulrich Zwingli, Swiss humanist and reformer, is born (d. 1531).

Sandro Botticelli, Italian painter (1444–1510), paints *The Birth of Venus*.

1485 Henry Tudor, Earl of Richmond, kills Richard III and succeeds him on the English throne as Henry VII.

1486 Johannes Eck is born (d. 1543). He will become a great Dominican theologian and opponent of Luther.

1489 More becomes a page to John Morton (d. 1500), archbishop of Canterbury and lord chancellor of England.

Thomas Cranmer, future English reformer, is born (d. 1556). He will be archbishop of Canterbury at the beginning of the English Reformation.

1490 Albert of Brandenburg, who will become a cardinal, is born (d. 1545). His administration as archbishop of Magdeburg and Mainz will be responsible for the sale of papal indulgences that precipitates Luther's famous protest in the form of Ninety-Five Theses affixed to the door of the Castle Church in Wittenberg in 1517.

1491 English King Henry VIII is born (d. 1547), as is Ignatius of Loyola (d. 1556), founder of the Jesuit order.

1492 More is nominated by Archbishop Morton for Canterbury College, Oxford, where he studies on scholarship for two years. The curriculum includes classical studies such as Aristotle's *Rhetoric* and disputations involving formal oratory and public debate.

Christopher Columbus (1452–1506), a Genoese supported by Isabella of Castile, Spain, sets sail west for India in the *Santa María,* landing instead in the Bahamas, October 12; in Cuba, October 18; and in Haiti, December 6. The *Santa María* goes down off Haiti December 25.

The Inquisition drives the Jews from Spain. Granada is taken from the Muslims by Spain, thus consolidating the monarchy of Ferdinand of Aragon and Isabella of Castile.

Roderigo Borgia (1430–1503), father of Cesare and Lucretia Borgia, becomes Pope Alexander VI following the death of Pope Innocent VIII.

Leonardo da Vinci (1452–1519) draws a flying machine.

1493 More leaves Oxford without a degree and studies at New Inn in London, where he enters the field of law. Gifted as an actor, expert at disputation, and skilled as an orator, More is richly endowed with the talents required for the practice of law.

Columbus returns to Spain, then leaves on a second voyage (September 25, 1493–June 11, 1496) and lands in Puerto Rico, Dominica, and Jamaica.

Maximilian I (1459–1519) becomes emperor of the Holy Roman Empire.

1494 Charles VIII of France invades Italy, sacks Rome, and forces the pope to take refuge in Castel Sant' Angelo, a Roman mausoleum built by Emperor Hadrian (d. A.D. 139).

1495 Charles VIII is crowned king of Naples, then returns to France. Ferdinand II reconquers Naples and expels the French. A syphilis epidemic, introduced by French soldiers, spreads from Naples all over Europe.

Jews who refuse to convert to Christianity are expelled from Portugal.

Hieronymus Bosch (1453–1516), of the Netherlands, paints *The Garden of Worldly Delights*.

Da Vinci paints *The Last Supper*.

John Tavener, English composer, is born (d. 1545).

The composer Josquin des Pres (c. 1450–1521) is appointed organist and choirmaster at Cambrai Cathedral.

1496 At Lincoln's Inn More's study of law involves the belief that judicial decisions are ultimately grounded in divine authority and as such foundational to human society. More accepts the priority given to law in the governance of human affairs and will defend it against the opposing case for private judgment that will be advanced by Luther.

1497 Philip Melancthon, German humanist, biblical scholar, and reformer, is born (d. 1560). He is to become a close associate of Luther. In 1530 he will compose the Lutheran formulation of faith known as the Augsburg Confession.

Girolamo Savonarola (1452–98), a Dominican prior in Florence, attempts to depose Pope Alexander VI for corruption, but instead is himself excommunicated.

John Cabot (1425–c. 1500) and his son, Sebastian, reach the east coast of North America. He is an Italian under commission to Henry VII of England.

1498 Desiderius Erasmus (1467–1536) of Rotterdam, a monk of the Augustinian Canons Regular, travels to England and teaches at Oxford. A humanist of great learning, Erasmus will come to insist on a Christianity purged of liturgical accretions and focused directly on a Gospel morality based on the Sermon on the Mount. He advocates a tolerant, humane ethos founded on a deep regard for human dignity and self-direction.

John Colet (1467?–1519) is ordained a priest and begins lecturing on the Epistles of Saint Paul at Oxford. He becomes a close associate of Erasmus and influences him to take up the study of Greek and the New Testament. Erasmus will write an account of Colet's life. Later on Colet becomes a spiritual advisor to More. He himself had been influenced on a trip to Italy by the fervor for reform of both Pico della Mirandola (1463–94) and Savonarola.

Savonarola is burned at the stake in Florence as a result of his revolutionary intransigence over reform of the papacy.

Charles VIII of France dies and is succeeded by Louis XII, Duke of Orleans.

Thomas Vasco da Gama (c. 1469–1525) of Portugal discovers the sea route to India, putting Asia in direct communication with Europe by sea.

Albrecht Dürer (1471–1528), German Renaissance genius, paints *Self-Portrait, Apocalypse,* and *The Knight, Death, and the Devil.*

Michelangelo Buonarroti (1475–1564) sculpts the *Pietà* for Saint Peter's in Rome.

1499 More and Erasmus meet for the first time. Their mutual interest in the "New Learning" (Renaissance humanism) provides the entry into a great, long friendship. In the summer they together make a social visit to Prince Henry of Wales (the future King Henry VIII).

Amerigo Vespucci (1454–1512) sails from Spain to South America.

War between the Turks and Venice; Lepanto, on the Gulf of Corinth, surrenders to the Sultan.

1500 Pope Alexander VI imposes a tithe for a crusade against the Turks. The Diet of Augsburg establishes the Council of Regency for administering the Holy Roman Empire.

Religious Formation

1501 More begins his close association with the Carthusian Charterhouse of London, where he will live for the next four years, participating in the monks' spiritual exercises of meditation and prayer, adopting their physical penances, and testing his possible vocation to the priesthood. It is here that More steeps himself in the piety of Walter Hilton's *Scale of Perfection* and Thomas à Kempis's *The Imitation of Christ.* He acquires a sense of the transience of the things of this world and the passing nature of ambition and success but nonetheless embraces life as an endeavor meriting one's best efforts.

More begins his own study of Greek and lectures on Augustine's *City of God* at the parish of Saint Lawrence Jewry in London. In this work Augustine describes two kinds of social orders: one based on love of self, even to the contempt of God; the other, heavenly in its focus on God, even to the abnegation of self. More will spend his own complicated life trying to reconcile these two loyalties.

During the period of his Charterhouse association, More translates and provides commentary for the biography of Pico della Mirandola (1463–94), an Italian Renaissance humanist who emphasized the dignity of the human person in his writings, especially *Oratio de hominis dignitate*. His *Life of John Picus* becomes a profound meditation on the suffering of Christ, who was ostracized and condemned for his virtues. The passion of Christ will be the mainstay of More's spiritual life throughout his career.

Erasmus publishes the *Enchiridion,* a moral treatise intended to promote spiritual reform in the Church. He emphasizes the inner, spiritual life of the Christian and derides the observances of monastic life.

Michelangelo executes the sculpture *David*.

1502 Martin Luther receives his bachelor's degree from Erfurt University.

Columbus makes his fourth and last voyage, this time to Honduras and Panama.

After he makes his second voyage, Vespucci realizes that South America is not identical with India but is rather a separate continent.

1503 More lectures on law at Furnivall's Inn for three years, through 1506.

Henry, Prince of Wales, is betrothed to Catherine of Aragon (1485–1536), daughter of Ferdinand of Aragon and Isabella of Castile, after obtaining a dispensation from Pope Julius II. It was granted because she had married Arthur, the eldest son of Henry the VII, in 1501, but he died the next year. King Henry VIII will repudiate both this marriage and papal supremacy in 1533 when he weds Anne Boleyn.

Venice signs a peace treaty with the Turks.

Pope Alexander VI dies and is succeeded by Pope Julius II (1443–1513), famous for his military prowess and patronage of the arts.

Matthias Grünewald (1470–1528), German painter and representative artist of the Reformation, paints *Crucifixion*. He is a close friend of Martin Luther.

Da Vinci paints the *Mona Lisa*.

Thomas Wyatt, English poet, is born (d. 1542).

1504 At age 27, More is elected to Parliament for one session.

Queen Isabella of Spain dies at age fifty-three, leaving King Ferdinand to lead Spain forward against French aggression in Italy, their common battleground.

Under the Treaty of Lyons, Louis XII cedes Naples to Ferdinand II, establishing Naples under Spanish control.

Maximilian I begins the transformation of the Holy Roman Empire into a universal Hapsburg monarchy.

Lucas Cranach the Elder (1472–1553), friend to Luther, paints *Rest on the Flight to Egypt*.

Dürer paints *Nativity*.

Raphael paints *Marriage of the Virgin*.

Marriage

1505 More determines that he is not called to a celibate, cloistered life and leaves the Charterhouse to follow a career in public life and to marry. He chooses for his wife Jane Colt, daughter of landowner John Colt of Essex. Jane is sixteen. They will have four children: Margaret (c. 1505–44), Elizabeth (c. 1506–?), Cecily (c. 1507–?), and John (c. 1508–47).

John Colet is made dean of Saint Paul's Cathedral, London. He will be a friend and spiritual advisor to More.

Martin Luther enters law school on May 20 but in July is caught in a terrifying lightning storm and vows to Saint Anne he will become a monk if he is spared. He is and consequently enters the monastery of the Augustinian Hermits at Erfurt.

Pope Julius II calls Michelangelo to Rome.

Thomas Tallis, English composer, is born (d. 1585).

1506 In Germany John Tetzel (1465–1519), a Dominican monk, begins selling indulgences.

1507 Martin Luther is ordained a priest on April 3.

1508 More goes abroad to visit the continental universities of Louvain and Paris, where he observes humanist methods of research and curriculum design. More is keenly interested in what is called "the New Learning," which stresses noble human values and the capacity of man to transform himself and societal structures. Fundamental is the Platonic ideal of virtue acquired through knowledge, particularly through a study of classical languages and literature.

Luther is called to the newly founded university in Wittenberg to lecture on the Bible.

Michelangelo begins to paint the ceiling of the Sistine Chapel in Rome.

Raphael enters the service of Julius II.

Law Career

1509 More becomes a member of the Mercers' Guild, an association of London tradesmen. His function is that of negotiator and orator, at both of which he excels.

Henry VII of England dies in April. Henry, Prince of Wales, succeeds his father as Henry VIII. He marries his brother's widow, Catherine of Aragon. As a representative of the Mercers, More composes coronation verses to celebrate the new age of justice, prosperity, piety, and scholarship that handsome young Henry is inaugurating.

John Fisher (1469–1535), bishop of Rochester, publishes *The Seven Penitential Psalms*. A prodigious scholar, he greatly encourages the work of Erasmus, is More's close friend and confidant, and will be a firm defender of Catholic doctrine against the Protestant teachings that begin to influence English university thinking.

Luther returns to Erfurt.

John Calvin is born (d. 1564). One of the major figures of the Reformation, he will center his activities in Geneva. He will be influenced by both Erasmus and Luther. '

France declares war on Venice and is victorious.

1510 More is appointed under-sheriff of the City of London, an office he will hold until 1518. In this capacity More deals with all manner of criminal offenses. He is also elected to Parliament as a representative of the City at Westminster. More's specially edited translation of the biography of Pico della Mirandola is published.

Titian Vecellio (c. 1488–1576), Italian, paints *The Gypsy Madonna*.

Louis Bourgeois, French musician, is born (d. 1561).

Widowed, More Marries Again

1511 More's wife, Jane, dies suddenly at the age of twenty-two from influenza, or possibly in childbirth. With four children between two and six years old to care for, More marries again within a month of Jane's death, this time to Alice Middleton. Dame Alice, widow and mother of several children, is relatively rich and possesses a practical, witty temperament. She is eight years older than More, but they are exceedingly well-matched in humor. Both are dedicated to the cultivation of a calm, pious family life. More institutes a regular life of prayer, Scripture study, and church attendance for his entire household. He builds for himself a small oratory, to which he retreats regularly on Friday of each week. He sets up a humanistic curriculum for his children, seeing to it that they become skilled in both Latin and Greek as well as English. There is also instruction in music and recreation in sports such as archery. More is very fond of animals and has a variety of pets, including a monkey, for the family's amusement. He is an affectionate, demonstrative father and delights in the accomplishments and charms of his children.

Now a doctor in Sacra Biblia, Luther is transferred from Erfurt to Wittenberg, where he lectures on Scripture for the next six years. These are called his "silent years."

The Holy League with Venice and Aragon is formed by Pope Julius II to drive the French out of Italy. Henry VIII joins the Holy League.

Dürer paints *Adoration of the Trinity*.

1512 More serves as governor and treasurer of Lincoln's Inn.

Threatened by the schismatic anti-papal council of Pisa, Pope Julius II convokes the Fifth Lateran Council, which will continue until 1517. It produces some little-heeded calls for reform and pronounces the dogma of the "Immortality of the Soul."

The French defeat Spain at Ravenna.

Michelangelo finishes work on the Sistine Chapel.

1513 Henry VIII reforms the Royal Navy and organizes an expedition against France in support of Pope Julius II. In accord with the Treaty of Mechlin, they join Ferdinand of Aragon and Maximilian I in an agreement to invade France.

Pope Julius II dies and is succeeded by Giovanni de'Medici (b. 1475), who is elected Pope Leo X. He begins the development of the sculpture gallery at the Vatican.

Luther begins lecturing in Latin on the Psalms. He sees Christ prefigured and speaking in the Psalms, which manifest His righteousness.

Vasco Núñez de Balboa (c. 1475–1517) discovers the Pacific. Juan Ponce de León discovers Florida.

1514 More is admitted to the Doctors' Commons, an association of lawyers who deal with international and maritime business. He also serves on the sewers commission. More writes *The History of Richard III,* an account of a ruthless and murderous man driven to vile acts by his evil ambitions.

An Anglo-French truce is achieved through the marriage of Louis XII to Mary Tudor, sister of Henry VIII.

Thomas Wolsey (1471–1530), a butcher's son, is made archbishop of York.

Albert of Brandenburg is named archbishop of Mainz. To pay the papal fees entailed on the honor, he borrows 30,000 ducats from the House of Fugger, a bank in Augsburg. To pay off the loan, he permits the sale in his archdiocese of indulgences granted by Pope Leo X to finance the building of Saint Peter's Basilica in Rome. Johann Tetzel preaches the indulgence sale.

Portuguese vessels sail as far as Chinese waters.

Antonio Allegri Carreggio (1494–1534), Italian painter, pioneers the use of *chiaroscuro,* the interplay of light and dark in pictorial composition.

Utopia

1515 More journeys to Bruges in the spring and Antwerp in the summer to help in the negotiation of commercial and diplomatic treaties. He begins work on *Utopia*. In it a traveler, Raphael Hythloday, gives an account of the people of Utopia, which he claims he encountered while journeying through the New World with Amerigo Vespucci. Similar to England in geography, it seems to be a country purified of the vices of greed and pride where harmony and good order reign. But do the Utopian policies truly guarantee an ideal society? There is much ambiguity about the work, and More's tone can be taken as highly ironic and satiric.

Thomas Wolsey is appointed cardinal and lord chancellor of England. He personifies corruption in high church office, seeking only secular advancement and political power. He will be disgraced in 1529 for his failure to help Henry VIII secure a divorce.

Louis XII of France dies and is succeeded by Francis I. He conquers Milan in the Battle of Marignano.

Luther undergoes his "tower experience" as he studies the Epistle to the Romans in a small third-story office at Wittenberg. Chapter 1, verse 17, becomes pivotal to his Reformation theology: "For the justice of God is revealed from faith to faith in that it is written, for the just shall live by faith." Luther emphasizes the word *live:* for him, faith gives life. He comes to understand the concept of God's *iustitia* (justice) as God's divine mercy. He and Erasmus will quarrel bitterly over this concept.

Philip Neri (d. 1595) is born in Florence. He is destined to become a leading figure of the Counter Reformation.

Raphael is appointed chief architect of Saint Peter's in Rome.

1516 More becomes a member of the Council of the Star Chamber, a council of the king headed by Wolsey that deals with property titles. John Colet, Dean of St. Paul's in London, is More's spiritual advisor and the court preacher. At Oxford Colet had lectured on the Epistles of Saint Paul using humanist methods of scholarship.

A daughter, Mary Tudor, is born (d. 1558) to Henry VIII and Queen Catherine. She is their only surviving child. She will take the throne of England in 1553.

The first edition of More's *Utopia* is published in Latin in Louvain, Belgium, having been edited by Erasmus.

Erasmus's *Novum instrumentum,* the first printed edition of the Greek New Testament with Latin translation and notes, appears. It will influence Luther's own German translation and other contemporary vernacular editions.

Corpus Christi College, Oxford, is founded by Richard Fox, and Saint John's College, Cambridge, by Bishop John Fisher.

Ferdinand II of Spain dies and is succeeded by King Charles, who later becomes Emperor Charles V (1500–58).

Raphael paints *The Sistine Madonna*.

Titian paints *The Assumption*.

Michelangelo finishes his sculpture *Moses*.

1517 More goes to Calais with Cardinal Wolsey in the fall to help settle commercial disputes between French and English merchants. A second edition of *Utopia* is published. More becomes a member of the king's Privy Chamber and is now in daily contact with Henry.

On October 31, which will eventually become known as Reformation Day, Luther posts his Ninety-Five Theses at Wittenberg against the indulgence that had been issued as a result of the arrangement between Pope Leo X, Archbishop Albert of Brandenberg, and the House of Fugger bank. Luther's theses are translated from Latin into German and sold far and wide. Luther stresses that the punishment for sin can be removed only by faith in the Gospel. One must repent, and no amount of money charitably donated can relieve one of this responsibility. His action marks the beginning of the Reformation in Germany.

Service to Henry VIII

1518 More becomes master of requests in Henry's service and resigns as under-sheriff of London.

The Peace of London Treaty is crafted by Cardinal Wolsey and signed by England, France, Emperor Maximilian I, the pope, and Spain.

Erasmus sends More a copy of what has become known as Luther's "Disputation."

Luther is summoned to the Diet of Augsburg by Cardinal Cajetan, papal legate to Germany, but refuses to recant his claims

or his published works. It is here that Luther expounds his fundamental creed, *sola scriptura* (Scripture alone), by which he asserts
that Christ speaks not through an institution but to the individual
heart. He rejects the teaching authority of the Church, the infalli-
bility of papal decisions, and papal primacy by divine right. This
puts Luther on a direct collision course with More, who will go to
his death for upholding the pope's supreme spiritual authority.
Elector Frederick the Wise of Saxony, which includes Wittenberg, acts as Luther's protector and refuses to allow him to be
either extradited to Rome or banished.

1519 On the death of Maximilian I, his grandson, Charles I of
Spain, becomes Holy Roman Emperor Charles V.

Ulrich Zwingli begins the Swiss Reformation while preaching
in Zurich. Like Luther, he sets Scripture as the sole guide of
belief, thus emphasizing individual religious experience. He and
Luther disagree over the Real Presence of Christ in the Eucharist,
which Luther affirms.

Hernán Cortés (1485–1547) of Spain conquers and destroys the
Aztec Empire in Mexico (1519–21). The Portuguese Ferdinand
Magellan (1480–1521) makes the first voyage around the world.

1520 Charles V is crowned Holy Roman Emperor at Aix-la-
Chapelle. More aids in the negotiations for Charles's visit to Canterbury and meets with Francis I in Calais on what is now called
"the Field of the Cloth of Gold" to settle the terms of the peace
treaty between France and England. In the fall of the year, More
is granted knighthood by the king.

William Tyndale (c. 1491–1536), priest and Scripture scholar at
Cambridge, translates the New Testament from Erasmus's Greek

version into English. His Bible translations will form the basis for the King James Version of the Bible (1611). He comes to share many views with Luther, whom he meets when he flees England under suspicion of heresy in 1524. Hunted down by previous order of Henry VIII, he will be executed in Brussels because of his anti-Roman tracts.

Luther receives the papal bull (a binding letter with papal lead seal, or "bull," attached) *Exsurge Domine,* which threatens him with excommunication. Luther burns both the bull and a copy of canon law before the Elster Gate in Wittenberg. In his reform tracts, *Address to the Christian Nobility of the German Nation, The Babylonian Captivity of the Church,* and *Freedom of the Christian,* Luther casts the pope as the Antichrist, the ruler of Babylon. He reduces the number of sacraments from seven to three (baptism, the Eucharist, and penance), and redefines the Mass. In his treatise *On Monastic Vows,* he rejects monasticism as a misguided attempt to please God. Many monks and nuns, on reading it, feel justified in leaving religious life.

Thomas Münzer (c. 1489–1525), a priest who becomes a radical German reformer and agitator in the Peasants' War, starts the Anabaptist movement, stressing adult baptism as an outward profession of faith. He emphasizes the rule of faith as purely the inspiration of the Holy Spirit needing no external authority, not even Scripture.

Magellan passes through the Straits of Magellan. He heads into the Pacific Ocean and sails for the Philippines.

Suleiman I the Magnificent (1497–1556), becomes Sultan of Turkey. Under him Turkish expansion reaches deep into Eastern Europe.

Knighthood

1521 More is knighted by Henry VIII and becomes under-treasurer. He goes on diplomatic missions to Bruges and Calais. His daughter Margaret marries William Roper (c. 1495–1578), who will write a sympathetic biography of his father-in-law after his death, but it will not be published until Catholicism is briefly restored in England under Queen Mary. (It is still in print. See p. 179.)

Henry VIII writes a rebuttal to Luther's *The Babylonian Captivity of the Church*. Pope Leo X confers the title "Defender of the Faith" on Henry for his anti-Luther tract, *Assertio septem sacramentorum* (*Defense of the Seven Sacraments*), edited by More. Luther will respond with a furious tirade, *Against Henry, King of the English,* stung that Henry has labeled him a heretic without considering that there might be truth in his stand against the Church. A pile of books by Luther are burned in public, with Cardinal Wolsey present. Bishop John Fisher preaches against Reformation principles on this occasion.

On January 3 Luther is excommunicated by Pope Leo X. In April Luther makes his stand at the Diet of Worms and refuses to recant. He is banned from the Holy Roman Empire but is hurried into protective custody at Wartburg Castle by his protector, Frederick the Wise, an influential elector of the Holy Roman Emperor. There he begins his German translation of the Bible. He finishes the New Testament in eleven weeks (and the Old Testament by 1534). Luther's translation of the Bible into High German marks one of the great milestones in the development of that language. Luther will be called "the father of the German language."

Philip Melancthon writes *Loci communes,* the first systematic survey of Evangelical (as it was first called, or Lutheran) theology.

The word *evangelical* designates those who accept the doctrine of justification by faith and thus distinguish themselves from the Catholic Church. He apprises Luther of the Anabaptist currents, which are gathering strength. Luther is infuriated by their insistence on adult baptism and denial of infant baptism, since he holds that a child is not baptized because of its faith (being too young for belief) but because of God's promise.

Ignatius of Loyola is wounded in battle defending Pamplona against the French. He undergoes conversion while convalescing. He then begins writing his *Spiritual Exercises,* in which he sets forth "Rules for Thinking with the Church."

Sultan Suleiman I defeats Belgrade and invades Hungary.

1522 More delivers a public oration to welcome Emperor Charles V. Now secretary to Henry VIII, More advises the king against warfare with France, but Henry is undeterred.

After the death of Leo X in December 1521, Adrian VI (1459–1523), a Dutchman, becomes pope. In his brief papacy, he favors reform but is generally ignored. Luther's German New Testament is published in September.

Speaker of the House of Commons

1523 More is elected Speaker of the House of Commons. He advocates the notion of free speech. More writes his first work of apologetics on Henry's behalf when he composes *Responsio ad Lutherum (Response to Luther)*, in which he insists on the divine origin of the papacy. Against the subjectivity of Luther's famous self-defense, "Here I stand," More invokes both the tradition and the historical identity of the Church. The vitriolic urgency of this tract is motivated by the heretical stance of young William Roper

(c. 1495–1578), husband of More's daughter Margaret, who is enthusiastic about Luther for a brief period of time.

Pope Adrian VI dies, and Giulio de'Medici becomes Pope Clement VII (1478–1534). A weak and indecisive man, he is unable to deal successfully with the reform movement provoked by Luther, the conflict between Francis I and Charles I for control of Europe, or the annulment proceedings begun by Henry VIII.

1524 More is appointed high steward at Oxford University. Through this office he is able to provide a readership for Juan Luis Vives (1492–1540), a Spanish humanist with whom he is friendly. Vives had recently published, with the help of Erasmus, a commentary on Saint Augustine's *City of God* and dedicated this work to Henry VIII. While at Oxford, Vives becomes secretary and advisor to Henry's wife, Queen Catherine of Aragon. Later he will displease Henry by opposing his divorce.

More invests in real estate with his augmented earnings and buys the land in Chelsea on which his great house is constructed. In concert with Cardinal Wolsey, he helps the king obtain funds for the war against France.

Erasmus of Rotterdam writes against Luther in *Concerning Free Will,* in which he objects to Luther's narrow understanding of Paul's justification by faith alone. Erasmus is far more optimistic than Luther about the capacity of the human spirit to respond to God's initiative.

The Peasants' Revolt begins in southern Germany under the leadership of Thomas Münzer, Florian Geyer, and Michael Gaismair. This war is connected to the Reformation in that the Gospel is invoked to justify the overthrow of existing authority. Luther takes the role of mediator between the peasants and the princes, but only at the outset.

Zwingli abolishes the Catholic Mass in Zurich.

The French are driven out of Italy.

1525 More acts as principal negotiator in a truce with France after King Francis I is defeated by the Germans and Spanish and is taken prisoner. More is made chancellor of the Duchy of Lancaster, where he adjudicates criminal cases. He also becomes high steward of Cambridge University. He keeps a vigilant eye on Hanseatic merchants who are importing books by Luther into England and investigates the dissemination of anti-Catholic tracts in the universities. The tides of heresy are swiftly rising in England.

Tyndale's English New Testament is published in Worms. More objects to this translation because of Tyndale's choice of vocabulary, e.g., substituting the word *congregation* for *church,* thereby implying a reformist theology.

Luther marries Katherine von Bora (1499–1552), a former nun. They produce six children, four of whom survive. Because Luther is a former monk and an ordained priest, his wedded state is a bold challenge to the ancient ideals of asceticism and virginity exalted by the Church. More considers that Luther "liveth under the name of wedlock in open, incestuous lechery without care or shame," doubtless because under Church law, the union of a monk and a nun was deemed incest.

Luther writes tracts against religious enthusiasts, rebellious peasants, and, particularly, against Erasmus. *Concerning the Bondage of the Will* is Luther's treatise expounding his belief that by itself the human will is completely helpless, "captive, subject, and slave either of the will of God or the will of Satan." Against Luther's insistence on predestination, Erasmus argues for man's free assent to God's saving grace. The break with Erasmus becomes bitter, total, and permanent.

The Peasants' Revolt is suppressed, with Luther's acquiescence. Münzer is executed.

Giovanni Pierluigi da Palestrina, Italian composer to the papal court (d. 1594), is born. His polyphonic style, which he develops as a corrective for using profane melodies as settings for liturgical texts, becomes the model, along with Gregorian chant, for liturgical music.

1526 More writes *Letter to Bugenhagen* against John Bugenhagen, one of Luther's closest associates. Though it is not published because Henry VIII's own letter to Luther takes precedence over it, it is a clear expression of More's outrage over the heretical teachings of Luther on the sacraments, celibacy, papal authority, and the Mass, and of his instigation of social disturbance (Peasants' Revolt). More encourages Erasmus to denounce Luther.

Dürer produces his last painting, *Four Apostles*. Dürer holds Luther in highest esteem and affection because he has rebuked the papacy and, in his opinion, rendered Christian doctrine in its purest and clearest form.

Hans Holbein the Younger (1497–1543), cosmopolitan German Renaissance painter, visits England for the first time, introduced to More by a letter from Erasmus. He becomes court painter to Henry VIII.

1527 Henry VIII's affair with Anne Boleyn begins and so does his exploration of the possibility of having his eighteen-year marriage to Catherine annulled. More and Cardinal Wolsey are both aware of Henry's intentions when they travel to France to ratify the peace agreement with Francis I. France and England are now in alliance against Emperor Charles V. Juan Luis Vives, More's friend and protégé, rallies to the side of Catherine.

Rome is sacked by a rogue army of Charles V composed of German and Spanish soldiers. Looting, burning, raping, and killing, for eight days they vent their hatred of all things Catholic. Four thousand people die, and the corpse of Pope Julius II is dug up and dragged through the streets. Pope Clement VII is imprisoned in Castel Sant' Angelo from May 6 to December 7.

The first Protestant university is founded in Marburg, Germany, and Lutheran reforms spread to Sweden.

Hans Holbein the Younger paints *Thomas More and His Family* at Chelsea and, later, a portrait of More as lord chancellor.

1528 Henry VIII addresses the English public to explain his motives for seeking a divorce from Catherine of Aragon.

Cuthbert Turnstall, archbishop of London and friend of More, urges More to defend the Church against Luther and Tyndale, who are gaining in popular appeal in England. More begins writing *Dialogue Concerning Heresies*. At this time Henry VIII reads an anonymous work titled *A Supplication for the Beggars* that alleges that the Church has usurped powers that rightly belong to the English crown. Tyndale soon asserts the same thesis in his *Obedience of a Christian Man*. Henry is inspired to consider the confiscation of Church property and to think of his primacy as king as superior to that of papal primacy. More struggles to support Henry's authority at the same time as he warns that the current heresies undermine all legitimate authority and could well lead to anarchy in the kingdom.

The Reformation begins in Scotland, introduced by merchants who bring Lutheran teachings with them from the Continent.

Lord Chancellor

1529 England joins Francis I and Charles V in the Treaty of Cambrai, which marks a peace agreement between France and Italy. More and Cuthbert Turnstall travel to Cambrai as ambassadors for Henry VIII to secure England's role as a European power and to ensure peace.

A special court, established to consider the validity of Henry's marriage to Catherine, meets at Blackfriars. Bishop John Fisher is Catherine's counsel, supported by More, who, on the mission to Cambrai, is absent from the session. Cardinal Wolsey is unsuccessful in getting a resolution favorable to the king, and Henry rids himself of the cardinal. Instead of appointing another clergyman, Henry names More, a layman, as lord chancellor. More is invested with the Great Seal of England. Wolsey dies before Henry can have him tried for treason. More takes on the task of trying to guide the conscience of the king.

Luther and Zwingli meet at Marburg to dispute the theology of the Eucharist. Luther considers Zwingli's teaching blasphemous because he rejects belief in the Real Presence of Christ in the elements of bread and wine.

Turkish forces attack Austria and lay siege to Vienna.

King Francis I founds the Collège de France.

Henry's "Great Matter"

1530 Acting as "the keeper of the king's conscience," More avoids signing the king's letter to Pope Clement VII in which Henry claims that a number of authorities have decided the marriage to Catherine is invalid. More issues a proclamation against heretics and compiles a list of heretical texts, ownership or sale of which is punished by a prison term. He extends help and encouragement to the besieged Catholic clergy.

In the summer, charges of violating the medieval statute *Praemunire* (which made it treasonous to refer appeals to Rome from Church courts in England) are filed on behalf of the king against fourteen clerics, including Bishop John Fisher. In the fall, Edward Fox and Thomas Cranmer hand to the king their research on the marriage questions, *Collectanea satis copiosa*. In it they suggest that the king vest all episcopal powers in the monarchy, thus giving himself the power to decide the validity of his marriage. Cranmer will become archbishop of Canterbury and lead Henry through his successive marriages and divorces.

The Augsburg Confession, a definitive formulation of Lutheran doctrine, is prepared by Melancthon and signed by the Protestant princes. Together they form the Schmalkaldic League of German princedoms and cities against Emperor Charles V and his Catholic allies. Western Christianity is henceforth divided. Charles V is crowned Holy Roman Emperor and king of Italy by Pope Clement VII.

Francis I marries Eleanor of Portugal, the sister of Charles V.

1531 Henry VIII invents a new title for himself: supreme head of the Church of England. The bishops agree to recognize Henry under this title with the careful proviso, "so far as the law of

Christ allows." More is so worried about the implications of this step that he wants to resign as lord chancellor. At the same time that More is vigorously pursuing heretics and even signing their death warrants, Henry is listening to Protestant arguments against the hierarchical structure of the Roman church.

During this period More writes *The Confutation of Tyndale's Answer*. In this text he addresses the conflict between Roman Catholicism and Protestant Lutheranism: inner prayer, faith alone, personal redemption through Christ, as opposed to the Catholic tradition of ritual worship, good works, and the sacramental system predicated on an ordained clergy. More insists on the "one, holy, Catholic Church" as the only true embodiment of Christ's mystical body on earth. More emphasizes the holiness of the Church in spite of the wickedness of some of its members and even hierarchy.

Henry VIII offers a pardon of sorts to the clerics accused of complicity with Cardinal Wolsey to work against the king's divorce from Catherine, but the pardon brings with it a fine of one hundred thousand pounds.

Zwingli is killed in the Battle of Kappel during the war in Switzerland between Protestant Zurich and the Catholic cantons.

Titian, Italian painter of the Venetian school, paints *The Magdalen*.

Halley's Comet arouses a wave of fear about the approaching end of the world.

Sir Thomas More Resigns as Lord Chancellor

1532 In late winter, Thomas Cromwell (1458–1540), master secretary to Henry VIII, accuses the clerical Canterbury Convocation of infringing upon the authority of the king and English law.
The bishops defend themselves, but Henry responds with
demands that all ecclesiastical legislation and statutes are to be at
the mercy of the king's authority. On May 16, a number of bishops and abbots sign their endorsement ("Submission of the
Clergy") with Cromwell as witness.

On the afternoon of May 16, More hands over the Great Seal of
England into Henry's hands as he resigns from the office of lord
chancellor.

The name of Thomas Cranmer is submitted to Rome as candi-
date to be named archbishop of Canterbury following the death
of Archbishop Warham.

Anne Boleyn travels with Henry VIII to France on a state visit
in the fall. By December she is pregnant.

John Calvin takes up studies in Latin, Greek, and Hebrew at
the new Collège de France.

François Rabelais (1494–1553), first a Franciscan, then a Benedictine, father of two children, finally a secular priest, publishes
the first book of his five-part satire, *The Histories of Gargantua
and Pantagruel*. Rabelais ridicules the clergy and savagely attacks
the abuses of the hierarchy, while affirming the fundamental
goodness of human nature and the power of common sense. His
protector is Marguerite of Angouleme, queen of Navarre (1492–
1549), sister of King Francis I. She is associated with the *Hep-*

tameron, a collection of bawdy tales in which the villains are frequently monks guilty of gluttony, greed, and rape.

The Religious Peace of Nuremberg grants Protestants free exercise of religion.

Niccolo Machiavelli's (1469–1527) *The Prince* is published. It is a study of politics as divorced from ethics, premised on the view that the end justifies any means.

1533 On January 25, Henry VIII marries Anne Boleyn without papal authorization. Under the new lord chancellor, Thomas Audley, and with the instigation of Cromwell, Parliament passes the Act in Restraint of Appeals, legislation which makes Catherine's appeals to Rome illegal.

Thomas Cranmer is consecrated archbishop and begins his annulment request on behalf of Henry in the spring. Bishop John Fisher opposes Cranmer, but on May 23, Henry's marriage to Catherine is declared invalid by Parliament, and his marriage to Anne Boleyn is recognized as legal. Henry's "Great Matter" is considered settled. Anne is crowned queen of England on June 1 in Westminster Abbey. More is absent from all the sumptuous royal festivities.

Excommunication of Henry VIII

In July Pope Clement VII declares the marriage of Henry and Anne to be invalid and threatens Henry with excommunication if he repudiates Catherine. Elizabeth I, daughter of Henry VIII and Anne Boleyn and future queen of England, is born (d. 1603).

More continues to write in defense of the Church and papal authority. He opposes a theory of the supremacy of the king over body and soul of his subjects propounded by Christopher Saint Germain, a brilliant English legal thinker, as well as Saint Germain's virulent anticlerical propaganda. To this end he produces *The Apology of Sir Thomas More, Knight*. Saint Germain is swift to respond with his dialogue, *Salem and Bizance*. More rebuts Saint Germain with *The Debellation of Salem and Bizance*. Against Protestant attacks on the true presence of Christ in the Eucharist, More writes *The Answer to a Poisoned Book*, a rebuttal to the anonymous heretical tract *The Supper of the Lord*.

On November 1, All Saints' Day, John Calvin hears Nicolas Cop, rector of the University of Paris, deliver a pro-Protestant address containing passages from Erasmus and Luther. Calvin determines to devote himself to the Protestant reform. He becomes its most formidable proponent after Luther himself.

1534 More is questioned by Cromwell regarding his association with Elizabeth Barton, the "Holy Maid of Kent" (c. 1506–34), a visionary Benedictine nun who prophesied disaster for Henry VIII if he persisted in his determination to divorce Catherine. She has many supporters, and the king is nervous about her influence. Convicted of treason, Barton is executed at Tyburn. Anyone who had communicated with her now faces the threat of the charge of treason. More is cleared of traitorous involvement with Barton, though Bishop John Fisher is deemed to be in collusion with her. More is, however, examined regarding his attitude toward Henry's marriage to Anne. He is offered a reinstatement to honor and wealth in exchange for his approval of the divorce. More refuses.

On March 23 Pope Clement VII formally pronounces the marriage of Henry VIII to Catherine of Aragon valid. Henry is ordered to give up Anne or be excommunicated. On March 30 Parliament passes the Succession Act, a statute that declares children born to Henry and Anne legitimate successors to the throne of England, repudiates the validity of the marriage to Catherine, and demands acknowledgment of Henry's absolute sovereignty. Anyone refusing to take the oath will be judged guilty of treason, for which the penalty is the combination of disemboweling, dismemberment, and beheading.

Sir Thomas More Is Charged with Treason

On April 12 More is summoned to appear at Lambeth Palace. On taking leave of his house the next day at Chelsea and fully aware of the imminent danger he is in, More remarks to his son-in-law, William Roper: "Son Roper, I thank our Lord the field is won."[1] It is now ultimately clear to More that the dictates of his conscience are against swearing the oath, though he will not judge anyone else who does swear allegiance to Henry as pope of the English church. Bishop John Fisher is also put to the test, refuses, and is arrested.

On April 17 More is imprisoned, along with his friend Fisher, in the Tower of London. Over the last fourteen months of his life, he writes *Treatise on the Passion, A Dialogue of Comfort Against Tribulation,* and *The Sadness of Christ.* His themes are Christ the Physician, who gives comfort and strength in tribulation; trust in the will of God, who seeks only what is good for us; and confidence in the promise of eternal life in the company of the saints. Meditating on the suffering and crucifixion of Christ gives More courage to face the prospect of his own impending torture and death.

Pope Clement VII dies and is succeeded by Pope Paul III.

1. Quoted in Peter Ackroyd, *The Life of Thomas More* (New York: Doubleday, 1998), p. 360.

Luther completes his translation of the entire Bible into German.

Anabaptists under John Leiden form the Kingdom of Zion at Münster. The Jesuit order is founded by Ignatius of Loyola. In addition to poverty, chastity, and obedience to their order, Jesuits take a unique fourth vow of direct obedience to the holy pontiff.

1535 In the spring Thomas Cromwell offers More another opportunity to reconsider his position. More again refuses.

On June 12 More is visited in his cell by Sir Richard Rich (1496–1567), a prominent lawyer working for Cromwell. On the basis of their conversation, as reported by Rich to Cromwell, More is officially charged with treason. More accuses Rich of perjury for misconstruing his words. All of More's writing materials are removed from his cell by Rich.

In May the imprisoned Bishop John Fisher is elevated to cardinal by Pope Paul III. This honor given by Rome to one declared a traitor infuriates King Henry. He is stripped of his post as bishop of Rochester, and on June 22, Fisher is beheaded before his cardinal's hat arrives in England. Fisher's naked body is displayed to the public and his head is piked on London Bridge, where its ruddy glow attracts the devotion of the crowds. Henry orders it to be pitched into the Thames.

Trial and Death

On July 1 More is tried for treason, found guilty, and sentenced to be hanged, cut down while still living, his bowels pulled from his body and burned in his sight, his genitals cut off, his head as well, and his body to be quartered and put on view to the public.

Just before the appointed time of his death, the sentence is commuted to beheading alone, as Henry fears the possible riot of commoners who love and respect More for his just and fair dealings with them.

On July 6 More is led to the scaffold at Tower Hill. He begs the assembled crowd to pray for him and to pray for the king as well, declaring that he dies "the king's good servant but God's first." Kneeling down, More prays the *Miserere* (Psalm 51, "Have mercy on me, O God"), kisses his executioner in an act of forgiveness, and then lays himself down for a single blow of the ax.

The body of More is buried in the chapel of Saint Peter in Chains, where he heard Mass while a prisoner in the Tower of London. His family is present. His head is parboiled before it is impaled on London Bridge. Ultimately More's beloved daughter Margaret claims his head, and it is buried with her when she dies in 1544.

In conversation with his daughter Margaret in August of 1534, which is recorded as a letter in dialogue form under a pseudonym, More confesses both his fear of death and his confidence in God as he contemplates the death he knows awaits him:

> "Mistrust him, Meg, I will not, though I feel myself faint, yea, and though I should feel my fear even at point to overthrow me too, yet shall I remember how Saint Peter, with a blast of wind, began to sink for his faint faith, and shall do as he did, 'call upon Christ and pray him to help.' And then I trust he shall set his holy hand unto me, and in the stormy seas, hold me up from drowning. . . . yet after shall I trust that his goodness will cast upon me his tender piteous eye, as he did upon Saint Peter, and make me stand up again and confess the truth of my conscience afresh, and abide the shame and harm here of mine own fault.

"But in good faith, Meg, I trust that his tender pity shall keep my poor soul safe and make me commend his mercy. And therefore mine own good daughter, never trouble thy mind for anything that ever shall hap me in this world. Nothing can come but that that God will.—trouble not yourself: as I shall full heartily pray for us all, that we may meet together once in heaven, where we shall make merry forever, and never have trouble after."[2]

After More's Death

1536 Catherine of Aragon dies. Queen Anne Boleyn is sent to the Tower of London and executed for treason on the charge of adultery. Thomas Cromwell is made vicar-general for church affairs and Lord Privy Seal. He devises a plan to pillage Church properties in England for the king's coffer, which is partially successful when implemented. Some 376 monasteries are dissolved by Henry's decree.

An act of Parliament declares all papal authority void in England.

Henry VIII marries Jane Seymour. Since Catherine of Aragon and Anne Boleyn are both dead, this marriage is valid, but Henry resists reconciliation with Rome. Cardinal Reginald Pole (1500–58), the last Catholic archbishop of Canterbury, who escapes imprisonment for treason because he is out of the country, writes *Pro ecclesiasticae unitatis defensione*. This attack on Henry's supremacy seals the breach with Rome.

Desiderius Erasmus dies.

Hans Holbein the Younger paints his portrait of Henry VIII.

2. Quoted in Alvaro de Silva, ed., *The Last Letters of Thomas More* (Grand Rapids, Mich.: William B. Eerdmans Publishing Co., 2000), pp. 88–89.

William Tyndale, English reformer, is burned as a heretic at Vilvorde in Brabrant.

John Calvin writes *Institutes of the Christian Religion,* the central work of Reformation theology.

The Reformation is introduced into Denmark by King Christian III.

Pope Paul III calls a council to be held in Mantua at Pentecost of 1537.

1557 The English writings of More, first collected by William Rastell, are published.

Canonization

1935 More and Bishop John Fisher are canonized by Pope Pius XI in Saint Peter's Basilica. Praising him as an example of Christian fortitude, the pope describes More as a "star of sanctity that traced a luminous path across that dark period of history."

Saint Thomas More and Saint John Fisher, martyrs for the faith, are honored together in the liturgy of the Church with feast days on June 22. More is designated the patron saint of lawyers, statesmen, and politicians.

The Sadness *of* Christ

The Sadness, the Weariness, the Fear, and the Prayer of Christ Before He Was Taken Prisoner.
Matthew 26, Mark 14, Luke 22, John 18.

"When Jesus had said these things, they recited the hymn and went out to the Mount of Olives."[1]

Though He had spoken at length about holiness during the supper with His apostles, nevertheless He finished His discourses with a hymn when He was ready to leave. Alas, how different we are from Christ, though we call ourselves Christians: our conversation during meals is not only meaningless and inconsequential (and even for such negligence Christ warned us that we will have to render an accounting)[2] but often our table talk is also vicious, and then finally, when we are bloated with food and drink, we leave the table without giving thanks to God for the banquets He has bestowed upon us, with never a thought for the gratitude we owe Him.

[Paul of Saint Mary, Archbishop of] Burgos,[3] a learned, holy man, and an outstanding investigator of sacred subjects, gives some convincing arguments to show that the hymn which Christ at that time recited with His apostles consisted of those six psalms which, taken together, are called by the Jews "The Great Alleluia"—namely Psalm 112 and the five following it. For from very ancient times the Jews have followed the custom of reciting these six psalms, under the name "Great Alleluia," as a prayer of thanksgiving at the Passover and certain other principal feasts, and even now they still go through the same hymn on the same feastdays.

1. Matt. 26 : 30. Here . . . More quotes from the *Monotessaron,* a gospel harmony by John Gerson (1363–1429), a French churchman and spiritual writer.
2. Matt. 12 : 36.
3. Usually called Burgensis. More refers to his *Additiones* to the *Postillae* of Nicholas de Lyra, both of which were included in the glossed Bibles of More's period.

But as for us, though we used to say different hymns of thanks-giving and benediction at meals according to the different times of the year, each hymn suited to its season, we have now permit-ted almost all of them to fall out of use, and we rest content with saying two or three words, no matter what, before going away, and even those few words we mumble merely for form's sake, muttering through our yawns.

"They went out to the Mount of Olives," not to bed. The prophet says, "I arose in the middle of the night to pay homage to you,"[4] but Christ did not even lie down in bed. But as for us, I wish we could truly apply to ourselves even this text: "I thought of you as I lay in my bed."[5]

Moreover, it was not yet summer when Christ left the supper and went over to the mount. For it was not that much beyond the vernal equinox, and that the night was cold is clearly shown by the fact that the servants were warming themselves around char-coal fires in the courtyard of the high priest.[6] But this was not the first time that Christ had done this, as the evangelist clearly testi-fies when he says "as He customarily did."[7]

He went up a mountain to pray, teaching us by this sign that, when we prepare ourselves to pray, we must lift up our minds from the bustling confusion of human concerns to the contempla-tion of heavenly things.

Mount Olivet itself also has a mysterious significance, planted as it was with olive trees. For the olive branch was generally used as a symbol of peace, which Christ came to establish between God and man after their long alienation. Moreover, the oil which is produced from the olive represents the anointing by the Spirit, for Christ came and then returned to His Father in order to send the Holy Spirit upon the disciples so that His anointing might

4. Ps. 118 : 62 (Authorized Version, hereafter *AV,* 119 : 62).
5. Ps. 62 : 7 (*AV,* 63 : 6).   6. John 18 : 18.   7. Luke 22 : 39.

then teach them what they would not have been able to bear had it been told them only a short time before.[8]

"Across the stream Cedron to the outlying estate named Gethsemane."[9]

The stream Cedron lies between the city of Jerusalem and the Mount of Olives, and the word "Cedron" in Hebrew means "sadness." The name "Gethsemane" in Hebrew means "most fertile valley" or "valley of olives." And so there is no reason for us to attribute it merely to chance that the evangelists recorded these place-names so carefully. For if that were the case, once they had reported that He went to the Mount of Olives, they would have considered that they had said quite enough, if it were not that God had veiled under these place-names some mysterious meanings which attentive men, with the help of the Holy Spirit, would try to uncover because the names were mentioned. And so, since not a single syllable can be thought inconsequential in a composition which was dictated by the Holy Spirit as the apostles wrote it, and since not a sparrow falls to the earth without God's direction,[10] I cannot think either that the evangelists mentioned those names accidentally or that the Jews assigned them to the places (whatever they themselves intended when they named them) without a secret plan (though unknown to the Jews themselves) of the Holy Spirit, who concealed in these names a store of sacred mysteries to be ferreted out sometime later.

But since "Cedron" means "sadness," and also "blackness," and since this same word is the name not only of the stream mentioned by the evangelists but also (as is sufficiently established) of the valley through which the stream flows and which separates the city from the estate Gethsemane, these names (if their effect is

8. John 16 : 12–13.   9. John 18 : 1, Matt. 26 : 36, and Mark 14 : 32.
10. Matt. 10 : 29.

not blocked by our drowsiness) remind us that while we are exiled from the Lord (as the apostle says)[11] we must surely cross over, before we come to the fruitful Mount of Olives and the pleasant estate of Gethsemane, an estate which is not gloomy and ugly to look at but most fertile in every sort of joy, we must (I say) cross over the valley and stream of Cedron, a valley of tears and a stream of sadness whose waves can wash away the blackness and filth of our sins. But if we get so weary of pain and grief that we perversely attempt to change this world, this place of labor and penance, into a joyful haven of rest, if we seek heaven on earth, we cut ourselves off forever from true happiness, and will drown ourselves in penance when it is too late to do any good and in unbearable, unending tribulations as well.

This, then, is the very salutary lesson contained in these place-names, so fittingly chosen are they. But as the words of holy scripture are not tied to one sense only but rather are teeming with various mysterious meanings, these place-names harmonize with the immediate context of Christ's passion very well, as if for that reason alone God's eternal providence had seen to it that these places should long beforehand have been designated by such names as would prove to be, some centuries later, preordained tokens of His passion, as the comparison of His deeds with the names would show. For, since "Cedron" means "blackened," does it not seem to recall that prediction of the prophet that Christ would work out His glory by means of inglorious torment, that He would be disfigured by dark bruises, gore, spittle, and dirt?— "There is nothing beautiful or handsome about his face."[12]

Then, too, the meaning of the stream He crossed—"sad"— was far from irrelevant as He Himself testified when He said, "My soul is sad unto death."[13]

11. 2 Cor. 5 : 6.   12. Isa. 53 : 2.   13. Matt. 26 : 38, Mark 14 : 34.

"And His disciples also followed Him."[14]

That is, the eleven who had remained followed Him. As for the twelfth, the devil entered into him after the morsel and made off with him,[15] so that he did not follow the master as a disciple but pursued Him as a traitor, and bore out only too well what Christ said: "He who is not with me is against me."[16] Against Christ he certainly was, since, at that very moment, he was preparing to spring his trap for Him, while the other disciples were following after Him to pray. Let us follow after Christ and pray to the Father together with Him. Let us not emulate Judas by departing from Christ, after partaking of His favors and dining excellently with Him, lest we should bear out that prophecy: "If you saw a thief you ran away with him."[17]

"Judas, who betrayed Him, also knew the place, because Jesus frequently went there with His disciples."[18]

Once again the evangelists take advantage of mentioning the betrayer to emphasize for us, and to recommend to us by such emphasis, Christ's holy custom of going together with His disciples to that place in order to pray. For if He had gone there only on some nights and not frequently, the betrayer would not have been so completely convinced he would find our Lord there that he could afford to bring the servants of the high priest and a Roman cohort there as if everything had been definitely arranged, for if they had found that it was not arranged, they would have thought he was playing a practical joke on them and would not have let him get away with it unscathed. Now where are those people who think they are men of stature, who are proud of themselves as if they had done something fine, if sometimes, on the vigil of a special feast, they either continue their

14. Luke 22 : 39.   15. John 13 : 27–30.   16. Matt. 12 : 30, Luke 11 : 23.
17. Ps. 49 : 18 (*AV,* 50 : 18).   18. John 18 : 2.

prayers a little longer into the night or get up earlier for their morning prayers? Our Savior Christ had the habit of spending whole nights without sleep in order to pray.

Where are those who called Him a glutton for food and wine because He did not refuse to go to the banquets of the publicans and did not think it beneath Him to attend the celebrations of sinful men?[19] Where are those who thought that, by comparison with the strict regimen of the pharisees, His morals were hardly better than those of the common rabble? But while these gloomy hypocrites were praying on the corners of the main thoroughfares so that they might be seen by men, He was eating lunch with sinners, calmly and kindly helping them to reform their lives. On the other hand, He used to spend the night praying under the open sky[20] while the hypocritical pharisee was snoring away in his soft bed. How I wish that those of us who are prevented by our own laziness from imitating the illustrious example of our Savior might at least be willing to call to mind His all-night vigils when we turn over on the other side in our beds, half asleep, and that we might then, during the short time before we fall asleep again, offer Him thanks, condemn our slothfulness, and pray for an increase of grace. Surely if we set out to make a habit of doing even the least little bit of good, I feel certain that God will soon set us forward a great way on the path of virtue.[21]

"And He said, 'Sit down here while I go over there to pray.' And He took Peter and the two sons of Zebedee with Him. He began to feel sorrow and grief and fear and weariness. Then He said to them, 'My soul is sad unto death. Stay here and keep watch with me.'"[22]

Commanding the other eight to stop somewhat lower down, He went further on, taking with Him Peter, John, and his

---

19. Cf. Matt. 11 : 19.   20. Luke 6 : 12.   21. Cf. Matt. 13 : 23.
22. Matt. 26 : 36–38, Mark 14 : 32–34.

brother James, the three whom He had always singled out from the rest of the apostles by a certain special privilege of intimacy. Now even if He had done this for no other reason than that He wanted to, no one ought to have been envious because of His generosity.[23] But still there were certain reasons for this which He might well have had in mind. For Peter was outstanding for his zealous faith and John for his virginity, and his brother James was to be the very first of all to suffer martyrdom in the name of Christ. Furthermore, these were the three to whom He had formerly granted the secret knowledge and open sight of His glorified body. It was only right, then, that those same three whom He had admitted to such an extraordinary vision and whom He had invigorated with a momentary flash of the eternal brilliance so that they ought to have been stronger than the others, should have assigned to them the role of His nearest supporters in the preliminary agony of His passion. But when He had gone on a little way, He suddenly felt such a sharp and bitter attack of sadness, grief, fear, and weariness that He immediately uttered, even in their presence, those anguished words which gave expression to His overburdened feelings: "My soul is sad unto death."[24]

For a huge mass of troubles took possession of the tender and gentle body of our most holy Savior. He knew that His ordeal was now imminent and just about to overtake Him: the treacherous betrayer, the bitter enemies, binding ropes, false accusations, slanders, blows, thorns, nails, the cross, and horrible tortures stretched out over many hours. Over and above these, He was tormented by the thought of His disciples' terror, the loss of the Jews, even the destruction of the very man who so disloyally betrayed Him, and finally the ineffable grief of His beloved mother. The gathered storm of all these evils rushed into His

23. Matt. 20 : 15.   24. Matt. 26 : 38.

most gentle heart and flooded it like the ocean sweeping through broken dikes.

Perhaps someone may wonder how it could be that our Savior Christ could feel sadness, sorrow, and grief, since He was truly God, equal to His all-powerful Father. Certainly He could not have felt them if He had been God (as He was) in such a way as not to be man also. But as a matter of fact, since He was no less really a man than He was really God, I see no reason for us to be surprised that, insofar as He was man, He had the ordinary feelings of mankind (though certainly no blameworthy ones)—no more than we would be surprised that, insofar as He was God, He performed stupendous miracles. For if we are surprised that Christ felt fear, weariness, and grief, simply on the grounds that He was God, why should we not also be surprised that He experienced hunger, thirst, and sleep, seeing that He was none the less divine for doing these things? But here, perhaps, you may object, "I am no longer surprised at His capacity for these emotions, but I cannot help being surprised at His desire to experience them. For He taught His disciples not to be afraid of those who can kill the body only and can do nothing beyond that;[25] and how can it be fitting that He Himself should now be very much afraid of those same persons, especially since even His body could suffer nothing from them except what He Himself allowed?

"Furthermore, since we know His martyrs rushed to their deaths eagerly and joyfully, triumphing over tyrants and torturers, how can it not seem inappropriate that Christ Himself, the very prototype and leader of martyrs, the standard-bearer of them all, should be so terrified at the approach of pain, so shaken, so utterly downcast? Shouldn't He rather have been especially careful to set a good example in this matter, just as He had always let His deeds precede His precepts,[26] so that others might learn from His own example to undergo death eagerly for truth's sake,

25. Cf. Luke 12 : 4, Matt. 10 : 28.   26. Cf. Acts 1 : 1.

and so that those who afterwards would suffer death for the faith with fear and hesitation might not indulge their slackness by imagining that they are following Christ's precedent?—whereas, actually, their reluctance would both detract a great deal from the glory of their cause and discourage others who observe their sadness and fear." Those who bring up these objections and others of the same sort do not scrutinize carefully enough all the facets of this problem and do not pay enough attention to what Christ meant when He forbad His followers to fear death. For He hardly intended it to mean that they should never under any circumstances recoil from a violent death, but rather that they should not, out of fear, flee from a death which will not last, only to run, by denying the faith, into one which will be everlasting. For He wished His followers to be brave and prudent soldiers, not senseless and foolish. The brave man bears up under the blows which beset him; the senseless man simply does not feel them when they strike. Only a foolish man does not fear wounds, but a prudent man does not allow any fear of suffering to divert him from a holy way of life for that would be to refuse lesser pains at the expense of plunging himself into far more bitter ones.

When an afflicted part of the body is to be cut or cauterized, the doctor does not try to persuade the sick man not to feel any mental anguish at the thought of the pain the cutting or burning will cause, but rather encourages him to bear up under it. He admits it will be painful, but stresses that the pain will be outweighed by the pleasure of health and the avoidance of even more horrible pain. Indeed, though our Savior Christ commands us to suffer death (when it cannot be avoided) rather than fall away from Him through a fear of death (and we do fall away from Him when we publicly deny our faith in Him), still He is so far from requiring us to do violence to our nature by not fearing death at all that He even leaves us free to flee from punishment (whenever this can be done without injury to His cause).

"If you are persecuted in one city," He says, "flee to another."[27] This permission, this cautious advice of a prudent master, was followed by almost all the apostles and by almost all the illustrious martyrs in the many succeeding centuries: there is hardly one of them who did not use it at some time or other to save his life and extend it, with great profit to himself and others, until such a time as the hidden providence of God foresaw was more fitting.

On the other hand, some brave champions have taken the initiative by publicly professing their Christianity, though no one was trying to discover it, and by freely exposing themselves to death, though no one was demanding it. Thus God chose, according to His pleasure, to increase His glory sometimes by concealing the riches of the faith, so that those who set clever traps for His believers might be duped, sometimes by displaying them, so that those who cruelly persecuted His followers might be incensed by seeing all their hopes frustrated and finding, much to their outrage, that all their ferocity could not overcome martyrs who met death willingly. But God in His mercy does not command us to climb this steep and lofty peak of bravery, and hence it is not safe for just anyone to go rushing on heedlessly to the point where he cannot retrace his steps gradually but may be in danger of falling head over heels into the abyss if he cannot make it to the summit. As for those whom God calls to do this, let them choose their goal and pursue it successfully and they will reign in triumph.[28] He keeps hidden the times, the moments,[29] the causes of all things, and when the time is right He brings forth all things from the secret treasure-chest of His wisdom, which penetrates all things irresistibly and disposes all things sweetly.[30]

And so, if anyone is brought to the point where he must either suffer torment or deny God, he need not doubt that it was God's

27. Matt. 10 : 23.   28. Cf. Ps. 44 : 5 (*AV,* 45 : 4).   29. Cf. Acts 1 : 7.
30. Cf. Sap. 8 : 1.

will for him to be brought to this crisis. Therefore, he has very
good reason to hope for the best. For God will either extricate
him from the struggle, or else He will aid him in the fight and
make him conquer so that He may crown him with the con-
queror's wreath. "For God is trustworthy," the apostle says. "He
does not allow you to be tempted beyond what you can stand, but
with the temptation He also gives a way out so that you may be
able to bear it."[31] Therefore, when things have come to the point
of a hand-to-hand combat with the prince of this world, the
devil,[32] and his cruel underlings, and there is no way left to withdraw without disgracing the cause, then I would think that a man
ought to cast away fear and I would direct him to be completely
calm, confident, and hopeful. "For," says the scripture, "whoever
lacks confidence on the day of tribulation, his courage will be lessened."[33]

But before the actual engagement, fear is not reprehensible, as
long as reason does not cease to struggle against fear—a struggle
which is not criminal or sinful but rather an immense opportunity for merit. For do you imagine that, since those most holy
martyrs shed their blood for the faith, they had no fear at all of
death and torments? On this point I will not pause to draw up a
list; to me Paul may stand for a thousand others. Indeed, if
David was worth ten thousand soldiers in the war against the
Philistines,[34] then certainly Paul can also be considered worth ten
thousand soldiers in the battle for the faith against faithless persecutors. And so this bravest of champions, Paul, who was so far
advanced in hope and the love of Christ that he had no doubts
about his heavenly reward, who said, "I have fought the good
fight, I have finished the race, and now there remains for me a
crown of justice,"[35] which he longed for so ardently that he said,

---

31. 1 Cor. 10 : 13.   32. John 12 : 31, 14 : 30, 16 : 11.   33. Prov. 24 : 10.
34. See 1 Kings 18 : 7–8, 21 : 11, 29 : 5.   35. 2 Tim. 4 : 7–8.

"To me to live is Christ and to die is gain"[36] and "I long to be dissolved and to be with Christ,"[37] nevertheless this very same Paul not only managed skillfully to escape from the snares of the Jews by means of the tribune,[38] but also freed himself from prison by declaring that he was a Roman citizen,[39] and once again he eluded the cruelty of the Jews by appealing to Caesar,[40] and he escaped the hands of the impious King Aretas by being let down from the wall in a basket.[41]

But if anyone should contend that he was looking to the fruit that was to be planted afterwards through his efforts, and that throughout these events he was not frightened by any fear of death, certainly I will freely grant the first point, but I would not venture to assert the second. For that most brave heart of the apostle was not impervious to fear, as he himself clearly shows when he writes to the Corinthians, "For even when we came to Macedonia, our flesh had no rest, but suffered all manner of affliction, conflicts without, fears within."[42] And in another place he wrote to the same persons: "I was with you in weakness and fear and much trembling."[43] And once again: "For we do not wish you, brethren, to be ignorant of the affliction which came upon us in Asia, since we were burdened beyond measure, beyond our strength, so that we were weary even of life."[44] In these passages do you not hear from Paul's own mouth his fear, his trembling, his weariness more unbearable than death itself, so that his experience seems to call to mind that agony of Christ and to present, as it were, an image of it? Go ahead now and deny if you can that Christ's holy martyrs felt fear at the terrible prospect of death. But, on the other hand, no amount of terror, however great, could deter this same Paul from his program of advancing the faith, and no advice from the disciples could persuade him not

36. Phil. 1 : 21.   37. Phil. 1 : 23.   38. Acts 23 : 6–10, 12–30.
39. Acts 22 : 25–29.   40. Acts 25 : 10–12.
41. 2 Cor. 11 : 32–33. Cf. Acts 9 : 25.   42. 2 Cor. 7 : 5.   43. 1 Cor. 2 : 3.
44. 2 Cor. 1 : 8.

to go to Jerusalem (to which he felt he was called by the Spirit of God), even though the prophet Agabus had foretold that chains and certain dangers were awaiting him there.[45]

And so the fear of death and torments carries no stigma of guilt but rather is an affliction of the sort Christ came to suffer, not to escape. We should not immediately consider it cowardice for someone to feel fear and horror at the thought of torments, not even if he prudently avoids dangers (provided he does not compromise himself); but to flee because of a fear of torture and death when the circumstances make it necessary to fight, or to give up all hope of victory and surrender to the enemy, that, to be sure, is a capital crime according to the military code.[46] But otherwise, no matter how much the heart of the soldier is agitated and stricken by fear, if he still comes forward at the command of the general, goes on, fights, and defeats the enemy, he has no reason to fear that his former fear might lessen his reward in any way. As a matter of fact, he ought to receive even more praise because of it, since he had to overcome not only the enemy but also his own fear, which is often harder to conquer than the enemy himself.

As for our Savior Christ, what happened a little later showed how far He was from letting His sadness, fear, and weariness prevent Him from obeying His Father's command and keep Him from carrying out with courage all those things which He had formerly regarded with a wise and wholesome fear. For the time being, however, He had more than one reason why He should choose to suffer fear, sadness, weariness, and grief—"choose" I say, not "be forced," for who could have forced God?[47] Quite the contrary, it was by His own marvelous arrangement that His divinity moderated its influence on His humanity for such a time and in such a way that He was able to yield to the passions of our frail humanity and to suffer them with such terrible intensity.

45. Acts 21 : 10–13.   46. *Codex Iustinianus* 12, 45, 1.
47. Cf. Isa. 53 : 7 and John 10 : 17–18.

But, as I was saying, Christ, in His wonderful generosity, chose to do this for a number of reasons.

First of all, in order to do that for which He came into the world—that is, to bear witness to the truth.[48] And then, although He was truly man and also truly God, still there have been some who, seeing the truth of His human nature in His hunger, thirst, sleep, weariness, and suchlike, have falsely persuaded themselves that He was not true God—I do not mean the Jews and gentiles of His time, who rejected Him, but rather the people of a much later time who even professed His name and His faith, namely heretics like Arius and his followers, who denied that Christ was of one nature with the Father and thus embroiled the church in great strife for many years. But against such plagues as this Christ provided a very powerful antidote, the endless supply of His miracles.

But there also arose an equal danger on the other side, just as those who escaped Scylla had to cope with Charybdis. For there were some who fixed their gaze so intently on the glory of His signs and powers that they were stunned and dazed by that immense brightness and went so far wrong as to deny altogether that He was truly a man. These people, too, growing from their original founder into a sect, did not hesitate to rend the holy unity of the Catholic Church and to tear it apart with their disgraceful sedition. This insane belief of theirs, which is no less dangerous than it is false, seeks to undermine and subvert completely (so far as lies within their power) the mystery of mankind's redemption, since it strives to utterly cut off and dry up the spring (as it were) from which the stream of our salvation flowed forth, namely the death and passion of our Savior. And so, to cure this very deadly disease, the best and kindest of physicians chose to experience sadness, dread, weariness, and fear of tortures and thus to show by these very real signs of human frailty that He was really a man.

48. John 18:37.

Moreover, because He came into the world to earn joy for us by
His own sorrow, and since that future joy of ours was to be fulfilled in our souls as well as our bodies, so too He chose to experience not only the pain of torture in His body but also the most
bitter feelings of sadness, fear, and weariness in His mind, partly
in order to bind us to Him all the more by reason of His greater
sufferings for us, partly in order to admonish us how wrong it is
for us either to refuse to suffer grief for His sake (since He freely
bore so many and such immense griefs for us) or to tolerate grudg-
ingly the punishment due to our sins, since we see our holy Savior
Himself endured by His own free choice such numerous and
bitter kinds of torment, both bodily and mental—and that not
because He deserved them through any fault of His own, but
rather in order to do away with the wicked deeds which we alone
committed.[49]

Finally, since nothing was hidden from His eternal foreknowl-
edge, He foresaw that there would be people of various temperaments in the church (which is His own mystical body)—that His
members (I say) would differ considerably in their makeup.[50]
And although nature alone, without the help of grace, is quite
incapable of enduring martyrdom (since, as the apostle says, "No
one can say 'Jesus is Lord' except in the Spirit"[51]), nevertheless
God does not impart grace to men in such a way as to suspend for
the moment the functions and duties of nature, but instead He
either allows nature to accommodate itself to the grace which is
superadded to it, so that the good deed may be performed with all
the more ease, or else, if nature is disposed to resist, so that this
very resistance, overcome and put down by grace, may add to the
merit of the deed because it was difficult to do.

Therefore, since He foresaw that there would be many people
of such a delicate constitution that they would be convulsed with

49. Cf. Isa. 53 : 5, 8, 12, and 2 Cor. 5 : 19–21.
50. See Eph. 4 : 4–16 and John 14 : 2.   51. 1 Cor. 12 : 3.

terror at any danger of being tortured, He chose to enhearten
them by the example of His own sorrow, His own sadness, His
own weariness and unequalled fear, lest they should be so disheartened as they compare their own fearful state of mind with
the boldness of the bravest martyrs that they would yield freely
what they fear will be won from them by force. To such a person
as this, Christ wanted His own deed to speak out (as it were) with
His own living voice: "O faint of heart, take courage and do not
despair.[52] You are afraid, you are sad, you are stricken with weariness and dread of the torment with which you have been cruelly
threatened. Trust me. I conquered the world,[53] and yet I suffered
immeasurably more from fear, I was sadder, more afflicted with
weariness, more horrified at the prospect of such cruel suffering
drawing eagerly nearer and nearer. Let the brave man have his
high-spirited martyrs, let him rejoice in imitating a thousand of
them. But you, my timorous and feeble little sheep, be content to
have me alone as your shepherd,[54] follow my leadership; if you do
not trust yourself, place your trust in me. See, I am walking ahead
of you along this fearful road. Take hold of the border of my garment and you will feel going out from it a power which will stay
your heart's blood from issuing in vain fears,[55] and will make
your mind more cheerful, especially when you remember that you
are following closely in my footsteps (and I am to be trusted and
will not allow you to be tempted beyond what you can bear, but I
will give together with the temptation a way out that you may be
able to endure it)[56] and likewise when you remember that this
light and momentary burden of tribulation will prepare for you a
weight of glory which is beyond all measure.[57] For the sufferings
of this time are not worthy to be compared with the glory to come

52. Cf. Isa. 35 : 4 and Ecclus. 7 : 9.   53. John 16 : 33.
54. Cf. Matt. 26 : 31, John 10 : 14–16, Jer. 17 : 16, and Zech. 13 : 7.
55. Mark 5 : 25–34, Luke 8 : 43–48.   56. 1 Cor. 10 : 13.   57. 2 Cor. 4 : 17.

which will be revealed in you.[58] As you reflect on such things, take heart, and use the sign of my cross to drive away this dread, this sadness, fear, and weariness like vain specters of the darkness. Advance successfully[59] and press through all obstacles, firmly confident that I will champion your cause[60] until you are victorious and then in turn will reward you with the laurel crown of victory."[61]

And so among the other reasons why our Savior deigned to take upon Himself these feelings of human weakness, this one I have spoken of is not unworthy of consideration—I mean that, having made Himself weak for the sake of the weak, He might take care of other weak men by means of His own weakness.[62] He had their welfare so much at heart that this whole process of His agony seems designed for nothing more clearly than to lay down a fighting technique and a battle code for the faint-hearted soldier who needs to be swept along, as it were, into martyrdom.

For, in order to teach anyone assailed by a fear of imminent danger that he should both ask others to watch and pray, and still place his trust in God alone apart from the others, and likewise in order to signify that He would tread the bitter winepress of His cross alone without any companion,[63] He commanded those same three apostles whom He had chosen from the other eight and taken on with Him almost to the foot of the mount, to stop there and to bear up and watch with Him; but He Himself withdrew from them about a stone's throw.[64]

"And going on a little way He fell face down on the earth and prayed that, if it were possible, the hour might pass from Him. And He said: 'Abba, Father, to you all things are possible. Take this

58. Rom. 8 : 18.   59. Cf. Ps. 44 : 5 (AV, 45 : 4).
60. Cf. Isa. 19 : 20 and 63 : 1.
61. Cf. 2 Tim. 2 : 5, 1 Cor. 9 : 25, 1 Cor. 15 : 57, Heb. 11 : 6.   62. 1 Cor. 9 : 22.
63. Isa. 63 : 3.   64. Luke 22 : 41.

cup away from me, but yet not what I will, but what you will. My Father, if it is possible, let this cup pass away from me; yet not as I will, but as you will.'"[65]

First of all Christ the commander teaches by His own example that His soldier should take humility as his starting point, since it is the foundation (as it were) of all the virtues from which one may safely mount to higher levels. For, though His divinity is equal and identical to that of God the Father, nevertheless because He is also man, He casts Himself down humbly as a man, face down on the earth before God the Father.[66]

Reader, let us pause for a little at this point and contemplate with a devout mind our commander lying on the ground in humble supplication. For if we do this carefully, a ray of that light which enlightens every man who comes into the world[67] will illuminate our minds so that we will see, recognize, deplore, and at long last correct, I will not say the negligence, sloth, or apathy, but rather the feeble-mindedness, the insanity, the downright blockheaded stupidity with which most of us approach the all-powerful God, and instead of praying reverently address Him in a lazy and sleepy sort of way; and by the same token I am very much afraid that instead of placating Him and gaining His favor we exasperate Him and sharply provoke His wrath.

I wish that sometime we would make a special effort, right after finishing our prayers, to run over in our minds the whole sequence of time we spent praying. What follies will we see there? How much absurdity, and sometimes even foulness will we catch sight of? Indeed we will be amazed that it was at all possible for our minds to dissipate themselves in such a short time among so many places at such great distance from each other, among so many different affairs, such various, such manifold,

65. Matt. 26 : 39, Mark 14 : 35–36.   66. Cf. Phil. 2 : 5–7.   67. John 1 : 9.

such idle pursuits. For if someone, just as an experiment, should make a determined effort to make his mind touch upon as many and as diverse objects as possible, I hardly think that in such a short time he could run through such disparate and numerous topics as the mind, left to its own devices, ranges through while the mouth negligently mumbles through the hours of the office and other much used prayers.

And so if anyone wonders or has any doubts about what the mind is doing while dreams take over our consciousness during sleep, I find no comparison that comes closer to the mark than to think that the mind is occupied during sleep in exactly the same way as are the minds of those who are awake (if those who pray in this way can be said to be awake) but whose thoughts wander wildly during prayers, frantically flitting about in a throng of absurd fantasies—with this difference, though, from the sleeping dreamer: some of the waking dreamer's strange sights, which his mind embraces in its foreign travels while his tongue runs rattling through his prayers as if they were mere sound without sense,[68] some these strange sights are such filthy and abominable monstrosities that if they had been seen during sleep, certainly no one, no matter how shameless, would have the nerve to recount such extravagant dreams after he woke up, not even in the company of stable-boys.

And undoubtedly that old saying is very true, that our looks are a mirror of our minds.[69] For certainly such a wild and deranged state of mind is distinctly reflected in the eyes, in the cheeks, eyelids, and eyebrows, in the hands, feet, and in short in the overall bearing of the entire body.[70] For just as our minds are inattentive when we set out to pray, so too we proceed to do so with an equally careless and sprawling deportment of our bodies.

68. Virgil, *Aeneid,* 10, 640.   69. Cicero, *De oratore,* 3, 59, 221.
70. Cf. Cicero, *Pis.,* 1, 1.

True, we do pretend that the worship of God is our reason for wearing better than everyday clothes on feast days, but the negligence with which most of us pray makes it utterly clear that we have utterly failed to conceal the real motive, namely a haughty desire to show off in the eyes of the world. Thus in our negligence we sometimes stroll around, sometimes sit down on a stool. And even when we kneel down, we either place our weight on one knee, raising up the other and resting it on our foot, or we place a cushion under our knees, and sometimes (if we are especially spoiled) we even support our elbows on a cushion, looking for all the world like a propped up house that is threatening to tumble down.

And then our actions too, in how many ways do they betray that our minds are wandering miles away? We scratch our heads, clean our fingernails with a pocketknife, pick our noses with our fingers, meanwhile making the wrong responses. Having no idea what we have already said and what we have not said, we make a wild guess as to what remains to be said. Are we not ashamed to pray in such a deranged state of mind and body—to beseech God's favor in a matter so crucial for us, to beg His forgiveness for so many monstrous misdeeds, to ask Him to save us from eternal punishment?—so that even if we had not sinned before, we would still deserve tenfold eternal torments for having approached the majesty of God in such a contemptuous fashion.

Imagine, if you will, that you have committed a crime of high treason against some mortal prince or other who has your life in his hands but who is so merciful that he is prepared to temper his wrath because of your repentance and humble supplication, and to commute the death sentence into a monetary fine or even to suspend it completely if you give convincing signs of great shame and sorrow. Now, when you have been brought into the presence of the prince, go ahead and speak to him carelessly, casually, without the least concern. While he stays in one place and listens attentively, stroll around here and there as you run through your plea. Then, when you have had enough of walking up and down, sit down on a chair, or if courtesy seems to require that you condescend to kneel down, first command someone to come and place a cushion beneath your knees, or, better yet, to bring a prie-dieu with another cushion to lean your elbows on. Then yawn, stretch, sneeze, spit without giving it a thought, and belch up the fumes of your gluttony. In short, conduct yourself in such a way that he can clearly see from your face, your voice, your gestures, and your whole bodily deportment that while you are addressing him you are thinking about something else. Tell me now, what success could you hope for from such a plea as this?

Certainly we would consider it quite mad to defend ourselves in this way before a mortal prince against a charge that carries the death penalty. And yet such a prince, once he had destroyed our bodies, could do nothing further. And do we think it is reasonable, when we have been caught committing a whole series of far more serious crimes, to beg pardon so contemptuously from the king of all kings,[71] God Himself, who, when He has destroyed our bodies, has the power to send both body and soul together to hell?[72]

Still I would not wish anyone to construe what I have said as meaning that I forbid anyone to pray while walking or sitting or even lying down. Indeed I wish that, whatever our bodies may be doing, we would at the same time constantly lift up our minds to God (which is the most acceptable form of prayer). For no matter where we may turn our steps, as long as our minds are directed to God, we clearly do not turn away from Him who is present everywhere.[73] But just as the prophet who says to God "I was mindful of you when I lay upon my bed"[74] did not rest content

71. Cf. 1 Tim. 6 : 15, Rev. 19 : 16.   72. Luke 12 : 4, Matt. 10 : 28.
73. Cf. Jer. 23 : 23–24.   74. Ps. 62 : 7 (AV, 63 : 6).

with that but also rose "in the middle of the night to pay homage to the Lord,"[75] so too I would require that, besides such prayers said while walking, we also occasionally say some prayers for which we prepare our minds more thoughtfully, for which we dispose our bodies more reverently, than we would if we were about to approach all the kings in the whole world sitting together in one place.

But of this much I can assure you: every time I think about this mental wandering, it vexes and plagues my mind.

Nevertheless, some ideas may be suggested to us during our prayers by an evil spirit or may creep into our imaginations through the normal functioning of our senses, and I would not assert that any one of these, not even if it is vile and quite horrible, must be immediately fatal, so long as we resist it and drive it away. But otherwise, if we accept it with pleasure or allow it through negligence to grow in intensity over a long period of time, I have not the slightest doubt that the force of it can become so aggravated as to be fatally destructive to the soul.

Certainly, when I consider the immeasurable glory of God's majesty, I am immediately compelled and forced to believe that if even these brief distractions of mind are not crimes punishable by death, it is only because God in His mercy and goodness deigns not to exact death for them, not because the wickedness inherent in their own nature does not deserve death—and for this reason: I simply cannot imagine how such thoughts can gain entrance into the minds of men when they are praying (that is, when they are speaking to God) unless it be through weakness of faith. Otherwise, since our minds do not go wool-gathering while we are addressing a mortal prince about some important matter or even speaking to one of his ministers who might be in a position of some influence with his master, certainly it could never happen that our minds should stray even the least bit while

75. Ps. 118 : 62 (AV, 119 : 62).

we are praying to God, certainly not, that is, if we believed with a strong and active faith that we are in the presence of God, who not only listens to our words and looks upon our facial features and bodily deportment as outward signs and indications from which our interior state of mind can be gathered, but who also pierces into the most secret and inward recesses of our hearts with a vision more penetrating than the eyes of Lynceus[76] and who illuminates everything with the immeasurable brightness of His majesty—it could not happen, I say, if we believed that God is present, God in whose glorious presence all the princes of the world in all their glory[77] must confess (unless they are out of their minds) that they are the merest mites and earth-creeping worms.

Therefore, since our Savior Christ saw that nothing is more profitable than prayer, but since He was also aware that this means of salvation would very often be fruitless because of the negligence of men and the malice of demons—so much so that it would very frequently be perverted into an instrument of destruction—He decided to take this opportunity, on the way to His death, to reinforce His teaching by His words and example, and to put the finishing touches on this most necessary point just as He did on the other parts of His teaching.

He wished us to know that we ought to serve God not only in soul but also in body, since He created both, and He wanted us to learn that a reverent attitude of the body, though it takes its origin and character from the soul, increases by a kind of reflex the soul's own reverence and devotion toward God. Hence He presented the most humble mode of subjection and venerated His heavenly Father in a bodily posture which no earthly prince has dared to demand, or even to accept if freely offered, except that drunken and debauched Macedonian [Alexander] and some other barbar-

76. Cf. 2 Par. 6 : 30 and Jer. 17 : 9–10. Lynceus, one of the Argonauts, was famed for the sharpness of his sight.
77. Cf. Matt. 6 : 29, Luke 12 : 27.

ians puffed up with success, who thought they ought to be venerated as gods.

For when He prayed He did not sit back or stand up or merely
kneel down, but rather He threw His whole body face-forward
and lay prostrate on the ground. Then, in that pitiable posture,
He implored His Father's mercy and twice called His Father by
name, begging Him that, since all things are possible to Him, He
might be moved by His prayers to take away the cup of His passion if this could be done, that is, if He had not imposed it on Him
by an immutable decree. But He also asked that His own will, as
expressed in this prayer, might not be granted, if something else
seemed better to His Father's will, which is absolutely best.

This passage should not lead you to think that the Son was
ignorant of the will of the Father. Rather, because He wanted to
instruct men, He also wanted to express the feelings of men. By
saying the word "Father" twice, He wanted to remind us that all
fatherhood proceeds from Him, both in heaven and on earth.[78]
Moreover, He also wanted to impress upon us that God the
Father is His father in a double sense—namely by creation,
which is a sort of fatherhood (for we come from God, who created us from nothing, more truly than we do from the human
father who begot us, since, in fact, God created beforehand that
begetter Himself and since He created and supplied beforehand
all the matter out of which we were begotten); but when Christ
acknowledged God as His Father in this sense, He did so as a
man. On the other hand, as God, He knows Him as His natural
and coeternal Father.

And yet another reason for His calling on His Father twice
may not be far from the truth: He intended not only to acknowledge that God the Father is His natural father in heaven, but also
to signify that He has no other father on earth, since He was con-

78. Eph. 3 : 15.

THE SADNESS OF CHRIST

ceived by a virgin mother according to the flesh, without any male seed, when the Holy Spirit came upon His mother—the Spirit, I say, both of the Father and of Himself, whose works coexist in identity and cannot be radically distinguished by any human insight.[79]

Moreover, this forceful repetition of His Father's name, since it expresses an intense desire to gain what He asked for, might serve to teach us a very wholesome lesson: that when we pray for something without receiving it we should not give up like King Saul, who, because he did not immediately receive a prophecy from God, resorted to witchcraft and went off to the woman with a spirit, engaging in a practice forbidden by the law and formerly suppressed by his own decree.[80]

Christ teaches us that we should persevere in our prayers without murmuring at all if we do not obtain what we seek—and for good reason, since we see that the son of God our Savior did not obtain the reprieve from death which He sought from His Father with such urgency, but always with the condition (and this is what we ought to imitate most of all) that His will was subject to the will of His Father.

"And He went to His disciples and found them sleeping."[81]

Notice here how much greater one love is than another. Notice how Christ's love for His own was much greater than the love they gave Him in return, even those who loved Him most. For even the sadness, fear, dread, and weariness which so grievously assailed Him as His most cruel torment drew near, could not keep Him from going to see them. But they, on the other hand, however much they loved Him (and undoubtedly they loved Him intensely), even at the very time when such an enormous

79. Cf. John 5 : 16–19.   80. 1 Kings 28 : 5–25 and 1 Par. 10 : 13–14.
81. Matt. 26 : 40, Mark 14 : 37, Luke 22 : 45.

danger was threatening their loving master, could still give in to sleep.

"And He said to Peter, 'Simon, are you sleeping? Could you not stay awake one hour with me? Stay awake and pray that you may not enter into temptation. For the spirit indeed is willing, but the flesh is weak.'"[82]

This short speech of Christ is remarkably forceful: the words are mild, but their point is sharp and piercing. For by addressing him as Simon and reproaching him under that name for his sleepiness, Christ tacitly lets it be known that the name Peter, which Christ had previously given him because of his firmness, would hardly be altogether appropriate now because of this infirmity and sleep. Moreover, not only was the failure to use the name Peter (or rather, Cephas) a barbed omission, but the actual use of the name Simon also carries a sting. For in Hebrew, the language in which Christ was speaking to him, "Simon" means "listening" and also "obedient." But in fact, he was neither listening nor obedient, since he went to sleep against Christ's express wishes.

Over and above these, our Savior's gentle words to Peter seem to carry certain other barbed implications, which if He were chiding him more severely, would be something like this: "Simon, no longer Cephas, are you sleeping? For how do you deserve to be called Cephas, that is, rock? I singled you out by that name because of your firmness,[83] but now you show yourself to be so infirm that you cannot hold out even for an hour against the inroads of sleep. As for that old name of yours, Simon, certainly you live up to that remarkably well: can you be called listening when you are sleeping this way? or can you be called obedient when in spite of my instructions to stay awake, I am no sooner

82. Matt. 26 : 40–41, Mark 14 : 37–38.   83. John 1 : 42.

gone than you relax and doze and fall asleep? I always made much of you Simon, and yet Simon are you sleeping? I paid you many high honors, and yet Simon are you sleeping? A few moment[s] ago you boasted that you would die with me,[84] and now Simon are you sleeping? Now I am pursued to the death by the Jews and the gentiles and by one worse than either of them, Judas, and Simon are you sleeping? Indeed, Satan is busily seeking to sift all of you like wheat,[85] and Simon are you sleeping? What can I expect from the others, when, in such great and pressing danger, not only to me but also to all of you, I find that you Simon, even you are sleeping?"

Then, lest this seem to be a matter which concerned Peter only, He turned and spoke to the others. "Stay awake and pray," He says, "that you may not enter into temptation. The spirit indeed is willing, but the flesh is weak."[86]

Here we are enjoined to be constant in prayer, and we are informed that prayer is not only useful but also extremely necessary—for this reason: without it, the weakness of the flesh holds us back, somewhat in the way a remora-fish retards a ship,[87] until our minds, no matter how willing to do good, are swept back into the evils of temptation. For whose spirit is more willing than Peter's was? And yet that he had great need of God's protection against the flesh is clear enough from this fact alone: when sleep kept him from praying and begging for God's help, he gave an opening to the devil, who not long afterwards used the weakness of Peter's flesh to blunt the eagerness of his spirit and impelled him to perjure himself by denying Christ.[88] Now if such things happened to the apostles, who were like flourishing green branches, that is, if they entered into temptation when they allowed

84. Mark 14 : 31, Luke 22 : 33.   85. Luke 22 : 31.   86. Matt. 26 : 41.
87. The remora (suck-fish) was thought to be able to stop a large ship simply by attaching itself to the hull.
88. Matt. 26 : 69–74, Mark 14 : 71.

sleep to interrupt their prayers, what will happen to us, who are like sapless sticks by comparison, if, when we are suddenly faced by danger (and when, I ask you, are we not in danger, since our enemy the devil constantly prowls like a roaring lion looking everywhere for someone who is ready to fall because of the weakness of the flesh, ready to pounce upon such a man and devour him[89]), in such great danger, I say, what will become of us if we do not follow Christ's advice by being steadfast in wakefulness and prayer?

Christ tells us to stay awake, but not for cards and dice, not for rowdy parties and drunken brawls, not for wine and women, but for prayer. He tells us to pray not occasionally, but constantly. "Pray," He says, "unceasingly."[90] He tells us to pray not only during the day (for it is hardly necessary to command anyone to stay awake during the day) but rather He exhorts us to devote to intense prayer a large part of that very time which most of us usually devote entirely to sleep. How much more, then, should we be ashamed of our miserable performance and recognize the enormous guilt we incur by saying no more than a short prayer or two, perhaps, during the day, and even those said as we doze and yawn. Finally our Savior tells us to pray, not that we may roll in wealth, not that we may live in a continuous round of pleasures, not that something awful may happen to our enemies, not that we may receive honor in this world, but rather that we may not enter into temptation. In fact, He wishes us to understand that all those worldly goods are either downright harmful, or else, by comparison with that one benefit, the merest trifles; and hence in His wisdom He placed this one petition at the end of the prayer which He had previously taught His disciples, as if it were a summary, in a way, of all the rest: "And lead us not into temptation, but deliver us from evil."[91]

*   *   *

89. 1 Pet. 5 : 8.   90. 1 Thess. 5 : 17. Cf. Luke 18 : 1.   91. Matt. 6 : 13.

"And again He went away, for the second time, and said the same prayer over again, in these words: 'My Father, if this cup cannot pass away without my drinking it, let your will be done.' And He came again and found them sleeping, for their eyes were heavy. And they did not know what answer to make to Him. And leaving them, He went away again and kneeling down said the same prayer, in these words: 'Father, if you are willing, take this cup from me. Yet not my will but yours be done.'"[92]

Thus, after He had given His disciples this warning, He went back to pray again, and He repeated the same prayer He had said before, but still in such a way as to commit the whole matter once more to the will of the Father. Thus He teaches us to make our petitions earnest without being absolutely definite, but rather to trust the whole outcome to God, who desires our welfare no less than we ourselves do[93] and who knows what is likely to produce it a thousand times better than we do.

"My Father," He says, "if this cup cannot pass away without my drinking it, let your will be done." That pronoun "my" has a twofold effect: for it expresses great affection, and it makes it clear that God the Father is the father of Christ in a singular way—that is, not only by creation (for in this way He is the father of all things), not by adoption (in this way He is the father of Christians), but rather by nature He is God the Father of God the Son. And then He teaches the rest of us to pray thus: "Our Father who art in heaven." By these words we acknowledge that we are all brothers who have one Father in common, whereas Christ Himself is the only one who can rightfully, because of His divinity, address the Father as He does here, "My Father." But if anyone is not content to be like other men[94] and is so proud as to imagine that he alone is governed by the secret Spirit of God and that he has a different status from other men, it certainly seems to

92. Mark 14 : 39–40, Matt. 26 : 42–44.   93. Cf. Matt. 6 : 26.
94. Cf. Luke 18 : 11.

me that such a person arrogates to himself the language of Christ and prays with the invocation "My Father" instead of "Our Father," since he claims for himself as a private individual the Spirit which God shares with all men. In fact, such a person is not much different from Lucifer, since he arrogates to himself God's language, just as Lucifer claimed God's place.[95]

Christ's language here—"If this cup cannot pass away without my drinking it, let your will be done"—also makes it perfectly clear on what basis He calls a thing possible or impossible, namely on no other basis than the certain, immutable, unconstrained decision of His Father concerning His death. For otherwise, if He had thought that He was ineluctably and necessarily destined to die, either because of the course of the heavenly bodies or because of some more abstract overall scheme of things such as fate, and if this had been the sense in which He said "If this cup cannot pass away without my drinking it," then it would have been completely pointless for Him to add the phrase "let your will be done." For how could He have left the matter to be decided by the Father if He believed that its outcome depended on something besides the Father, or if He thought that the Father had to make a certain choice necessarily, that is, willy-nilly?

But at the same time, while we examine the words with which Christ begged His Father to avert His death and humbly submitted everything to the will of His Father, we must also constantly bear in mind that, though He was both God and man, He said all these things not as God, but insofar as He was man. We ourselves provide a parallel: because we are composed of body and soul, we sometimes apply to our whole selves things which actually are true only of the soul and on the other hand we sometimes speak of ourselves when strict accuracy would require us to speak of our bodies alone. For we say that the martyrs go straight to heaven

95. Cf. Isa. 14 : 13–14.

when they die, whereas actually only their souls are taken up to heaven. And, on the other hand, we say that men, however proud they may be, are still only dust and ashes and that when they have finished with this brief life they will rot in a common ordinary grave. We constantly talk this way, even though the soul does not enter into the grave or undergo death but rather outlives the body, either in miserable torment if it lived badly while in the body, or else in perpetual well-being if it lived well.

In a similar fashion, then, Christ speaks of what He did as God and what He did as man, not as if He were divided into two persons but as one and the same person, and that rightly, since He was one person; for in the omnipotent person of Christ humanity and divinity were joined and made one no less closely than His immortal soul was united to a body which could die. Thus because of His divinity He did not hesitate to say "I and the Father are one"[96] and "Before Abraham came to be, I am."[97] Moreover, because of both His natures, He said, "I am with you all days even to the end of the world."[98] And, conversely, because of His humanity alone He said, "The Father is greater than I"[99] and "A little while I am with you."[100] It is true, of course, that His glorious body is really present with us, and always will be till the end of the world, under the appearance of bread in the venerable sacrament of the eucharist; but that bodily form in which He once associated with His disciples (and this is the kind of presence He had in mind when He said, "A little while I am with you") was taken away after Christ's ascension, unless He Himself chooses to show it to someone, as He sometimes does.

Therefore, in this passage about Christ's agony, whichever of these deeds, sufferings, or prayers of His are so lowly that they seem quite incompatible with the lofty height of divinity, let us

96. John 10 : 30.   97. John 8 : 58.   98. Matt. 28 : 20.
99. John 14 : 28.   100. John 13 : 33.

remember that the same Christ performed them as a man. Indeed some of them had their origin only in the lower part of His humanity. I mean the part concerned with sensation; and these served to proclaim the genuineness of His human nature and to relieve the natural fears of other men in later times. Nothing, then, in these words or in any of all the other things that the sequence of His agony presented as signs of His afflicted humanity, was considered by Christ to be unworthy of His glory; indeed so little did He think so that He Himself took special care to see that they became widely known.

For, though everything written by all the apostles was dictated throughout by one and the same spirit of Christ, still I find it hard to recall any of His other deeds which He took such particular pains to preserve in the memories of men. To be sure, He told His apostles about His intense sadness, so that they might be able to hand it down from Him to posterity. But the words of His prayer to His Father they could hardly have heard even if they had been awake (since the nearest of them were a stone's throw away), and even if they had been present when it happened, they still could not have heard because they were asleep. Certainly they would have been even less able, at that time of night, to make out when He knelt down or when He threw Himself face forward on the ground. As for those drops of blood which flowed like sweat from His whole body,[101] even if they had later clearly seen the stain left on the ground, I think they would have drawn almost any number of conclusions without guessing the right one, since it was an unprecedented phenomenon for anyone to sweat blood.

Yet in the ensuing time before His death it seems unlikely that He spoke of these things either to His mother or to the apostles, unless one is willing to believe that He told the apostles the whole story of His agony when He left off praying and came back to

101. Luke 22 : 44.

them—that is, while they were either still sleeping or barely awake and quite drowsy—or else that He told them at the very time when the troops were at hand. The remaining alternative, then, and the one that seems most likely to be true, is that, after He rose from the dead and there could no longer be any doubt that He was God, His most loving mother and beloved disciples heard from His own most holy lips this detailed account, point by point, of His human suffering, the knowledge of which would benefit both them and (through them) others who would come after them, and which no one could have recounted except Christ Himself. Therefore, to those whose hearts are troubled, meditation on this agony provides great consolation, and rightly so, since it was for this very purpose, to console the afflicted, that our Savior in His kindness made known His own affliction, which no one else knew or could have known.

Some may be concerned about another point: when Christ came back from that prayer to see His apostles and found them sleeping and so startled by His arrival that they did not know what to say, He left them, so that it might seem He had come only for the purpose of finding out whether they were awake, whereas He could not have lacked this knowledge (insofar as He was God) even before He came.

The answer to such persons, if there are any, should be this: nothing that *He* did was done in vain. It is true that His coming into their presence did not rouse them to complete vigilance but only to such a startled, half-waking drowsiness that they hardly raised their eyes to look at Him, or else (what is worse yet) if His reproaches did wake them up completely, still they slipped back into sleep the moment He went away. Nevertheless, He Himself both demonstrated His anxious concern for His disciples and also by His example gave to the future pastors of His church a solemn injunction not to allow themselves the slightest wavering, out of sadness or weariness or fear, in their diligent care of their flock, but rather to conduct themselves so as to prove in actual fact that they are not so much concerned for themselves as for the welfare of their flock.

But perhaps some meticulous fussy dissector of the divine plan might say: "Either Christ wished the apostles to stay awake or He did not. If He did not, why did He give such an explicit command? If He did, what use was there in going back and forth so often? Since He was God, could He not at one and the same time speak the command and insure its execution?"

Doubtless He could have, my good man, since He was God, who carried out whatever He wished, who created all things with a word:[102] He spoke and it was done, He commanded and they were created.[103] He opened the eyes of a man blind from birth,[104] and could He not, then, find a way to open the eyes of a man who was asleep? Clearly, even someone who was not God could easily do that. For anyone can see that if you merely prick the eyes of sleepy men with a tiny pin they will stay awake and will certainly not go right back to sleep.

Doubtless Christ could have caused the apostles not to sleep at all but to stay awake, if that had been what He wished in an absolute and unqualified sense. But actually His wish was modified by a condition—namely that they themselves wish to do so, and wish it so effectually that each of them do his very best to comply with the outward command Christ Himself gave and to cooperate with the promptings of His inward assistance. In this way He also wishes for all men to be saved[105] and for no one to suffer eternal torment, that is, always provided that we conform to His most loving will and do not set ourselves against it through our own willful malice. If someone stubbornly insists on doing this, God does not wish to waft him off to heaven against his will, as if He were in need of our services there and could not continue

102. Cf. Sap. 9 : 1.   103. Ps. 32 : 9 (AV, 33 : 9).   104. John 9 : 32.
105. 1 Tim. 2 : 4.

His glorious reign without our support. Indeed, if He could not reign without us, He would immediately punish many offenses which now, out of consideration for us, He tolerates and overlooks for a long time to see if His kindness and patience will bring us to repent. But we meanwhile abuse this great mercy of His by adding sins to sins,[106] thus heaping up for ourselves (as the apostle says) a treasure of wrath on the day of wrath.[107]

Nevertheless, such is God's kindness that even when we are negligent and slumbering on the pillow of our sins, He disturbs us from time to time, shakes us, strikes us, and does His best to wake us up by means of tribulations. But still, even though He thus proves Himself to be most loving even in His anger, most of us, in our gross human stupidity, misinterpret His action and imagine that such a great benefit is an injury, whereas actually (if we have any sense) we should feel bound to pray frequently and fervently that whenever we wander away from Him He may use blows to drive us back to the right way, even though we are unwilling and struggle against Him.

Thus we must first pray that we may see the way and with the church we must say to God, "From blindness of heart, deliver us, O Lord."[108] And with the prophet we must say, "Teach me to do your will"[109] and "Show me your ways and teach me your paths."[110] Then we must intensely desire to run after you eagerly, O God, in the odor of your ointments,[111] in the most sweet scent of your Spirit. But if we grow weary along the way (as we almost always do) and lag so far behind that we barely manage to follow at a distance,[112] let us immediately say to God, "Take my right hand"[113] and "Lead me along your path."[114]

---

106. Cf. Ecclus. 5 : 5 and Isa. 30 : 1.   107. Rom. 2 : 5.
108. Part of the litany of the saints in the breviary of Salisbury.
109. Ps. 142 : 10 (AV, 143 : 10).   110. Cf. Ps. 24 : 4 (AV, 25 : 4).
111. Cf. Cant. 1 : 3.   112. Matt. 26 : 58, Mark 14 : 54, Luke 23 : 54.
113. Cf. Ps. 72 : 24 (AV, 73 : 23), Isa. 42 : 6 and 45 : 1.
114. Cf. Ps. 5 : 9 (AV, 5 : 8), 26 : 11 (AV, 27 : 11), 138 : 24 (AV, 139 : 24).

Then if we are so overcome by weariness that we no longer have the heart to go on, if we are so soft and lazy that we are about to stop altogether, let us beg God to drag us along[115] even as we struggle not to go. Finally, if we resist when He draws us on gently, and are stiffnecked against the will of God, against our own salvation, utterly irrational like horses and mules which have no intellects,[116] we ought to beseech God humbly in the most fitting words of the prophet, "Hold my jaws hard, O God, with a bridle and bit when I do not draw near to you."[117]

But then, since fondness for prayer is the first of our virtues to go when we are overtaken by sloth, and since we are reluctant to pray for anything (however useful) that we are reluctant to receive, certainly if we have any sense at all we ought to take this weakness into account well in advance, before we fall into such sick and troubled states of mind—we ought, in other words, to pour out to God unceasingly such prayers as I have mentioned, and we should humbly implore Him that, if at some later time we should ask for anything untoward—allured perhaps by the enticements of the flesh or seduced by a longing for worldly things or overthrown by the clever snares of the devils—He may be deaf to such prayers and avert what we pray for, showering upon us instead those things He knows will be good for us, however much we beg Him to take them away. In fact, this is the way we normally act (if we are wise) when we are expecting a fever: we give advance warning to those who are to take care of us in our sickness that, even if we beg them, they should not give us any of those things which our diseased condition makes us perversely long for, though they are harmful to our health and only make the disease worse.

And when we are so fast asleep in our vices that even the calls and stirrings of divine mercy do not make us willing to rouse our-

115. Cf. Cant. 1 : 3, John 6 : 44, 12 : 32.   116. Tob. 6 : 17, Ps. 31 : 9 (AV, 32 : 9).
117. Ps. 31 : 9 (AV, 32 : 9).

selves and wake up to virtuous living, we ourselves sometimes supply the reason why God goes away and leaves us to our vices; some He leaves so as never to come back again, but others He lets sleep only until another time, according as He sees fit in His wondrous kindness and the inscrutable depths of His wisdom.

Christ's action provided a sort of paradigm of this fact: when He went back to check on the apostles, they were unwilling to stay awake but rather went right on sleeping, and so He went away and left them. For "leaving them He went away again and kneeling down said the same prayer, in these words: 'Father, if you are willing, take this cup from me. Yet not my will but yours be done.'"[118]

Notice how He again asks the same thing, again adds the same condition, again sets us an example to show that when we fall into great danger, even for God's sake, we should not think we are not allowed to beg God urgently to provide us a way out[119] of that crisis. For one thing, it is quite possible that He permits us to be brought into such difficulties precisely because fear of danger makes us grow fervent in prayer when prosperity has made us cold, especially when it is a question of bodily danger—for most of us are not very warmly concerned about danger to our souls. Now as for those who are concerned (as they ought to be) about their souls, unless someone is strengthened and inspired by God to undergo martyrdom—a condition which must be either directly experienced in an unexplainable way or else judged by appropriate indications—apart from such a case everyone has sufficient grounds to be afraid that he may grow weary under his burden and give in. Hence everyone, to avoid such overconfidence as Peter's,[120] ought to pray diligently that God in His goodness may deliver him from such a great danger to his soul. But it must be stressed again and again that no one should pray to

118. Matt. 26 : 42, Mark 14 : 39.   119. Cf. 1 Cor. 10 : 13.
120. Matt. 26 : 33–35.

escape danger so absolutely that he would not be willing to leave the whole matter up to God, ready in all obedience to endure what God has prepared for him.

These are some of the reasons, then, why Christ provided us with this salutary example of prayer, not that He Himself was in any need of such prayer—nothing could be further from the truth. For, insofar as He was God, He was not inferior to the Father. Insofar as He was God, not only His power but also His will was the same as the Father's.[121] Certainly insofar as He was man, His power was infinitely less,[122] but then all power, both in heaven and on earth, was finally given to Him by the Father.[123] And though His will, insofar as He was man, was not identical with the Father's, still it was in such complete conformity with the will of the Father that no disagreement was ever found between them.[124]

Thus the reasoning power of His soul, in obedience to the will of the Father, agrees to suffer that most bitter death, while at the same time, as a proof of His humanity, His bodily senses react to the prospect with revulsion and dread. His prayer expresses vividly both the fear and the obedience: "Father," He said, "if you are willing, take this cup from me. Yet not my will but yours be done."

His deeds, however, present this dual reaction even more clearly than His words. That His reasoning faculties never drew back from such horrible torture but rather remained obedient to the Father even to death, even to the death of the cross,[125] was demonstrated by the succeeding events of the passion. And that His feelings were overwhelmed by an intense fear of His coming passion is shown by the words which come next in the gospel.

*   *   *

121. John 5 : 17–18.   122. John 14 : 28.   123. Matt. 11 : 27, 28 : 18.
124. Cf. John 5 : 30.   125. Cf. Phil. 2 : 8.

"And there appeared to Him an angel from heaven to strengthen Him."[126]

Do you realize how intense His mental anguish must have been, that an angel should come from heaven to strengthen Him?

But when I consider this passage, I cannot help wondering what pernicious nonsense has gotten into the heads of those who contend that it is futile for anyone to seek the intercession of any angel or departed saint, namely on the grounds that we can confidently address our prayers to God Himself, not only because He alone is more present to us than all the angels and all the saints put together but also because He has the power to grant us more, and a greater desire to do so, than any of the saints in heaven, of whatever description.

With such trivial and groundless arguments as these, they express their envious displeasure at the glory of the saints, who are in turn equally displeased with such men; for they strive to undermine the loving homage we pay to the saints and the saving assistance they render to us. Why should these shameless men not follow the same line of reasoning here and argue that the angel's effort to offer consolation to our Savior Christ was utterly pointless and superfluous? For what angel of them all was as powerful as He Himself or as near to Him as God, since He Himself was God? But in fact, just as He wished to undergo sadness and anxiety for our sake, so too for our sake He wished to have an angel console Him, for a number of reasons: both to refute the foolish arguments of such men, and to make it clear that He was truly man (for just as angels ministered to Him as God when He had triumphed over the temptations of the devil, so too an angel came to console Him as man while He was making His lowly progress toward death) and moreover to give us hope that if we direct our prayers to God when we are in danger we cannot lack consola-

126. Luke 22 : 43.

tion, always provided we do not pray in a lazy and perfunctory way, but rather imitate Christ in this passage by sighing and praying from the bottom of our hearts.

"For in His agony He prayed more earnestly, and His sweat became like drops of blood running down to the ground."[127]

Most scholars affirm that what Christ suffered for us was more painful than the suffering of any of all the martyrs, of whatever time or place, who underwent martyrdom for the faith. But others disagree, because there are various other sorts of torture than those to which Christ was subjected and some torments have been extended over a period of several days, a longer time than those of Christ lasted. Then, too, they think that, since one drop of Christ's precious blood, because of His infinite divinity, would have been far more than enough to redeem all mankind, therefore His ordeal was not ordained by God according to the standards of anyone else's suffering, but according to the proper measure of His own unfathomable wisdom. And since no one can know this measure with certainty, they hold that it is not prejudicial to the faith to believe that Christ's pain was less than that of some of the martyrs. But as for me, apart from the widespread opinion of the church which fittingly applies to Christ Jeremiah's words about Jerusalem ("O all you who pass by the way, look and see if there is any sorrow like mine"[128]), certainly I find that this passage also provides very convincing reasons to believe that no martyr's torments could ever be compared with Christ's suffering, even on this point of the intensity of the pain.

Even if I should grant what I have good reasons to think need not be granted, namely that any of the martyrs was subjected to more kinds of torture, and greater ones, even (if you like) longer

127. Luke 22 : 44.
128. Lam. 1 : 12. The text was recited at matins and lauds of Good Friday; there the words are imagined as spoken by Christ rather than by Jerusalem.

ones than Christ endured, still I find it not at all hard to believe that tortures which to all appearances may be considerably less fierce actually caused Christ to suffer more excruciating pain than someone might feel from tortures that seem much more grievous, and for this reason: I see that Christ, as the thought of His coming passion was borne in upon Him, was overwhelmed by mental anguish more bitter than any other mortal has ever experienced from the thought of coming torments. For who has ever felt such bitter anguish that a bloody sweat broke out all over his body and ran down in drops to the ground? The intensity of the actual pain itself, therefore, I estimate by this standard: I see that even the presentiment of it before it arrived was more bitter to Christ than such anticipation has ever been to anyone else.

Nor could this anguish of the mind ever have grown to sufficient intensity to cause the body to sweat blood if He had not, of His own free will, exercised His divine omnipotence, not only to refrain from alleviating this painful pressure, but even to add to its force and strength. This He did in order to prefigure the blood which future martyrs would be forced to pour forth on the ground, and at the same time to offer this unheard of, this marvelous example of profound anguish as a consolation to those who would be so fearful and alarmed at the thought of torture that they might otherwise interpret their fear as a sign of their downfall and thus yield to despair.

At this point, if someone should again bring up those martyrs who freely and eagerly exposed themselves to death because of their faith in Christ, and if he should offer his opinion that they are especially worthy of the laurels of triumph because with a joy that left no room for sorrow they betrayed no trace of sadness, no sign of fear, I am perfectly willing to go along with him on that point, so long as he does not go so far as to deny the triumph of those who do not rush forth of their own accord but who nevertheless do not hang back or withdraw once they have been seized, but rather go on in spite of their fearful anxiety and face the terrible prospect out of love for Christ.

Now if anyone should argue that the eager martyrs receive a greater share of glory than the others, I have no objection—he can have the argument all to himself. For I rest content with the fact that in heaven neither sort of martyr will lack a glory so great that while they were alive their eyes never saw the like, nor did their ears ever hear it, nor did it ever enter into their hearts [to conceive of it].[129] And even if someone does have a higher place in heaven, no one else envies him for it—quite the opposite, everyone enjoys the glory of everyone else because of their mutual love.

Besides, just who outranks whom in the glory assigned by God in heaven is not, I think, quite crystal-clear to us, groping as we are in the darkness of our mortality.

For, though I grant that God loves a cheerful giver,[130] still I have no doubt that He loved Tobias, and holy Job, too. Now it is true that both of them bore their calamities bravely and patiently, but neither of them, so far as I know, was exactly jumping with joy or clapping his hands out of happiness.

To expose one's self to death for Christ's sake when the case clearly demands it or when God gives a secret prompting to do so, this, I do not deny, is a deed of preeminent virtue. But otherwise I do not think it very safe to do so, and among those who willingly suffered for Christ we find outstanding figures who were very much afraid, who were deeply distressed, who even withdrew from death more than once before they finally faced it bravely.

Certainly I do not mean to derogate from God's power to inspire martyrs; indeed I believe that He exercises it on occasion (either granting this favor to holy persons as a reward for the labors of their past lives or giving it purely and simply out of His own generosity) by filling the whole mind of a martyr with

129. 1 Cor. 2 : 9.   130. 2 Cor. 9 : 7.

such joy that he not only wards off those grievous emotional dis-
turbances but also keeps himself completely free from what the
Stoics call "incipient emotions," freely admitting that even their
factitious wise men are susceptible to them.

Since we often see it happen that some men do not feel wounds
inflicted in battle until their awareness, which had been displaced
by strong feeling, returns to them and they notice the injury,[131]
certainly there is no reason why I should doubt that a mind exulting in the high hopes of approaching glory can be so rapt and
transported beyond itself that it neither fears death nor feels torments.

But still, even if God did give someone this gift, I would certainly be inclined to call it an unearned felicity or the recompense
of past virtue, but not the measure of future reward in heaven.
Now I might have believed that this future reward corresponds
to the pain suffered for Christ except that God in His generosity
bestows it in such good measure—so full, so concentrated, so
overflowing[132]—that the sufferings of this time are by no means
worthy to be compared to that future glory which will be
revealed in those[133] who loved God so dearly that they spent their
very life's blood for His glory, with such mental agony and bodily
torment. Besides is it not possible that God in His goodness
removes fear from some persons not because He approves of or
intends to reward their boldness, but rather because He is aware
of their weakness and knows that they would not be equal to facing fear. For some have yielded to fear, even though they won out
later when the actual tortures were inflicted.

Now as for the point that those who eagerly suffer death
encourage others by their example, I would not deny that for
many they provide a very useful pattern. But on the other hand,
since almost all of us are fearful in the face of death, who can

131. Cf. Cicero, *Tusculan Disputations,* 2, 24, 58–59.   132. Luke 6 : 38.
133. Rom. 8 : 18.

know how many have also been helped by those whom we see face death with fear and trembling but whom we also observe as they break bravely through the hindrances blocking their path, the obstacles barring their way with barriers harder than steel, that is, their own weariness, fear, and anguish, and by bursting these iron bars and triumphing over death take heaven by storm?[134] Seeing them, will not weaklings who are, like them, cowardly and afraid take heart so as not to yield under the stress of persecution even though they feel great sadness welling up within them, and fear and weariness and horror at the prospect of a ghastly death?

Thus the wisdom of God, which penetrates all things irresistibly and disposes all things sweetly,[135] foreseeing and contemplating in His ever-present sight how the minds of men in different places would be affected, suits His examples to various times and places, choosing now one destiny, now another, according as He sees which will be most profitable. And so God proportions the temperaments of His martyrs according to His own providence in such a way that one rushes forth eagerly to his death, another creeps out hesitantly and fearfully, but for all that bears his death none the less bravely—unless someone perhaps imagines he ought to be thought less brave for having fought down not only his other enemies but also his own weariness, sadness, and fear—most strong feelings and mighty enemies indeed.

But the whole drift of the present discussion finally comes to this: we should admire both kinds of most holy martyrs, we should venerate both kinds, praise God for both, we should imitate both when the situation demands it, each according to his own capacity and according to the grace God gives to each.

But the person who is conscious of his own eagerness needs not so much encouragement to be daring as perhaps a reminder to be afraid lest his presumption, like Peter's,[136] lead to a sudden

134. Cf. Matt. 11 : 12.   135. Sap. 8 : 1.   136. Matt. 26 : 33–35, 69–75.

relapse and fall. But if a person feels anxious, heavy-hearted, fearful, certainly he ought to be comforted and encouraged to take heart. For both sorts of martyrs this anguish of Christ is most salutary: it keeps the one from being over-exultant and it makes the other be of good hope when his spirit is crestfallen and downcast. For if anyone feels his mind swelling with ungovernable enthusiasm, perhaps when he recalls this lowly and anguished bearing of his commander, he will have reason to fear lest our sly enemy is lifting him up on high for a while so that a little later he can dash him to the ground all the harder.[137] But whoever is utterly crushed by feelings of anxiety and fear and is tortured by the fear that he may yield to despair, let him consider this agony of Christ, let him meditate on it constantly and turn it over in his mind, let him drink deep and health-giving draughts of consolation from this spring. For here he will see the loving shepherd lifting the weak lamb on his shoulders,[138] playing the same role as he himself does, expressing his very own feelings, and for this reason: so that anyone who later feels himself disturbed by similar feelings might take courage and not think that he must despair.

Therefore let us give Him as many thanks as we can (for certainly we can never give Him enough); and in our agony remembering His (with which no other can ever be compared), let us beg Him with all our strength that He may deign to comfort us in our anguish by an insight into His; and when we urgently beseech Him, because of our mental distress, to free us from danger, let us nevertheless follow His own most wholesome example by concluding our prayer with His own addition: "Yet not as I will but as you will." If we do these things diligently, I have no doubt at all that, just as an angel brought Him consolation in answer to His prayer, so too each of our angels will bring us from His Spirit consolation that will give us the strength to persevere in those deeds

137. Cf. Job 30 : 22 and Ps. 101 : 11 (AV, 102 : 10). Cf. Claudian, *In Rufinum,* I, 22.
138. Cf. Luke 15 : 5 and John 10 : 14.

that will lift us up to heaven. And in order to make us completely confident of this fact, Christ went there before us by the same method, by the same path. For after He had suffered this agony for a long time, His spirits were so restored that He arose, returned to His apostles, and freely went out to meet the traitor and the tormentors who were seeking Him to make Him suffer. Then, when He had suffered (as was necessary) He entered into His glory,[139] preparing there a place also for those of us who follow in His footsteps.[140] And lest we should be deprived of it by our own dullness, may He Himself because of His own agony deign to help us in ours.

"And when He had arisen from prayer and come to His disciples, He found them sleeping for sadness, and He said to them, 'Why are you sleeping?[141] Sleep on now and take your rest. That is enough. Get up and pray that you may not enter into temptation. Behold, the hour is coming when the Son of Man will be betrayed into the hands of sinners. Get up, let us go. Behold, the one who will betray me is near at hand.'"[142]

See now, when Christ comes back to His apostles for the third time, there they are, buried in sleep, though He commanded them to bear up with Him and to stay awake and pray because of the impending danger; but Judas the traitor at the same time was so wide awake and intent on betraying the Lord that the very idea of sleep never entered his mind.

Does not this contrast between the traitor and the apostles present to us a clear and sharp mirror image (as it were), a sad and terrible view of what has happened through the ages from those times even to our own? Why do not bishops contemplate in this scene their own somnolence? Since they have succeeded in the place of the apostles, would that they would reproduce their

---

139. Luke 24 : 26.   140. John 14 : 2, 1 Pet. 2 : 21.   141. Luke 22 : 45–46.
142. Matt. 26 : 45–46, Mark 14 : 41–42.

virtues just as eagerly as they embrace their authority and as faithfully as they display their sloth and sleepiness! For very many are sleepy and apathetic in sowing virtues among the people and maintaining the truth, while the enemies of Christ in order to sow vices[143] and uproot the faith (that is, insofar as they can, to seize Christ and cruelly crucify Him once again) are wide awake—so much wiser (as Christ says) are the sons of darkness in their generation than the sons of light.[144]

But although this comparison of the sleeping apostles applies very well to those bishops who sleep while virtue and the faith are placed in jeopardy, still it does not apply to all such prelates at all points. For some of them—alas, far more than I could wish—do not drift into sleep through sadness and grief as the apostles did. Rather they are numbed and buried in destructive desires; that is, drunk with the new wine[145] of the devil, the flesh, and the world,[146] they sleep like pigs sprawling in the mire. Certainly the apostles' feelings of sadness because of the danger to their master were praiseworthy, but for them to be so overcome by sadness as to yield completely to sleep, that was certainly wrong. Even to grieve because the world is perishing or to weep because of the crimes of others bespeaks a reverent outlook, as was felt by the writer who said "I sat by myself and groaned"[147] and also by the one who said "I was sick at heart because of sinners abandoning your law."[148] Sadness of this sort I would place in the category of which he says[149]   But I would place it there only if the feeling, however good, is checked by the rule and guidance of reason. For if this is not the case, if sorrow so grips the mind that its strength is sapped and reason gives up the reins,[150] if a bishop is so

143. Cf. Matt. 13 : 24–29, Luke 8 : 5–15.   144. Luke 16 : 8.
145. Cf. Acts 2 : 13.   146. Cf. 1 John 2 : 15–16.   147. Lam. 3 : 28.
148. Ps. 118 : 53 (AV, 119 : 53).
149. For the blank space after this word More may have intended to quote 2 Cor. 7 : 10.
150. Plato, *Phaedrus,* 246, 254.

overcome by heavy-hearted sleep that he neglects to do what the duty of his office requires for the salvation of his flock—like a cowardly ship's captain who is so disheartened by the furious din of a storm that he deserts the helm, hides away cowering in some cranny, and abandons the ship to the waves—if a bishop does this, I would certainly not hesitate to juxtapose and compare his sadness with the sadness that leads, as[151]   says, to hell; indeed, I would consider it far worse, since such sadness in religious matters seems to spring from a mind which despairs of God's help.

The next category, but a far worse one, consists of those who are not depressed by sadness at the danger of others but rather by a fear of injury to themselves, a fear which is so much the worse as its cause is the more contemptible, that is, when it is not a question of life or death but of money.[152]

And yet Christ commands us to contemn the loss of the body itself for His sake. "Do not be afraid," He says, "of those who destroy the body and after that can do nothing further. But I will show you the one you should fear, the one to fear: fear him who, when He has destroyed the body, has the power to send the soul also to hell. This, I tell you, is the one you must fear."[153]

And though He lays down this rule for everyone without exception when they have been seized and there is no way out, He attaches a separate charge over and above this to the high office of prelates: He does not allow them to be concerned only about their own souls or merely to take refuge in silence until they are dragged out and forced to choose between open profession or lying dissimulation, but He also wished them to come forth if they see that the flock entrusted to them is in danger and to face the danger of their own accord for the good of their flock. "The good shepherd," says Christ, "lays down his life for his sheep."[154]

---

151. Left blank in the manuscript. More perhaps intended "Paul," referring to 2 Cor. 7 : 10.
152. Cf. Terence, *Phormio,* 631.   153. Luke 12 : 4–5, Matt. 10 : 28.
154. John 10 : 11.

But if every good shepherd lays down his life for his sheep, certainly one who saves his own life to the detriment of his sheep is not fulfilling the role of a good shepherd.

Therefore, just as one who loses his life for Christ (and he does this if he loses it for the flock of Christ entrusted to him) saves it for life everlasting, so too one who denies Christ (and this he does if he fails to profess the truth when his silence injures his flock) by saving his life, he actually proceeds to lose it.[155] Clearly, it is even worse if, driven by fear, he denies Christ openly in words and forsakes Him publicly. Such prelates do not sleep like Peter, they make his waking denial. But under the kindly glance of Christ most of them through His grace will eventually wipe out that failure and save themselves by weeping, if only they respond to His glance and friendly call to repentance with bitterness of heart[156] and a new way of life, remembering His words and contemplating His passion and leaving behind the shackles of evil which bound them in their sins.

But if anyone is so set in evil that he does not merely neglect to profess the truth out of fear but like Arius and his ilk preaches false doctrine, whether for sordid gain or out of a corrupt ambition, such a person does not sleep like Peter, does not make Peter's denial, but rather stays awake with wicked Judas and like Judas persecutes Christ. This man's condition is far more dangerous than that of the others, as is shown by the sad and horrible end Judas came to.[157] But since there is no limit to the kindness of a merciful God, even this sort of sinner ought not to despair of forgiveness. Even to Judas God gave many opportunities of coming to his senses. He did not deny him His companionship. He did not take away from him the dignity of his apostleship. He did not even take the purse-strings from him, even though he was a thief.[158] He admitted the traitor to the fellowship of His beloved

155. Matt. 10 : 33, 39, Mark 8 : 35, Luke 9 : 24.   156. Cf. Luke 22 : 61–62.
157. Matt. 27 : 5, Acts 1 : 18.   158. John 12 : 6, 13 : 29.

disciples at the last supper. He deigned to stoop down at the feet of the betrayer and to wash with His innocent and most sacred hands Judas' dirty feet, a most fit symbol of his filthy mind.[159] Moreover, with incomparable generosity, He gave him to eat, in the form of bread, that very body of His which the betrayer had already sold; and under the appearance of wine, He gave him that very blood to drink which, even while he was drinking it, the traitor was wickedly scheming to broach and set flowing.[160] Finally when Judas, coming with his crew to seize Him, offered Him a kiss, a kiss that was in fact the terrible token of his treachery, Christ received him calmly and gently.[161] Who would not believe that any one of all these could have turned the traitor's mind, however hardened in crime, to better courses? Then too, even that beginning of repentance, when he admitted he had sinned, and gave back the pieces of silver, and threw them away when they were not accepted, crying out that he was a traitor and confessing that he had betrayed innocent blood[162]—I am inclined to believe that Christ prompted him thus far so that He might if possible (that is, if the traitor did not add despair to his treachery) save from ruin the very man who had so recently, so perfidiously betrayed Him to death.

Therefore, since God showed His great mercy in so many ways even toward Judas, an apostle turned traitor, since He invited him to forgiveness so often and did not allow him to perish except through despair alone, certainly there is no reason why, in this life, anyone should despair of any imitator of Judas. Rather, according to that holy advice of the apostle "Pray for each other that you may be saved,"[163] if we see anyone wandering wildly from the right road, let us hope that he will one day return to the

---

159. John 13 : 4–11.   160. Luke 22 : 21.
161. Matt. 26 : 48–50, Luke 22 : 47–48.   162. Matt. 27 : 3–5.
163. James 5 : 16.

path, and meanwhile let us pray humbly and incessantly that God will hold out to him chances to come to his senses, and likewise that with God's help he will eagerly seize them, and having seized them will hold fast and not throw them away out of malice or let them slip away from him through wretched sloth.

And so when Christ had found His apostles sleeping for the third time, He said to them, "Why are you sleeping?"[164] as if to say: "Now is not the time to sleep. Now is the crucial time for you to stay awake and pray, as I myself have already warned you twice before, only a little while ago." And as for them, since they did not know what to reply to Him[165] when He found them sleeping for the second time, what suitable excuse could they possibly have devised now that they had been so quickly caught in the same fault for the third time? Could they use as an excuse what the evangelist mentions—that is, could they say they were sleeping because of their sadness? Certainly the fact is mentioned by Luke,[166] but it is also quite clear that he does not praise it. It is true, he does suggest that their sadness itself was praiseworthy, as it certainly was. Still, the sleep that followed from it was not free of moral blame. For the sort of sadness that is potentially worthy of great reward sometimes tends toward great evil. Certainly it does if we are so taken up by it that we render it useless—that is, if we do not have recourse to God with our petitions and prayers and seek comfort from Him, but instead, in a certain downcast and desperate frame of mind, try to escape our awareness of sadness by looking for consolation in sleep. Nor will we find what we are looking for: losing in sleep the consolation we might have obtained from God by staying awake and praying, we feel the weary weight of a troubled mind even during sleep itself and also we stumble with our eyes closed into temptations and the traps set by the devil.

164. Luke 22 : 46.   165. Mark 14 : 40.   166. Luke 22 : 45.

And so Christ, as if He intended to preclude any excuse for this sleepiness, said: "'Why are you sleeping?[167] Sleep on now and take your rest. That is enough. Get up and pray that you may not enter into temptation. Behold, the hour has almost come when the Son of Man will be betrayed into the hands of sinners. Get up, let us go. Behold, the one who will betray me is near at hand.' And while Jesus was still speaking, behold Judas Iscariot, etc."[168]

Immediately after He had aroused the sleeping apostles for the third time, He undercut them with irony, not indeed that trivial and sportive variety with which idle men of wit are accustomed to amuse themselves, but rather a serious and weighty kind of irony. "'Sleep on now,' He said, 'and take your rest. That is enough. Get up and pray that you may not enter into temptation. Behold, the hour has almost come when the Son of Man will be betrayed into the hands of sinners. Get up, let us go. Behold, the one who will betray me is near at hand.' And while He was still speaking, Judas, etc."

Notice how He grants permission to sleep in such a way as clearly shows He means to take it away. For He had hardly said "Sleep" before He added "That is enough," as if to say: "Now there is no need for you to sleep any longer. It is enough that throughout the whole time you ought to have been staying awake, you have been sleeping—and that even against my direct orders. Now there is no time left to sleep, not even to sit down. You must get up immediately and pray that you may not enter into temptation, the temptation, perhaps, of deserting me and giving great scandal by doing so. Otherwise, so far as sleep is concerned, sleep on now and take your rest—you have my permission—that is, if you can. But you will certainly not be able to. For there are people coming—they are almost here—who will shake the yawning sleepiness out of you. For behold the hour has almost come when the Son of Man will be betrayed into the hands of sin-

167. Luke 22 : 46.   168. Matt. 26 : 45–47, Mark 14 : 41–43.

ners and behold the one who will betray me is near at hand." And He had hardly finished these few admonitions and was still speaking when, behold, Judas Iscariot, etc.

I am not unaware that some learned and holy men do not allow this interpretation, though they admit that others, equally learned and holy, have found it agreeable. Not that those who do not accept this interpretation are shocked by this sort of irony, as some others are—also pious men to be sure, but not sufficiently versed in the figures of speech which sacred scripture customarily takes over from common speech. For if they were, they would have found irony in so many other places that they could not have found it offensive here.

What could be more pungent or witty than the irony with which the blessed apostle gracefully polishes off the Corinthians?—I mean where he asks pardon because he never burdened any of them with charges and expenses: "For how have I done any less for you than for the other churches, except this, that I have never been a burden to you? Pardon me for this injustice."[169] What could be more forceful or biting than the irony with which God's prophet ridiculed the prophets of Baal as they called upon the deaf statue of their god: "Call louder," he said, "for your god is asleep or perhaps has gone somewhere on a trip."[170] I have taken this occasion to bring up these instances in passing, because some readers, out of a certain pious simplicity, refuse to accept in sacred scripture (or at least do not notice there) these universally used forms of speech, and by neglecting the figures of speech they very often also miss the real sense of scripture.

Now concerning this passage St. Augustine says that he finds the interpretation I have given to be not unacceptable but also not necessary. He claims that the plain meaning without any figure is adequate. He presents such an interpretation of this passage in the work he wrote entitled *The Harmony of the Gospels*. "It

169. 2 Cor. 12 : 13.   170. 3 Kings 18 : 27.

seems," he says, "that the language of Matthew here is self-contradictory. For how could He say 'Sleep on now and take your rest' and then immediately add 'Get up, let us go'? Disturbed by this seeming inconsistency some try to set the tone of the words 'Sleep on now and take your rest' as reproachful rather than permissive. And this would be the right thing to do if it were necessary. But Mark reports it in such a way that when Christ had said 'Sleep on now and take your rest,' He added 'That is enough' and then went on to say 'The hour has come when the Son of Man will be betrayed.' Therefore it is surely at least implied that after He had said 'Sleep and take your rest' the Lord was silent for a while so that they could do what He had allowed them to do, and that He then went on to say 'Behold, the hour has almost come.' That is the reason why Mark includes 'That is enough,' that is, 'You have rested long enough.'"[171]

Subtle indeed this reasoning of the most blessed Augustine, as he always is; but I imagine that those of the opposite persuasion do not find it at all likely that, after Christ had already reproached them twice for sleeping when His capture was imminent, and after He had just rebuked them sternly by saying "Why are you sleeping?" He should then have granted them time to sleep, especially at the very time when the danger which was the reason they ought not to have slept before, was now pounding on the door, as they say. But now that I have presented both interpretations, everyone is free to choose whichever he likes. My purpose has been merely to recount both of them; it is not for such a nobody as me to render a decision like an official arbitrator.

"Get up and pray that you may not enter into temptation."[172]

Before, He ordered them to watch and pray.[173] Now that they

171. More quotes Augustine's *De consensu evangelistarum (Corpus Scriptorum Ecclesiasticorum Latinorum 43,* 282–83) from the *Catena aurea* of Aquinas.
172. Luke 22 : 46.   173. Matt. 26 : 41, Mark 14 : 38.

have twice learned by experience that the drowsy position of sitting lets sleep gradually slip up on them, He teaches an instant remedy for that sluggish disease of somnolence, namely to get up. Since this sort of remedy was handed down by our Savior Himself, I heartily wish that we would occasionally be willing to try it out at the dead of night. For here we would discover not only that well begun is half done (as Horace says),[174] but that once begun is all done.

For when we are fighting against sleep, the first encounter is always the sharpest. Therefore, we should not try to conquer sleep by a prolonged struggle, but rather we should break with one thrust the grip of the alluring arms with which it embraces us and pulls us down, and we should dash away from it all of a sudden. Then, once we have cast off idle sleep, the very image of death,[175] life with its eagerness will resume its sway. Then, if we devote ourselves to meditation and prayer, the mind, collected and composed in that dark silence of the night,[176] will find that it is much more receptive to divine consolation than it is during the daytime, when the noisy bustle of business on all sides distracts the eyes, the ears, and the mind, and dissipates our energy in manifold activities, no less pointless than they are divers. But Lord spare us, though thoughts about some trifling matter, some worldly matter at that, may sometimes interrupt our sleep and keep us awake for a long time and hardly let us go back to sleep at all, prayer does not keep us awake: in spite of the immense loss of spiritual benefits, in spite of the many traps set for us by our deadly enemy, in spite of the danger of being utterly undone, we do not wake up to pray, but lie in a drugged sleep watching the dream-visions induced by mandragora.

But we must continually keep in mind that Christ did not command them simply to get up, but to get up in order to pray. For it

174. Horace, *Epistulae,* 1, 2, 40.   175. Cf. Ovid, *Amores,* 2, 9, 41.
176. Cf. Virgil, *Aeneid,* 4, 123.

is not enough to get up if we do not get up for a good purpose. If we do not, there would be far less sin in losing time through slothful drowsiness than in devoting waking time to the deliberate pursuit of malicious crimes.

Then, too, He does not merely order them to pray but shows them the need for it and teaches what they should have prayed for: "Pray," He says, "that you may not enter into temptation." Again and again He drove home this point to them,[177] that prayer is the only safeguard against temptation and that if someone refuses it entrance into the castle of his soul and shuts it out by yielding to sleep, through such negligence he permits the besieging troops of the devil (that is, temptations to evil) to break in.

Three times He admonished them verbally to pray. Then, to avoid the appearance of teaching merely by these words and in order to teach them by His example as well, He Himself prayed three times, suggesting in this way that we ought to pray to the Trinity, namely to the unbegotten Father, to the coequal Son begotten by Him, and to the Spirit equal to each and proceeding from each of them. From these three we should likewise pray for three things: forgiveness for the past, grace to manage the present, and a prudent concern for the future. But we should pray for these things not lazily and carelessly but incessantly and fervently. Just how far from this kind of prayer nearly all of us are nowadays, everyone can judge privately from his own conscience and we may all publicly learn (God forbid) by the decreasing fruits of prayer, falling off gradually from day to day.

Nevertheless, since a little earlier I bore down on this point as vigorously as I could by attacking that sort of prayer in which the mind is not attentive but wandering and distracted among many ideas, it would be well at this point to propose an emollient from

177. Matt. 6 : 13. Christ's command appears once in Matt. (26 : 41), once in Mark (14 : 38), and twice in Luke (22 : 40, 46).

Gerson[178] to alleviate this sore point, lest I seem to be like a harsh surgeon touching this common sore too roughly, bringing to many tender-souled mortals not a healing medicine but rather pain, and taking away from them hope of attaining salvation. In order to cure these troublesome inflammations of the soul, Gerson uses certain palliatives which are analogous to those medications which doctors use to relieve bodily pain and which they call "anodynes."

And so this John Gerson, an outstanding scholar and a most gentle handler of troubled consciences, saw (I imagine) some people whom this distraction of mind made so terribly anxious that they repeated the individual words of their prayers one after the other with a belabored sort of babbling, and still got nowhere and sometimes were even less pleased with their prayer the third time than the first time. He saw that such people, through sheer weariness, lost all sense of consolation from their prayers and that some of them were ready to give up the habit of prayer as useless (if they were to pray in this way) or even harmful (as they feared). This kind man, then, in order to relieve them of their troublesome difficulty, pointed out three aspects of prayer: the act, the virtue, and the habit.

But to make his meaning clearer, he explains it by the example of a person setting out from France on a pilgrimage to St. James [of Compostella].[179] For such a person sometimes goes forward on his journey and at the same time meditates on the holy saint and the purpose of the pilgrimage. And so this man throughout this whole time continues his pilgrimage by a double act, namely (and I shall use Gerson's own words) by a "natural continuity" and a "moral continuity": natural, because he actually and in fact pro-

178. In what follows More paraphrases John Gerson's seventh "consideration" in *De oratione et ejus valore.*
179. Compostella is a city in northwest Spain traditionally supposed to be the place of burial of St. James the Greater.

ceeds toward that place; moral, because his thoughts are occupied with the matter of his pilgrimage. By "moral" he refers to that moral intention by which the act of setting out, otherwise indifferent, is perfected by the pious reason for setting out.

Sometimes, however, the pilgrim goes his way considering other matters, without thinking anything about the saint or the place, thinking perhaps about something even holier, such as God Himself. In such a case he continues the act of his pilgrimage on a natural, but not a moral level. For though he actually moves his feet along, he does not actually think about the reason for setting out nor perhaps even about the way he is going. But though the moral act of his pilgrimage does not continue, its moral virtue does. For that whole natural act of walking is informed and imbued with a moral virtue because it is silently accompanied by the pious intention formed at the beginning, since all this motion follows from that first decision just as a stone continues in its course because of the original impetus, even though the hand which threw it has been withdrawn.

Sometimes, however, the moral act takes place when there is no natural act, as, for example, whenever the person thinks about his pilgrimage when he is perhaps sitting and not walking. Finally, it often happens that both kinds of act are missing, as, for example, when we are sleeping, for then the pilgrim neither performs the natural act of walking nor the moral act of thinking about the pilgrimage; but still in the meantime the moral virtue, so long as it is not deliberately renounced, remains and persists habitually.

And so this pilgrimage is never truly interrupted in such a way that its merit does not continue and persist at least habitually, unless an opposite decision is made, either to give up the pilgrimage completely or at least to put it off until another time. And so by means of this comparison he draws the same conclusions about prayer, namely that once it has been begun attentively it can never

afterwards be so interrupted that the virtue of the first intention
does not remain and persist continuously—that is, either actually
or habitually—so long as it is not relinquished by making a decision to stop nor cut off by turning away to mortal sin.

Hence he says that those words of Christ "You should pray
always and not cease"[180] were not spoken figuratively but in a
simple and straightforward sense, and that in fact they are actually and literally fulfilled by good men. He supports his opinion
with that well-known adage of learned men—"Whoever lives well
is always praying"—which is true, because whoever does everything according to the apostle's precept for the glory of God,[181]
once he has begun praying attentively, never afterwards inter-
rupts his prayer in such a way that its meritorious virtue does not
persist, if not actually then at least habitually.

This is the explanation given by that most learned and virtuous
man John Gerson in his short treatise entitled *Prayer and Its Value*.
But nevertheless he intends it as a consolation for those who are
troubled and saddened because their attention slips away from
them unawares during prayer, even though they are earnestly trying to pay attention; he does not intend that it should provide a
flattering illusion of safety for those who out of careless laziness
make no effort to think about their prayers. For when we per-
form such a grave duty negligently, we say prayers indeed, but we
do not pray, and we do not (as I said before) render God favorable
to us but drive Him far from us in His wrath.

And why should anyone be surprised if God is angry when He
sees Himself addressed so contemptuously by a lowly human
creature? And how can we imagine that a person does not
approach and address God contemptuously when he says to God
"O God, hear my prayer"[182] while his own mind all the time is

180. Luke 18 : 1.   181. 1 Cor. 10 : 31.
182. Ps. 54 : 2 (AV, 55 : 1) and 63 : 2 (AV, 64 : 1).

turned away to other matters—vain and foolish and, would that they were not, sometimes also wicked matters—so that he does not even hear his own voice but murmurs his way by rote through well-worn prayers, his mind a complete blank, emitting (as Virgil says) sounds without sense.[183] Thus when we have finished our prayers and gone our way, very often we are immediately in need of other prayers to beg forgiveness for our former carelessness.

And so when Christ had said to His apostles "Get up and pray that you may not enter into temptation," He immediately warned them how great the impending danger was, in order to show that no drowsy or lukewarm prayer would suffice: "Behold," He said, "the hour has almost come when the Son of Man will be betrayed into the hands of sinners,"[184] as if to include the following implications: "I predicted to you that I must be betrayed by one of you—you were shocked at the very words.[185] I foretold to you that Satan would seek you out to sift you like wheat—you heard this carelessly and made no response, as if his temptation were not much to be reckoned with.[186] So that you might know that temptation is not at all to be contemned, I predicted that you would all be scandalized because of me—you all denied it. To him who denied it most of all, I predicted that he would deny me three times before the cock crowed—he absolutely insisted it would not be so and that he would rather die with me than deny me, and so you all said.[187] Lest you should consider temptation a thing to be taken lightly, I again and again commanded you to watch and pray lest you enter into temptation—but you were always so far from recognizing the strength of temptation that you took no pains to pray against it or even to stay awake.

"Perhaps you were encouraged to scorn the power of the devil's temptation by the fact that before, when I sent you out two by two to preach the faith, you came back and reported to me that even

---

183. Virgil, *Aeneid,* 10, 640.   184. Matt. 26 : 45, Mark 14 : 41.
185. Matt. 26 : 21–22.   186. Luke 22 : 31–34.   187. Matt. 26 : 31–35.

the demons were subject to you. But I, to whom the nature of demons, as well as your own nature, is more deeply known than either is to you, since indeed I established each of them, I immediately cautioned you not to glory in such vanity, because it was not your power that subjected the demons but rather I myself did it, and I did it not for your sakes but for the sake of others who were to be converted to the faith; and I admonished you rather to glory in a real source of joy, namely that your names are written in the book of life.[188] This really and truly belongs to you because once you have attained that joy you can never lose it, though all the ranks of the demons should struggle against you. But still the power you exerted against them at that time gave you such high confidence that you seem to scorn their temptations as matters of little moment.

"And so, though I foretold that there was danger impending on this very night, up to now you have still viewed these temptations as it were from a distance. But now I warn you that not only the very night but even the very hour is at hand. For behold, the hour has almost come when the Son of Man will be betrayed into the hands of sinners. Now, therefore, there is no more chance to sit and sleep. Now you will be forced to stay awake, and there is hardly a moment left to pray. Now, therefore, I no longer foretell future events, but I say to you right now, at this present moment: Get up, let us go—behold, the one who will betray me is at hand. If you are not willing to stay awake so that you might be able to pray, at least get up and go away quickly lest you be unable to escape. For, behold, the one who will betray me is at hand"— unless perhaps He did not say "Get up, let us go" as intending that they should run away in fear, but rather that they should go forward with confidence. For He himself did so: He did not turn back in another direction but even as He spoke He freely went on to encounter those butchers who were making their way toward

188. Luke 10 : 17–20.

Him with murder in their hearts: "While Jesus was still saying these things, behold, Judas Iscariot, one of the twelve, and with him a large crowd with swords and clubs, sent by the chief priests and the scribes and the elders of the people."[189]

Although nothing can contribute more effectively to salvation, and to the implanting of every sort of virtue in the Christian breast, than pious and fervent meditation on the successive events of Christ's passion, still it would certainly be not unprofitable to take the story of that time when the apostles were sleeping as the Son of Man was being betrayed, and to apply it as a mysterious image of future times. For Christ, to redeem man truly became a son of man—that is, although He was conceived without male seed, He was nevertheless really descended from the first men and therefore truly became a son of Adam, so that by His passion He might restore Adam's posterity, lost and cast off into wretchedness through the fault of our first parents, to a state of happiness even greater than their original one.[190]

This is the reason that, in spite of His divinity, He constantly called Himself the Son of Man (since He was also really a man), thus constantly suggesting, by mentioning that nature which alone was capable of death, the benefit we derive from His death. For, though God died, since He who was God died, nevertheless His divinity did not undergo death, but only His humanity, or actually only His body, if we consider the fact of nature more than the custom of language. For a man is said to die when the soul leaves the dead body, but the soul which departs is itself immortal. But since He did not merely delight in the phrase describing our nature but was also pleased to take upon Himself our nature for our salvation, and then finally to unite with Himself, in the structure of one body[191] (as it were), all of us whom He regenerated by His saving sacraments and by faith, granting us a share

---

189. Matt. 26 : 47, Mark 14 : 43.   190. Cf. Rom. 5 : 12–21.
191. Cf. Jer. 13 : 11.

even of His names (since scripture calls all the faithful both gods[192] and Christs[193]), I think we would not be far wrong if we were to fear that the time approaches when the Son of Man, Christ, will be betrayed into the hands of sinners, as often as we see an imminent danger that the mystical body of Christ,[194] the church of Christ, namely the Christian people, will be brought to ruin at the hands of wicked men. And this, alas, for some centuries now we have not failed to see happening somewhere, now in one place, now in another, while the cruel Turks invade some parts of the Christian dominion and other parts are torn asunder by the internal strife of manifold heretical sects.

Whenever we see such things or hear that they are beginning to happen, however far away, let us think that this is no time for us to sit and sleep but rather to get up immediately and bring relief to the danger of others in whatever way we can, by our prayers at least if in no other way. Nor is such danger to be taken lightly because it happens at some distance from us. Certainly if that saying of the comic poet is so highly approved, "Since I am a man, I consider nothing human to be foreign to me,"[195] how could it be anything but disgraceful for Christians to snore while other Christians are in danger? In order to suggest this, Christ directed His warning to watch and pray not only to those He had placed nearby but also to those He had caused to remain at some distance. Then, too, if we are perhaps unmoved by the misfortunes of others because they are at some distance from us, let us at least be moved by our own danger. For we have reason to fear that the destructive force will make its way from them to us, taught as we are by many examples how rapid the rushing force of a blaze can be and how terrible the contagion of a spreading plague. Since, therefore, all human safeguards are useless without the help of God to ward off evils, let us always remember these

192. E.g., John 10 : 34–35 (quoting Ps. 81 : 6, *AV,* 82 : 6), Exod. 22 : 8–9.
193. E.g., Mark 9 : 40, 1 Par. 16 : 22, Ps. 104 : 15 (*AV,* 105 : 15).
194. Cf. 1 Cor. 12 : 27.   195. Terence, *Heautontimorumenos,* 77.

words from the gospel and let us always imagine that Christ Himself is again addressing to us over and over those words of His: "Why are you sleeping? Get up and pray that you may not enter into temptation."

At this juncture another point occurs to us: that Christ is also betrayed into the hands of sinners when His most holy body in the sacrament is consecrated and handled by unchaste, profligate, and sacrilegious priests. When we see such things happen (and they happen only too often, alas), let us imagine that Christ Himself again says to us "Why are you sleeping? Stay awake, get up, and pray that you may not enter into temptation, for the Son of Man is betrayed into the hands of sinners." From the example of bad priests the contamination of vice spreads easily among the people. And the less suitable for obtaining grace those persons are whose duty it is to watch and pray for the people, the more necessary it is for the people to stay awake, get up, and pray all the more earnestly for themselves—and not only for themselves but also for priests of this sort. For it will be much to the advantage of the people if bad priests improve.

Finally, Christ is betrayed into the hands of sinners in a special way among those of a certain sect: these people, though they receive the venerable sacrament of the eucharist more frequently and wish to give the impression of honoring it more piously by receiving it under both species (contrary to public custom, without any necessity, but not without a great affront to the Catholic Church), nevertheless these people blaspheme against what they have received under a show of honor, some them by calling it true bread and true wine, some of them—and this is far worse—by calling it not only true but also mere bread and wine. For they altogether deny that the real body of Christ is contained in the sacrament, though they call it by that name [corpus Christi]. When at this late date they set out to do such a thing, against the most open passages of scripture, against the clearest interpretations of all the saints, against the most constant faith of the whole church for so many centuries, against the truth most amply witnessed to by so many thousands of miracles—this group that labors under the second kind of infidelity (by far the worse), how little difference is there, I ask you, between them and those who took Christ captive that night? How little difference between them and those troops of Pilate who in jest bent their knees before Christ as if they were honoring Him while they insulted Him and called Him the king of the Jews, just as these people kneel before the eucharist and call it the body of Christ—which according to their own profession they no more believe than the soldiers of Pilate believed Christ was a king.

Therefore, whenever we hear that such evils have befallen other peoples, no matter how distant, let us immediately imagine that Christ is urgently addressing us: "Why are you sleeping? Get up and pray that you may not enter into temptation." For the fact is that wherever this plague rages today most fiercely, everyone did not catch the disease in a single day. Rather the contagion spreads gradually and imperceptibly while those persons who despise it at first, afterwards can stand to hear it and respond to it with less than full scorn, then come to tolerate wicked discussions, and afterwards are carried away into error, until like a cancer (as the apostle says) the creeping disease finally takes over the whole country.[196] Therefore let us stay awake, get up, and pray continually that all those who have fallen into this miserable folly through the wiles of Satan may quickly come to their senses and that God may never suffer us to enter into this kind of temptation and may never allow the devil to roll the blasts of this storm of his to our shores. But so much for my digression into these mysteries; let us now return to the historical events.

*   *   *

196. 2 Tim. 2 : 17.

"Judas, therefore, when he had received a cohort from the chief priests and servants from the pharisees, came there with lanterns and torches.[197] And while Jesus was still speaking, behold, Judas Iscariot, one of the twelve, and with him a large crowd with swords and clubs, sent by the chief priests and scribes and elders of the people. The traitor, however, had given them a sign, etc."[198]

I tend to believe that the cohort which, according to the accounts of the evangelists, was handed over to the traitor by the high priests, was a Roman cohort assigned to the high priests by Pilate. To it the pharisees, scribes, and elders of the people had added their own servants, either because they did not have enough confidence in the governor's soldiers or because they thought extra numbers would help prevent Christ from being rescued through some sudden confusion caused by the darkness, or perhaps for another reason, their desire to arrest at the same time all the apostles, without letting any of them escape in the dark. They were prevented from executing this part of their plan by the power of Christ Himself, who was Himself captured only because He, and He alone, wished to be taken.

They carry smoking torches and dim lanterns so that they might be able to discern through the darkness of sin the bright sun of justice,[199] not that they might be enlightened by the light of Him who enlightens every man that comes into this world,[200] but that they might put out that eternal light of His which can never be darkened. And like master like servant, for those who sent them strove to overthrow the law of God for the sake of their traditions. Even now some still follow in their footsteps and persecute Christ by striving mightily to overshadow the splendor of God's glory for the sake of their own glory. But in this passage it is worthwhile to pay close attention to the constant revolutions and vicissitudes of the human condition. For not six days before, even

197. John 18 : 3.   198. Matt. 26 : 47–48, Mark 14 : 43–44.   199. Mal. 4 : 2.
200. John 1 : 9.

the gentiles had been eager to get a look at Christ, because of His remarkable miracles, together with the great holiness of His life.[201] But the Jews had welcomed Him with truly extraordinary reverence as He rode into Jerusalem. But now the Jews, joining forces with the gentiles, had come to arrest Him like a thief; and not merely among them but at their head was a man worse than all the gentiles and Jews put together, Judas. Thus in His death Christ took care to provide this contrast as a notable warning to all men that no one should expect blind Fortune to stand still for him, and that no Christian especially, as one who hopes for heaven, should pursue the contemptible glory of this world.

The persons responsible for sending the crowd after Christ were priests—and not merely that, but princes of the priests— pharisees, scribes, and elders of the people. Here we see that whatever is best by nature turns out in the end to be the worst, once it begins to reverse its direction. Thus Lucifer, created by God as the most eminent among the angels in heaven, became the worst of the demons after he yielded to the pride which brought his downfall. So too, not the dregs of the crowd but the elders of the people, the scribes, pharisees, priests, and high priests, the princes of the priests, whose duty it was to see that justice was done and to promote the affairs of God, these were the very ring-leaders in a conspiracy to extinguish the sun of justice[202] and to destroy the only begotten son of God—to such insane extremes of perversity were they driven by avarice, arrogance, and envy.

Another point should not be passed over lightly but should be given careful consideration: Judas, who in many other places is called by the infamous name "traitor," is here also disgraced by the lofty title "apostle." "Behold," he says, "Judas Iscariot, one of the twelve," Judas Iscariot—who was not one of the unbelieving pagans, not one of the Jewish enemies, not one of Christ's ordinary disciples (and even that would have been incredible enough),

201. John 12 : 20–22.   202. Mal. 4 : 2.

but (O the shame of it!) one of Christ's chosen apostles—can bear to hand over his Lord to be captured, and even to be the leader of the captors himself.

There is in this passage a lesson to be learned by all who exercise high public office: when they are addressed with solemn titles, they do not always have reason to be proud and congratulate themselves; rather, such titles are truly fitting only if those who bear them know in their hearts that they have in fact lived up to such honorific names by conscientiously performing their duties. For otherwise, they may very well be overcome with shame (unless they find pleasure in the empty jingle of words), since wicked men in high office—whether they be great men, princes, great lords, emperors, priests, bishops, it makes no difference as long as they are wicked—certainly ought to realize that whenever men titillate their ears by crooning their splendid titles of office, they do not do so sincerely, in order to pay them true honor, but rather to reproach them freely by seeming to praise those honors which they bear in so unpraiseworthy a fashion. So too, in the gospel, when Judas is celebrated under his title of apostle in the phrase "Judas Iscariot, one of the twelve," the real intent is anything but praise, as is clear from the fact that in the next breath he is called a traitor. "For the traitor," according to the account, "had given them a signal, saying, 'Whomever I kiss, that is the one. Seize him.'"[203]

At this point the usual question is why it was necessary for the traitor to give the crowd a signal identifying Jesus. To this some answer that they agreed on a signal because more than once before Christ had suddenly escaped from the hands of those who were trying to apprehend Him. But since this usually happened in the daytime, when He was escaping from the hands of those who already recognized Him, and since He did it by employing His divine power, either to disappear from their sight or to pass

203. Matt. 26 : 48, Mark 14 : 44.

from their midst while they were in a state of shock, against this sort of escape giving a signal to identify Him could not be of any use.

And so others say that one of the two Jameses looked very much like Christ—and for that reason, they think, he was called the brother of Christ[204]—so much so that unless you looked at them closely you could not tell them apart. But since they could have arrested both of them and taken both away with them to be identified later at their leisure by comparing them at close quarters, what need was there to worry about a signal?

The gospel makes it clear that the night was far advanced, and, although daybreak was drawing near, it was still nighttime and quite dark, as is evident from the torches and lanterns they carried, which gave enough light to make them visible from some distance but hardly enough for them to discern anyone else from afar. And, although on that night they perhaps had the advantage of some faint light from the full moon, it could only have been enough to make out the shapes of bodies in the distance, not to get a good view of facial features and distinguish one person from another. Hence, if they went rushing in at random in the hope of capturing all of them at once, each man choosing his victim without knowing who he was, they were afraid, and rightly so, that out of so many some (by all odds) might perhaps get away and that one of the fugitives might well be the very man they had come for. For those who are in the greatest danger are likely to be the quickest to look out for themselves.

Thus, whether they thought of this or whether Judas himself suggested it, they set their trap by having the betrayer go on ahead to single out the Lord by embracing and kissing Him. In this way, when they had all fixed their eyes on Him alone, each and every one of them could try to get his hands on Him. After that, if any of the others got away, it would not be such a dangerous matter.

204. Gal. 1 : 19.

"Therefore the traitor had given them a signal, saying, 'Whomever I kiss, that is the one. Seize him and take him away carefully.'"[205]

O the lengths to which greed will go! Couldn't you be satisfied, you treacherous scoundrel, with betraying your Lord (who had raised you to the lofty office of an apostle) into the hands of impious men by the signal of a kiss, without also being so concerned that He should be taken away carefully, lest He might escape from His captors? You were hired to betray Him; others were sent to take Him, to guard Him, to produce Him in court. But you, as if your role in the crime were not important enough, go on to meddle in the duties of the soldiers; and as if the villainous magistrates who sent them had not given them adequate instructions, there was a need for a circumspect man like you to add your own gratuitous cautions and commands, that they must lead Him away carefully once He is captured. Were you afraid that, even though you had fully performed your criminal task by betraying Christ to His assassins, still if the soldiers had somehow been so remiss that Christ escaped through their carelessness or was rescued by force against their will—were you afraid that then your thirty pieces of silver, that illustrious reward of your heinous crime, would not be paid? Have no fear, they will be paid. But believe me, you are no more eager and greedy to get them now than you will be impatient and anxious to throw them away once you have gotten them. Meanwhile you will go on to complete a deed that brings pain to your Lord and death to you, but salvation to many.

"He went ahead of them and came up to Jesus to kiss Him. And when he had come, he went right up to Him and said 'Rabbi, hail Rabbi' and he kissed Him. Jesus said to Him, 'Friend, why have

205. Mark 14 : 44.

you come?[206] Judas, are you betraying the Son of Man with a kiss?'"[207]

Though Judas really did, as a matter of historical fact, precede the crowd, still this also means in a spiritual sense that among those who share in the same sinful act, the one who has most reason to abstain takes precedence in God's judgment of their guilt.

"And he came up to Him to kiss Him. And when he had come, he went right up to Him and said 'Rabbi, hail Rabbi.' And he kissed Him." In this same way Christ is approached, greeted, called "Rabbi," kissed, by those who pretend to be disciples of Christ, professing His teaching in name but striving in fact to undermine it by crafty tricks and stratagems. In just this way Christ is greeted as "Rabbi" by anyone who calls Him master and scorns His precepts. In just this way is He kissed by those priests who consecrate the most holy body of Christ and then put to death Christ's members, Christian souls, by their false teaching and wicked example. In just this way is Christ greeted and kissed by those who demand to be considered good and pious because at the persuasion of bad priests, they, though laymen, receive the sacred body and blood of Christ under both species, without any real need for it, but not without great contempt for the whole Catholic Church and therefore not without grave sin. And this these latter-day saints do against the long-standing practice and custom of all Christians. And not only do they themselves do it (that we could somehow manage to put up with) but they condemn everyone who receives both substances under only one of the two species—that is, apart from themselves, all Christians everywhere for these many years. And still, though they hotly insist that both species are necessary for the laity, most of them—both laymen and priests—eliminate the reality, that is the body and blood, from both species, keeping only the words "body" and

206. Matt. 26 : 49–50; cf. Mark 14 : 45.   207. Luke 22 : 48.

"blood." In this respect, indeed, they are not unlike Pilate's guards, who mocked Christ by kneeling before Him and saluting Him as the king of the Jews. For these men likewise genuflect in veneration of the eucharist and call it the body and blood of Christ though they no more believe it is the one or the other than the soldiers of Pilate believed Christ was a king.

Now all these groups which I have enumerated certainly bring to our minds the traitor Judas in that they combine a greeting and a kiss with treachery. But just as they renew an action of the past, so Joab (2 Kings 20) once provided a prophetic figure of the future: for "when he had greeted Amasa thus, 'Greetings, my brother,' and had caressed Amasa's chin with his right hand" as if he were about to kiss him, he stealthily unsheathed a hidden sword and killed him with one stroke through his side,[208] and by a similar trick he had formerly killed Abner,[209] but later (as was only right) he justly paid with his life for his heinous deception.[210] Judas rightly calls to mind and represents Joab, whether you consider the status of the persons involved or the deceitful treachery of the crime, or the vengeance of God and the bad end both came to— with this difference, that Judas surpassed Joab in every respect.

Joab enjoyed great favor and influence with his prince; Judas had even more with an even greater prince. Joab killed Amasa who was his friend; Judas killed Jesus who was an even closer friend, not to say also his Lord. Joab was motivated by envy and ambition because he had heard that the king would promote Amasa above him;[211] but Judas, enticed by greed for a miserable reward, for a few pieces of silver, betrayed the Lord of the world to His death. In the same degree, therefore, as Judas' crime was worse, the vengeance exacted from him was the more devastating. For Joab was killed by another, but the most wretched Judas hanged himself with his own hand.

208. 2 Kings 20 : 8–10. 209. 2 Kings 3 : 26–30. 210. 3 Kings 2 : 28–35.
211. 2 Kings 19 : 13.

But in the treacherous pattern of their deception, there is a nice equivalence between the crimes of Joab and Judas. For just as Joab kills Amasa in the very act of courteously greeting him and preparing to kiss him, so too Judas approaches Christ affably, greets Him reverently, kisses Him lovingly and all the time the villainous wretch has nothing else in mind than to betray his Lord to His death. But Joab was able to deceive Amasa by flattery; not so Judas with Christ. He receives his advances, listens to his greeting, does not refuse his kiss, and, though aware of his abominable treachery, He nevertheless acted for a while as if He were completely ignorant of everything. Why did He do this? Was it to teach us to feign and dissemble, and with polite cunning to turn the deception back upon the deceiver? Hardly, but rather to teach us to bear patiently and gently all injuries and snares treacherously set for us, not to smolder with anger, not to seek revenge, not to give vent to our feelings by hurling back insults, not to find an empty pleasure in tripping up an enemy through some clever trick, but rather to set ourselves against deceitful injury with genuine courage, to conquer evil with good[212]—in fine, to make every effort by words both gentle and harsh, to insist both in season and out of season,[213] that the wicked may change their ways to good, so that if anyone should be suffering from a disease that does not respond to treatment, he may not blame the failure on our negligence but rather attribute it to the virulence of his own disease.

And so Christ as a most conscientious physician tries both ways of effecting a cure. Employing first of all gentle words, He says, "Friend, why have you come?" When he heard himself called "friend," the traitor was left hanging in doubt. For, since He was aware of his own crime, he was afraid that Christ used the title "friend" as a severe rebuke for his hostile unfriendliness. On the other hand, since criminals always flatter themselves with the

212. Rom. 12 : 21.   213. Cf. 2 Tim. 4 : 2.

hope that their crimes are unknown, he was blind and mad enough to hope (even though he had often learned by personal experience that the thoughts of men lay open to Christ[214] and though his own treachery had been touched upon at the [last] supper),[215] nevertheless, I say, he was so demented and oblivious to everything as to hope that his villainous deed had escaped Christ's notice.

But because nothing could be more unwholesome for him than to be duped by such a futile hope (for nothing could work more strongly against his repentance than this), Christ in His goodness no longer allows him to be led on by a deceptive hope of deceiving but immediately adds in a grave tone, "Judas, do you betray the Son of Man with a kiss?" He addresses him by the name He had ordinarily used—and for this reason, so that the memory of their old friendship might soften the heart of the traitor and move him to repent. He openly rebukes his treachery lest he should believe it is hidden and be ashamed to confess it. Moreover, He reviles the impious hypocrisy of the traitor: "With a kiss," He says, "do you betray the Son of Man?"

Among all the circumstances of a wicked deed it is not easy to find one more hateful to God than the perversion of the real nature of good things to make them into the instruments of our malice. Thus lying is hateful to God because words, which are ordained to express the meaning of the mind, are twisted to other deceitful purposes. Within this category of evil, it is a serious offense against God if anyone abuses the law to inflict the very injuries it was designed to prevent. And so Christ reproaches Judas sharply for this detestable kind of sin: "Judas," He says, "do you betray the Son of Man with a kiss? Either be in fact as you wish to seem or else show yourself openly as you really are. For whoever commits such an unfriendly misdeed under the guise of a friend is a villain who compounds his villainy. Were you not sat-

214. See, e.g., Matt. 9 : 4 and 12 : 25.   215. Matt. 26 : 21–25.

isfied, Judas, with betraying the Son of Man—indeed, I say, the son of that man through whom all men would have perished if this Son of Man, whom you imagine you are destroying, had not redeemed those who wish to be saved—was it not enough for you, I say, to betray this Son of Man without doing it with a kiss, thus turning the most sacred sign of charity into an instrument of betrayal? Certainly I am more favorably disposed toward this mob which attacks me with open force than toward you, Judas, who betray me to the attackers with a false kiss."

And so when Christ saw no sign of repentance in the traitor, wishing to show how much more willing He was to speak with open enemies than with a secret foe, having made it clear to the traitor that He cared not a whit for all his wicked stratagems, He immediately turned away from him and made His way, unarmed as He was, toward the armed crowd. For so the gospel says: "And then Jesus, knowing everything that was to happen to Him, went forward and said to them, 'Whom do you seek?' They replied to Him, 'Jesus of Nazareth.' Jesus said to them, 'I am He.' Now Judas, who betrayed Him, was also standing with them. When, therefore, He said to them, 'I am He,' they drew back and fell to the ground."[216]

O saving Christ, only a little while ago, you were so fearful that you lay face down in a most pitiable attitude and sweat blood as you begged your Father to take away the chalice of your passion. How is it that now, by a sudden reversal, you leap up and spring forth like a giant running his race[217] and come forward eagerly to meet those who seek to inflict that passion upon you? How is it that you freely identify yourself to those who openly admit they are seeking you but who do not know that you are the one they are seeking? Hither, hither let all hasten who are faint of heart. Here let them take firm hold of an unwavering hope when they feel themselves struck by a horror of death. For just as they share

216. John 18 : 4–6.   217. Cf. Ps. 18 : 6 (AV, 19 : 5).

Christ's agony, His fear, grief, anxiety, sadness, and sweat (provided that they pray, and persist in prayer, and submit themselves wholeheartedly to the will of God), they will also share this consolation, undoubtedly they will feel themselves helped by such consolation as Christ felt; and they will be so refreshed by the spirit of Christ that they will feel their hearts renewed as the old face of the earth is renewed by the dew from heaven,[218] and by means of the wood of Christ's cross let down into the water of their sorrow, the thought of death, once so bitter, will grow sweet,[219] eagerness will take the place of grief, mental strength and courage will replace dread, and finally they will long for the death they had viewed with horror, considering life a sad thing and death a gain, desiring to be dissolved and to be with Christ.[220]

"And so Christ coming up close to the crowd asks, 'Whom do you seek?' They replied to Him 'Jesus of Nazareth.' Now Judas, who betrayed Him, was standing with them. And Jesus said to them, 'I am He.' When, therefore, Jesus said to them, 'I am He,' they drew back and fell to the ground." If Christ's previous fear and anxiety lessened His standing in anyone's mind, the balance must now be redressed by the manly courage with which He fearlessly approaches that whole mass of armed men and, though He faces certain death ("for He knew everything which was to happen to Him"),[221] betrays Himself by His own act to those villains, who did not even know who He was, and thus offers Himself freely as a victim to be cruelly slaughtered.

Certainly this sudden and drastic change would rightly be considered marvelous viewed simply as occurring in His venerable human nature. But what sort of estimate of Him, how intense a reaction to Him must be produced in the hearts of all the faithful by the force of divine power flashing so wonderfully through the

---

218. Ps. 103 : 30 (AV, 104 : 30). Cf. Exod. 16 : 13–14, Ps. 132 : 3 (AV, 133 : 3), Prov. 19 : 12, Mic. 5 : 7.
219. See Exod. 15 : 23–25.   220. Phil. 1 : 21–23.   221. John 18 : 4.

weak body of a man? For how was it that none of His pursuers recognized Him when He came up close to them? He had taught in the temple. He had overturned the tables of the moneychangers, He had driven out the moneychangers themselves,[222] He had carried out His activities in public, He had confuted the pharisees,[223] He had satisfied the sadducees,[224] He had refuted the scribes,[225] He eluded by a prudent answer the trick question of the Herodian soldiers,[226] He had fed seven thousand men with five loaves,[227] He had healed the sick, raised the dead, made Himself available to all sorts of men, pharisees, tax-gatherers, the rich, the poor, just men, sinners, Jews, Samaritans, and gentiles, and now in this whole large crowd there was no one who recognized Him by His face or voice as He addressed them near at hand, as if those who sent them had taken special care not to send anyone along who had ever seen beforehand the person they were then seeking.

Had no one even singled out Christ from His meeting with Judas, from the embrace and the sign Judas gave with a kiss? Even more, the traitor himself, who was at that time standing together with them, did he suddenly forget how to recognize the very person he had just betrayed by singling Him out with a kiss? What was the source of this strange happening? Indeed, no one was able to recognize Him for the very same reason that a little later Mary Magdalen, though she saw Him, did not recognize Him until He revealed Himself, and likewise neither one of the two disciples, though they were talking with Him, knew who He was until He let them know, but rather the two disciples thought that He was a traveller and she thought He was a gardener.[228] Finally, then, if you want to know how it was that no one could

---

222. Mark 11 : 15.   223. See, e.g., John 8 : 21–47.   224. Matt. 22 : 23–33.
225. E.g., Mark 2 : 6–12.   226. Matt. 22 : 15–22.
227. In all the gospel accounts the five loaves were distributed to 5,000 men. See Matt. 14 : 16–21, Mark 6 : 38–44, Luke 9 : 13–17, John 6 : 8–13.
228. See John 20 : 14–16 and Luke 24 : 16–31.

recognize Him when He came up to them, you should undoubtedly attribute it to the same cause you use to explain the fact that when He spoke no one could remain standing: "But when Jesus said, 'I am He,' they drew back and fell to the ground."

Here Christ proved that He truly is that word of God which pierces more sharply than any two-edged sword.[229] Thus a lightning bolt is said to be of such a nature that it liquefies a sword without damaging the sheath.[230] Certainly the mere voice of Christ, without damaging their bodies, so melted their souls that it deprived them of the strength to hold up their limbs.

Here the evangelist relates that Judas was standing together with them. For when he heard Jesus rebuke him openly as a traitor, whether overcome with shame or struck with fear (for he was acquainted with Peter's impulsiveness), he immediately withdrew and returned to his own kind. Thus the evangelist tells us he was standing together with them so that we may understand that like them he also fell down. And certainly the character of Judas was such that there was in that whole crowd no one worse or more worthy of being cast down. But the evangelist wished to impress upon everyone generally that they must be careful and cautious about the company they keep, for there is a danger that if they take their place with wicked men they will also fall together with them. It rarely happens that a person who is foolish enough to cast his lot with those who are headed for shipwreck in an unseaworthy vessel gets back to land alive after the others have drowned in the sea.

No one, I suppose, doubts that a person who could throw them all down with one word could easily have dashed them all down so forcibly that none of them could have gotten back up again. But Christ, who struck them down to let them know that they could inflict no suffering upon Him against His will, allowed them to get up again so that they could accomplish what He

229. Heb. 4 : 12.   230. Cf. Seneca, *Naturales Quaestiones*, 2, 31.

wished to endure: "And so, when they had gotten up, He asked them once more, 'Whom do you seek?' And they said to Him, 'Jesus of Nazareth.'"[231]

Here, too, anyone can see that they were so daunted, stunned, and stupefied by their meeting with Christ that they seem almost to be out of their minds. For they might very well have known that at that time of night and in that place they would not find anyone who was not one of Christ's band of followers or else a friend of His and that the last thing in the world such a person would do would be to lead them to Christ. And yet, suddenly meeting a person whose identity was unknown to them as well as the reason for His question, right away they foolishly blurt out the heart of the whole affair, which they ought to have kept carefully concealed until they had carried it out. For as soon as He asked, "Whom do you seek?" they replied, "Jesus of Nazareth." Jesus answered, "I have told you I am He. If, therefore, you seek me, let these men go their way"[232]—as if to say: If you are looking for me, now that I have approached you and let you know who I am by my own admission, why do you not arrest me on the spot? Surely the reason is that you are so far from being able to take me against my will that you cannot even remain standing at my mere words, as you have just learned by falling backwards. But now, if you have forgotten it so quickly, I again remind you that I am Jesus of Nazareth. "If, therefore, you seek me, let these men go their way."

By throwing them down, Christ made it very clear, I think, that His words, "Let these men go their way," did not constitute a request. But sometimes it happens that those who are planning some great piece of villainy are not content with the bare crime alone but with perverse wantonness make a practice of adding certain trimmings, as it were, beyond what is required by the scope of the crime itself. Moreover, there are some ministers of

231. John 18 : 7.   232. John 18 : 8.

crime who are so preposterously faithful that, to avoid the risk of omitting any evil deed that has been entrusted to them, they will add something extra on their own for good measure. Christ implicitly refers to each of these two types: "If you seek me," He says, "let these go their way." If my blood is what the chief priests, the scribes, pharisees, and the elders of the people are longing to drain away with such an eager thirst, behold, when you were seeking me I came to meet you; when you did not know me, I betrayed myself to you; when you were prostrate, I stood nearby; now that you are arising, I stand ready to be taken captive; and finally I myself hand myself over to you (which the traitor was not able to do) to keep my followers and you from imagining (as if it were not crime enough to kill me) that their blood must be added over and above mine. Therefore, "if you seek me, let these men go their way."

He commanded them to let them go, but He also forced them to do so against their will, and by seeing to it that all were saved by flight He frustrated their efforts to capture them. An indication of this outcome was what He intended by this prophetic statement of His—"Let these men go their way"—so that those words He had spoken might be fulfilled: "Of those you have given me, I have not lost anyone."[233] The words of Christ which the evangelist is talking about here are those words He spoke to His Father that same night at supper: "Holy Father, preserve in your name those whom you have given to me."[234] And afterwards: "I have guarded those whom you gave to me, and none of them has perished except the son of perdition, that the scripture might be fulfilled."[235] See how Christ here, as He foretells that the disciples will be saved when He is taken captive, declares that He is their guardian. Hence the evangelist recalls this to the minds of his readers, wishing them to understand that, in spite of His words to the crowd—"Let these men go their way"—He Himself by His hidden power had opened up a way for their escape.

233. John 18 : 9.   234. John 17 : 11.   235. John 17 : 12.

The place in scripture which predicts that Judas would perish is in Psalm 108, where the psalmist prophesies in the form of a prayer: "May his days be few and may another take over his ministry."[236] Although these prophetic words were spoken about the traitor Judas such a long time before the event, nevertheless it would be hard to say whether anyone, apart from the psalmist himself, knew that they referred to Judas until Christ made this clear and the event itself bore out the words. Even the prophets themselves did not see everything foreseen by other prophets. For the spirit of prophecy is measured out individually.[237] Certainly it seems clear to me that no one understands the meaning of all scriptural passages so well that there are not many mysteries hidden there which are not yet understood, whether concerning the times of the Antichrist or the last judgment by Christ, and which will remain unknown until Elias returns to explain them.[238] Therefore it seems to me that I can justly apply the apostle's exclamation about God's wisdom to holy scripture (in which God has hidden and laid up the vast stores of His wisdom): "O the depth of the riches of the wisdom and knowledge of God! How incomprehensible are His judgments and how unsearchable His ways!"[239]

And nevertheless nowadays, first in one place, then in another, there are springing up from day to day, almost like swarms of wasps or hornets, people who boast that they are "autodidacts" (to use St. Hierome's word) and that, without the commentaries of the old doctors, they find clear, open, and easy all those things which all the ancient fathers confessed they found quite difficult—and the fathers were men of no less talent or training, of tireless energy, and as for that "spirit" which these moderns have as often on their lips as they do rarely in their hearts, here the fathers surpassed them no less than in holiness of life. But now

236. Ps. 108 : 8 (AV, 109 : 8).   237. Cf. Ephes. 4 : 7.   238. Mal. 4 : 5.
239. Rom. 11 : 33.

these modern men, who have sprouted up overnight as theologians professing to know everything, not only disagree about the meaning of scripture with all those men who led such heavenly lives, but also fail to agree among themselves concerning great dogmas of the Christian faith. Rather, each of them, whoever he may be, insisting that he sees the truth, conquers the rest and is in turn conquered by them. But they all are alike in opposing the Catholic faith and all are alike in being conquered by it. He who dwells in the heavens laughs to scorn these wicked and vain attempts of theirs.[240] But I humbly pray that He may not so laugh them to scorn as to laugh also at their eternal ruination, but rather that He may inspire in them the health-giving grace of repentance, so that these prodigal sons[241] who have wandered so long, alas, in exile may retrace their steps to the bosom of mother church, and so that all of us together, united in the true faith of Christ and joined in mutual charity as true members of Christ, may attain to the glory of Christ our head,[242] which no one should ever be foolish enough to hope to arrive at outside the body of Christ and without the true faith.

But, to return to what I was saying, the fact that this prophetic utterance applies to Judas was suggested by Christ,[243] was made clear by Judas' suicide, was afterwards made quite explicit by Peter,[244] and was fulfilled by all the apostles when Matthias was chosen by lot[245] to take his place and thus another took over his ministry. And to make the matter even clearer, after Matthias took Judas' place, no replacement was ever taken into that group of twelve (although bishops succeed in the place of the apostles in an uninterrupted line), but rather, as the apostleship was transmitted gradually to more persons, that sacred number came to an end once the prophecy had been fulfilled.

Therefore, when Christ said, "Let these men go their way," He

---

240. Ps. 2 : 4.   241. Cf. Luke 15 : 11–32.   242. Cf. Ephes. 4 : 1–16.
243. John 17 : 12.   244. Acts 1 : 20.   245. Acts 1 : 26.

was not begging for their permission, but rather declaring in veiled terms that He Himself granted His disciples the power to leave, that He might fulfill those words He had spoken: "Father, I have guarded those whom you gave to me, and none of them has perished except the son of perdition."[246] I think it worthwhile to consider here for a moment how strongly Christ foretold in these words the contrast between the end of Judas and the end of the rest, the ruination of the traitor Judas and the success of the others. For He asserts each future outcome with such certainty that He announces them not as future happenings but as events that have already definitely taken place. "I have guarded," He says, "those whom you gave to me." They were not defended by their own strength, nor were they preserved by the mercy of the Jews, nor did they escape through the carelessness of the cohort, but rather "I guarded them. And none of them perished except the son of perdition." For he, too, Father, was among those whom you gave to me. Chosen by me, he received me, and to him as well as to the rest who received me I had given the power to become a son of God.[247] But when in his insane greed he went over to Satan, leaving me, betraying me treacherously, refusing to be saved, then he became a son of destruction in the very act of pursuing my destruction, and perished like a wretch in his wretchedness.

Infallibly certain about the fate of the traitor, Christ expresses his future ruin with such certainty that He asserts it as if it had already come to pass. And for all that, as Christ is being arrested, the unhappy traitor stands there as the ferocious leader and standard-bearer of Christ's captors, rejoicing and exulting, I imagine, in the danger of his fellow-disciples and his master, for I am convinced he desired and hoped that all of them would be arrested and put to death. The raving madness and perversity of ingratitude manifests itself in this peculiarity: the ingrate desires the death of the very victim he has unjustly injured. So too, the

246. John 17 : 12.   247. Cf. John 1 : 12.

person whose conscience is full of guilty sores is so sensitive that he views even the face of his victim as a reproach and shrinks from it with dread. Thus as the traitor rejoiced in the hope that all of them would be captured together, he was so stupidly sure of himself that nothing was further from his mind than the thought that the death sentence passed on him by God was hanging over his head like a dreadful noose ready to fall around his neck at any moment.

In this connection I am struck by the lamentable obscurity of the miserable human condition: often we are distressed and fearful, ignorant all the while that we are quite safe; often, on the other hand, we act as if we had not a care in the world, unaware that the death-dealing sword hangs over our heads. The other apostles were afraid they would be seized together with Christ and put to death, whereas actually they were all to escape. Judas, who had no fears for himself and took pleasure in their fears, perished only a few hours later. Cruel is the appetite which feeds on the misery of others. Nor is there any reason why a person should rejoice and congratulate himself on his good fortune because he has it in his power to cause another man's death, as the traitor thought he had by means of the cohort that had been delivered to him. For though a man may send someone else to his death, he himself is sure to follow him there. Even more, since the hour of death is uncertain, he himself may precede the very person he arrogantly imagines he has sent to death ahead of him.

Thus the death of the wretched Judas preceded that of Christ, whom he had betrayed to His death—a sad and terrible example to the whole world that the wrongdoer, however he may flout his arrogant impenitence, ought not to think he is safe from retribution. For against the wicked all creatures work together in harmony with their creator.[248] The air longs to blow noxious vapors

248. Cf. Sap. 5 : 21–24, 16 : 16–17; Cicero, *De Finibus,* 1, 16, 50–51; Ariosto, *Orlando Furioso,* 6, 1.

against the wicked man, the sea longs to overwhelm him in its waves, the mountains to fall upon him, the valleys to rise up against him, the earth to split open beneath him, hell to swallow him up after his headlong fall, the demons to plunge him into gulfs of ever-burning flames. All the while the only one who preserves the wretch is the God whom he deserted.

But if anyone is such a persistent imitator of Judas that God finally decides not to offer any longer the grace which has been offered and refused so often, this man is really and truly wretched: however he may flatter himself in the delusion that he is floating high in the air on the wings of felicity, he is actually wallowing in the utter depths of misery and calamity. Therefore let each of us pray to the most merciful Christ, each praying not only for himself but also for others, that we may not imitate Judas in his stubbornness but rather may eagerly accept the grace God offers us and may be restored once more to glory through penance and mercy.

THE SEVERING OF MALCHUS' EAR, THE FLIGHT OF THE APOSTLES, AND THE CAPTURE OF CHRIST

The severing of Malchus' ear

The apostles had previously heard Christ foretelling the very things they were now seeing happen.[249] On that occasion, though they were saddened and grieved, they treated the matter with much less concern than now when they see it happening before their very eyes. Now that they see the whole cohort standing there and openly admitting that they are seeking Jesus of Nazareth, there is no more room for doubt that they are seeking Him to take Him captive.

249. Matt. 16 : 21. Cf. John 16 : 6, 22.

When the apostles saw what was about to happen, their minds were overwhelmed by a sudden welter of different feelings: anxiety for their Lord whom they loved, fear for their own safety, and finally shame for that high-sounding promise[250] of theirs that they would all rather die than fail their master. Thus their impulses were divided between conflicting feelings. Their love of their master urged them not to flee; their fear for themselves, not to remain. Fear of death impelled them to run away; shame for their promise, to stand fast.

Moreover, they remembered what Christ had said to them that very night: He told them that, whereas before He had forbidden any of them to carry so much as a staff to defend himself with,[251] now whoever did not have a sword should even sell his tunic to buy one.[252] Now they were struck with great fear as they saw massed against them the Roman cohort and the crowd of Jews, all of them armed with weapons, whereas there were only eleven of them, and even of those none had any weapons (apart perhaps from table knives) except two had swords. Nevertheless, they remembered that when they had said to Christ, "Look, here are two swords," He had replied, "That is enough."[253] Not understanding the great mystery contained in this reply, they suddenly and impulsively ask Him whether He wants them to defend Him with the sword, saying, "Lord, shall we strike with the sword?"[254]

But Peter's feelings boiled over so that he did not wait for a reply, but drew his sword, struck a blow at the servant of the high priest, and cut off his right ear—perhaps simply because this man happened to be standing near to Peter, perhaps because his fierce and haughty bearing made him conspicuous among the rest. At any rate he certainly seems to have been a notoriously wicked man, for the evangelists mention that he was the servant of the high priest, the chief and prince of all the priests. "The greater the

250. Matt. 26 : 33–35.   251. Matt. 10 : 10.   252. Luke 22 : 35–36.
253. Luke 22 : 38.   254. Luke 22 : 49.

house, the prouder the servants," as the satirist says,[255] and men know from experience that everywhere in the world the servants of great lords are more arrogant and overbearing than their masters. That we might know that this man had some standing with the high priest and was for that reason all the more egregiously proud, John immediately adds his name. "The servant's name," he says, "was Malchus."[256] The evangelist does not ordinarily provide such information everywhere or without some special reason.

I imagine that this rascal, displaying such fierceness as he thrust himself forward, irked Peter, who chose this enemy to open the fight and who would have pressed the attack vigorously if Christ had not checked his course. For Christ immediately forbad the others to fight, declared Peter's zeal ineffectual, and restored the ear of this miserable creature. These things He did because He came to suffer death, not to escape it; and even if He had not come to die, He would not have needed such assistance. To make this more manifest, He first gave His reply to the question put by the other apostles: "Let them go this far."[257] Still give them leave for a while. For I cast them all down with a mere word, and yet even I, as you see, allowed them to get up so that for the present they may accomplish whatever they wish. Since, then, I allow them to go so far, you must do the same. The time will shortly come when I will no longer allow them any power against me. Even now, in the meantime, I do not need your help.

Thus to the others He answered only "Let them go this far." But turning to Peter separately, He said, "Put your sword away"[258]—as if to say: I do not wish to be defended with the sword, and I have chosen you for the mission of fighting not with such a sword but with the sword of the word of God.[259] Therefore return the sword of iron to the sheath where it belongs—that is, to the hands of worldly princes to be used against evildoers. You

255. Juvenal, 5, 66.   256. John 18 : 10.   257. Luke 22 : 51.
258. Matt. 26 : 52, John 18 : 11.   259. Cf. Eph. 6 : 17.

who are the apostles of my flock have yet another sword far more terrible than any sword of iron, a sword by which a wicked man is sometimes cut off from the church (like a rotten limb[260] removed from my mystical body) and handed over to Satan for the destruction of the flesh to save the spirit[261] (provided only that the man is of a mind to be healed) and to enable him once more to be joined and grafted into my body—though it sometimes happens that a man suffering from a hopeless disease is also handed over to the invisible death of the soul, lest he should infect the healthy members with his disease. But I am so far from wishing you to make use of that sword of iron (whose proper sheath, you must recognize, is the secular magistrate) that I do not think even that spiritual sword, whose use properly pertains to you, should be unsheathed very often. Rather, wield with vigor that sword of the word,[262] whose stroke, like that of a scalpel, lets the pus out and heals by wounding. As for that other heavy and dangerous sword of excommunication, I desire that it be kept hidden in the sheath of mercy unless some urgent and fearful necessity requires that it be withdrawn.

In answering the other apostles Christ contented Himself with three words, because they were more temperate, or perhaps merely more tepid, than Peter; but Peter's fiery and wild assault He controlled and checked at greater length. He not only ordered him to put up his sword, but also added the reason why He did not approve of his zeal, however pious. "Do you not wish me," He said, "to drink the chalice my Father gave me?"[263] Some time ago Christ had predicted to the apostles that "it would be necessary for Him to go to Jerusalem and to suffer many things from the elders and scribes and princes of the priests, and to be killed and to rise on the third day. And taking Him aside, Peter began to chide Him, saying, 'Far be it from you, O Lord. This will not

260. Cf. Matt. 5 : 29–30.   261. 1 Cor. 5 : 5.   262. Eph. 6 : 17.
263. John 18 : 11.

happen to you.' Christ turned and said to Peter, 'Get thee behind me, Satan, for you do not understand the things of God.'"[264] Notice how severely Christ here rebuked Peter.

Shortly before, when Peter had professed that Christ was the Son of God, Christ had said to him, "Blessed are you, Simon bar Jona, for flesh and blood have not revealed this to you, but rather my Father who is in heaven. And I say to you that you are Peter and upon this rock I will build my church, and the gates of hell shall not prevail against it. And to you I will give the keys of heaven, and whatever you bind on earth will also be bound in heaven, etc."[265] But here He almost rejects this same Peter and thrusts him behind Him and declares that he is a stumbling-block to Him and calls him Satan and asserts that he does not understand the things of God but rather those of men. And why does He do all this? Because Peter tried to persuade Him not to die. Then He showed that it was necessary for Him to follow through to His death, which was irrevocably decreed for Him by His own will; and hence not only did He not want them to hinder His death, He even wanted them to follow Him along the same road. "If anyone wishes to come after me," He said, "let him deny himself and take up his cross and follow me."[266] Not satisfied even with this, He went on to show that if anyone refuses to follow Him on the road to death when the case requires it, he does not avoid death, but incurs a much worse death; on the other hand, whoever gives up his life does not lose it but exchanges it for a more vital life.[267] "Whoever wishes to save his life," He says, "will lose it. But whoever loses his life for my sake will find it. For what does it profit a man if he gain the whole world but suffer the loss of his own soul? Or what will a man give in exchange for his soul? For the Son of Man is to come with His angels in the glory of His Father, and then He will render to everyone according to his deeds."[268]

264. Matt. 16 : 21–23.   265. Matt. 16 : 17–19.   266. Matt. 16 : 24.
267. Cf. Cicero, *De amicitia*, 6, 22.   268. Matt. 16 : 25–27.

Perhaps I have devoted more time to this passage than was necessary. But I ask you, who would not be led beyond the pale, as they say, by these words of Christ, so severe and threatening but also so effective in creating hope of eternal life? But the relevance of these words to the passage under discussion is this: here we see Peter earnestly admonished not to be misled by his zeal into further hindering the death of Christ. And yet see now how Peter is again carried away by this same zeal to oppose Christ's death, except that this time he does not limit himself to verbal dissuasion but tries to ward it off by fierce fighting. Still, because Peter meant well when he did what he did, and also because Christ bore Himself with humility toward everyone as He drew near to His passion, Christ chose not to reprove Peter sharply. Rather, He first rebuked him by giving a reason, then He declared Peter's act to be sinful, and finally He announced that even if He wished to avoid death He would not need Peter's protection or any other mortal assistance, since if He wished help He had only to ask His Father, who would not fail to aid Him in His danger by sending a mighty and invincible array of angels against these puny mortals who were coming to take Him captive.

First of all, then, as I said, He checks Peter's zeal to strike out by presenting a rational argument. He says, "Do you not wish me to drink the chalice which my Father gave me?" My whole life up to this point has been a pattern of obedience and a model of humility. What lessons have I taught more frequently or more forcefully than that magistrates ought to be obeyed,[269] that parents should be honored,[270] that what is Caesar's should be rendered to Caesar, what is God's to God.[271] And now, when I ought to be applying the finishing touches to bring my work to full per-

---

269. In the gospels Christ does not have much to say about obeying magistrates, but More would assume that Paul (Rom. 13 : 4–7) and Peter (1 Pet. 2 : 17) were transmitting Christ's teaching.

270. Cf. Exod. 20 : 12, Eph. 6 : 1, and Col. 3 : 20.

271. Matt. 22 : 21, Mark 12 : 17, Luke 20 : 25.

fection, now can you wish that I should refuse the chalice extended to me by my Father, that the Son of Man should disobey God the Father, and thus unravel in a single moment all of that most beautiful fabric I have spent such a long time weaving?

Then He teaches Peter that he committed a sin by striking with the sword, and this He does by a parallel from the civil law. "For everyone who takes up the sword," He says, "will perish by the sword."[272] According to the Roman law, which also applied to the Jews at that time, any person discovered wearing a sword without legitimate authority for the purpose of killing a man was placed in almost the same category as the man who had killed his victim.[273] Naturally, therefore, a person who not only wore a sword but also drew it and struck a blow was in even greater legal jeopardy. Nor do I think that Peter, in that moment of confusion and alarm, was so self-possessed that he deliberately avoided hitting Malchus' head and aimed only at his ear, so as merely to frighten him but not kill him.

But if someone should perhaps maintain that everyone has the right even to use force in order to protect an innocent person from criminal assault, this objection would require a longer discussion than I could conveniently introduce in this place. This much is certain: however much Peter's offense was mitigated by his loyal affection for Christ, nevertheless, his lack of any legitimate authority to fight is made quite clear by the fact that on a previous occasion Christ had sharply warned him not to try to prevent His passion and death, not even by verbal dissuasion, much less by actual fighting.

Next He checks Peter's attack by making another point: Peter's protection is quite unnecessary. "Do you not know," He says, "that I could ask my Father for help and He would immediately deliver to me more than twelve legions of angels?"[274]

272. Matt. 26 : 52.   273. *Corpus Juris Civilis, Digesta,* 48, 8, 1.
274. Matt. 26 : 53.

About His own power He says nothing, but glories that He enjoys the favor of His Father. For as He drew near to His death, He wished to avoid lofty statements about Himself or any assertion that His own power was equal to that of the Father. Rather, wishing to make it clear that He had no need of help from Peter or any other mortal, He declares that the assistance of the heavenly angels (if He chose to ask for it) would immediately be at hand, sent by His omnipotent Father. "Do you not know," He says, "that I could ask my Father for help and He would immediately deliver to me more than twelve legions of angels?"—as if to say: You have just seen before your very eyes how I threw down, with a mere word, without even touching them, this whole crowd, such a large crowd that it would be sheer folly for you to think you are strong enough to defend me against them. If that could not convince you that I do not need your help, consider at least whose son you proclaimed me to be when I put the question "Who do you say I am?" and you immediately gave that heaven-inspired reply, "You are Christ, the Son of the living God."[275] Therefore, since you know from God's own revelation that I am the Son of God, and since you must know that mortal parents do not fail their children, do you imagine that, if I were not going to my death of my own free will, my heavenly Father would choose to fail me? Do you not know that, if I chose to ask Him, He would deliver to me more than twelve legions of angels, and that He would do so forthwith, without hesitation or delay? Against so many legions of angels, what resistance could be offered by this miserable cohort of puny mortals? Ten times twelve legions of creatures such as these would not dare even to look upon the angry frown of a single angel.

Then Christ returns to His first point, as the one closest to the central issue. "How, then," He says, "will the scriptures be fulfilled that say this is the way it must be?"[276]

275. Matt. 16:15–17.   276. Matt. 26:54.

The scriptures are full of prophecies concerning Christ's death, full of the mysteries of His passion and of mankind's redemption which would not have happened without that passion. Therefore, lest Peter or anyone else should mutter under his breath, "If you can obtain so many legions from your Father, Christ, why don't you ask for them?"—to counter this, Christ says, "How, then, will the scriptures be fulfilled that say this is the way it must be?" Since you understand from the scriptures that this is the only way chosen by the most just wisdom of God to restore the human race to its lost glory, if I should now successfully implore my Father to save me from death, what would I be doing but striving to undo the very thing I came to do? To call down from heaven angels to defend me, what effect would that have but precisely to exclude from heaven the whole human race, which I come to redeem and restore to the glory of heaven? With your sword, therefore, you are not fighting against the wicked Jews but rather attacking the whole human race, inasmuch as you are setting yourself against the fulfillment of the scriptures and desiring me not to drink the chalice given to me by my Father, that chalice by which I myself (unstained and undefiled) will wipe away that defiling stain of fallen nature.

But now behold the most gentle heart of Christ, who did not think it enough to check Peter's strokes but also touched the severed ear of His persecutor and made it sound again, in order to give us an example of rendering good for evil.

No one's body, I think, is so fully pervaded by his soul as the letter of holy scripture is pervaded by spiritual mysteries. Indeed, just as one cannot touch any part of the body in which the soul does not reside, providing life and sensation to even the smallest part, so too no factual account in all of scripture is so gross and corporeal (so to speak) that it does not have life and breath from some spiritual mystery. Therefore, in considering how Malchus' ear was cut off by Peter's sword and restored by the hand of Christ, we should not feel bound to consider only the facts of the account, though even these can teach us salutary lessons, but let us look further for the saving mystery of the spirit veiled beneath the letter of the story.

Thus Malchus, whose name is the Hebrew word for "king," can appropriately be taken as a figure of reason. For in man reason ought to reign like a king, and it does truly reign when it makes itself loyally subject to faith and serves God. For to serve Him is to reign. The high priest, on the other hand, together with his priests, with the pharisees, scribes, and elders of the people, was given over to perverse superstitions, which he mixed into the law of God, and he used piety as a pretext to oppose piety and sought eagerly to eliminate the founder of true religion. Hence he together with his accomplices may rightly be taken to represent wicked heresiarchs, the chief priests of pernicious superstition, together with their followers.

And so whenever the rational mind rebels against the true faith of Christ and devotes itself to heresies, it becomes a fugitive from Christ and a servant of the heresiarch whom it follows, led astray by the devil and wandering down the byways of error. Keeping, therefore, its left ear, with which it listens to sinister heresies, it loses its right ear, with which it ought to listen to the true faith. But this does not always happen from the same motivation or with the same effect. For some minds turn to heresies out of determined malice. Then the ear is not cut off by a swift stroke but rots slowly and gradually as the devil infuses his venom, until finally the purulent parts harden and block the passages with a clot so that nothing good can penetrate within. Such persons, alas, are hardly ever restored to health. For the parts eaten away by the ravaging cancer are completely gone and there is nothing left which can be put back in place.

But the ear cut off by a sudden stroke and sent whirling in one piece to the ground because of imprudent zeal, stands for those who turn from the truth to a false appearance of the truth because they are overcome by a sudden impulse; or it also represents those who are deceived by a well-meaning zeal, concerning whom Christ says, "The time will come when everyone who etc.   performing a service for God."[277] Of this kind of person the apostle Paul was a typical figure.[278] Some of these, because their minds are confused by earthly feelings, allow the ear which has been cut off from heavenly doctrine to remain lying on the earth. But Christ often takes pity on the misery of such persons and with His own hand picks up from the earth the ear which has been cut off by a sudden impulse or by ill-considered zeal and with His touch fastens it to the head again and makes it once more capable of listening to true doctrine. I know that the ancient fathers elicited various mysteries from this one passage, as each one, aided by the grace of the Holy Spirit, made his own particular discovery. But it is no part of my plan to review them all here because to do so would make too long an interruption in the account of the historical events.

"But Jesus said to those princes of the priests and magistrates of the temple and elders who had come, 'You have come out with swords and clubs to seize me as if I were a robber, though I was with you every day in the temple, and I sat teaching there and you did not detain me—you made no move to lay hands on me. But this is your hour and the power of darkness.'"[279]

Christ said this to those princes of the priests and magistrates of the temple and elders who had come. But here some readers are puzzled because the evangelist Luke reports that Jesus said these things to the princes of the priests and the magistrates of the temple and the elders of the people, while the other evangelists write in their accounts that these persons did not come themselves but sent the cohort and their servants.

277. John 16 : 2. The words More merely indicated by "etc." and a blank space are "kills you will think he is."
278. Acts 9 : 1–2.   279. Luke 23 : 52–53; cf. Matt. 26 : 55, Mark 14 : 48–49.

Some solve the problem by saying that Jesus may indeed be said to have spoken to these persons because He spoke to those whom they had sent. In this sense princes ordinarily speak to one another through their ambassadors, and private persons everywhere speak to each other through messengers. Thus whatever we tell a servant who has been sent to us, we say to his master who sent him, for such servants will repeat to their master what they have been told.

Though I do not deny such a solution, I am certainly much more inclined to the opinion of those who think that Christ spoke face to face with the princes of the priests, magistrates of the temple, and elders of the people. For Luke does not say that Christ said these things to all the princes of the priests, or to all the magistrates of the temple, or to all the elders of the people, but only to those "who had come." These words seem to indicate rather clearly that, although the cohort and servants had been commissioned to seize Christ in the name of the whole assembly gathered together in council, still some members of each group—elders, pharisees, and princes—also went along with them. This opinion agrees exactly with Luke's words and does not contradict the accounts of the other evangelists.

Addressing, therefore, the princes of the priests, the pharisees, and the elders of the people, Christ implicitly reminds them that they should not attribute His capture to their own strength or adroitness and should not foolishly boast of it as a clever and ingenious achievement (according to that unfortunate tendency of those who are fortunate in evil). He lets them know that the foolish contrivances and maneuvers by which they labored to suppress the truth were powerless to accomplish anything against Him, but rather the profound wisdom of God had foreseen and set the time when the prince of this world[280] would be justly

280. John 12:31, 14:30, 16:11.

tricked into losing his ill-gotten prey, the human race, even as he strove by unjust means to keep it. If this were not the case, Christ explains to them, there would have been no need at all for them to pay for the services of the betrayer, to come at night with lanterns and torches, to make their approach surrounded by the dense ranks of the cohort and armed with swords and clubs, since they had previously had many opportunities to arrest Him as He sat teaching in the temple, and then they could have done it without expense, without any special effort, without spending a sleepless night, without any saber-rattling at all.

But if they should take special credit for their prudent foresight and say that the arrest of Christ was no easy matter, as He claimed, but rather quite difficult because it necessarily brought with it the great danger of a popular uprising,[281] this difficulty, for the most part, had arisen only recently, after the resurrection of Lazarus.[282] Before that event, it had happened more than once that, in spite of the people's great love of His virtues and their profound respect for Him, He had had to use His own power to escape from their midst.[283] On those occasions anyone attempting to capture and kill Him would not have been in the least danger from the crowd but would have found them to be willing accomplices in crime. So unfailingly unreliable is the common herd, always ready at a moment's notice to take the wrong side. Finally, what happened a little later showed how easy it is to brush aside the people's favor toward a person, and any fear that might arise from it; as soon as He was arrested, the people were no less furious at him as they cried out, "Away with him! Crucify him!" than they had formerly been eager to honor Him when they cried, "Blessed is He who comes in the name of the Lord!" and "Hosanna in the highest!"

281. See, e.g., Matt. 21 : 46 and Luke 20 : 19.   282. John 11 : 45–48.
283. Luke 4 : 28–30.

And so up to that time God had caused the would-be captors of Christ to imagine purely fictitious grounds for fear and to tremble with dread where there was no reason to be afraid. But now that the proper time had come for all men (all, that is, who truly desire it) to be redeemed by the bitter death of one man[284] and be restored to the sweetness of eternal life, these puny creatures stupidly imagined that they had achieved by clever planning what as a matter of fact God in His omnipotent providence (without which not a sparrow falls to earth)[285] had mercifully prescribed from all eternity. To show them how very wrong they were and to let them know that, without His own consent, the deceitfulness of the betrayer and their own cleverly laid snares and the power of the Romans would have been utterly ineffectual, Christ said, "But this is your hour and the power of darkness." These words of Christ are grounded firmly by what the evangelist says: "But all this was done so that the writings of the prophets might be fulfilled."[286]

Predictions of Christ's death are very frequent throughout the prophets: "He was led like a lamb to the slaughter, and His cry was not heard in the streets,"[287] "They have pierced my hands and my feet,"[288] "I was struck with these blows in the home of those who loved me,"[289] "And He was reckoned among the wicked,"[290] "Truly He bore our infirmities,"[291] "By His bruises we have been healed,"[292] "He has been brought to His death by the wickedness of my people."[293] The prophets are full of very clear predictions of the death of Christ. In order that these might not remain unfulfilled, it was necessary that the matter depend not on human planning but rather on Him who foresaw and prearranged from

284. Cf. Rom. 5 : 12–19.   285. Matt. 10 : 29.   286. Matt. 26 : 56.
287. More seems to have conflated Isa. 53 : 7 (cited also in Acts 8 : 32) and Ps. 143 : 14 (AV, 144 : 14).
288. Ps. 21 : 17 (AV, 22 : 16).   289. Zech. 13 : 6.
290. Luke 22 : 37, citing Isa. 53 : 12.   291. Isa. 53 : 4.
292. Isa. 53 : 5. Cf. 1 Pet. 2 : 24.
293. Apparently a conflation of Isa. 53 : 8 and 12.

all eternity what would happen (that is, on the Father of Christ, and likewise on Christ Himself, and on the Holy Spirit of both of them, for the actions of these three are always so harmoniously unified that there is no exterior act of any one of them that does not belong equally to all three). The most suitable times of fulfillment, then, were already foreseen and prescribed. Therefore, while the high priests and the princes of the priests, the scribes, pharisees and elders of the people, in short, all these accursed and wicked magistrates, were taking pride in their masterful plan for capturing Christ cleverly, they were nothing more than tools of God, eager in their ignorance, blind instruments of the most excellent and unchangeable will of almighty God, not only of the Father and the Holy Spirit, but also of Christ Himself; thus, foolish and blind with malice, they did great harm to themselves and great good to others, they inflicted a temporary death on Christ but contributed to a most happy life for the human race, and they enhanced the everlasting glory of Christ.

And so Christ said to them, "This is your hour and the power of darkness." In the past, although you hated me intensely, although you longed to destroy me, although you could have done so at that time with less trouble (except that heavenly power prevented it), yet you did not detain me in the temple—you did not even make a single move to lay hands on me. Why was this? It was because the time and the hour had not yet come, the hour fixed not by the heavenly bodies, not by your cleverness, but rather by the unsearchable plan of my Father, to which I too had given my consent. Would you like to know when He did this? Not only as long ago as the times of Abraham, but from all eternity. For from all eternity, together with the Father, before Abraham came to be, I am.[294]

And so this is your hour and the power of darkness. This is the short hour allowed to you and the power granted to darkness, so

294. John 8 : 58.

that now in the dark you might do what you were not permitted to do in the daylight, flying in my face like winged creatures from the Stygian marsh, like harpies, like horned owls and screech-owls, like night-ravens and bats and night-owls, futilely swarming in a shrill uproar of beaks, talons, and teeth. You are in the dark when you ascribe my death to your strength. So too the governor Pilate will be in the dark when he takes pride in possessing the power to free me or to crucify me. For, even though my people and my high priests are about to hand me over to him, he would not have any power over me if it were not given to him from above. And for that very reason, those who will hand me over to him are the greater sinners.[295]

But this is the hour and the brief power of darkness. A man who walks in the dark does not know where he is going.[296] You also do not see or know what you are doing, and for that reason I myself will pray that you may be forgiven for what you are scheming to do to me.[297] But not everyone will be forgiven. Blindness will not be an excuse for everyone. For you yourselves create your own darkness, you put out the light, you blind your own eyes first and then the eyes of others so that you are the blind leading the blind until both fall into a ditch.[298] This is your short hour. This is that mad and ungovernable power which brings you armed to take an unarmed man, which brings the fierce against the gentle, criminals against an innocent man, a traitor against his lord, puny mortals against God.

But this hour and this power of darkness are not only given to you now against me, but such an hour and such a brief power of darkness will also be given to other governors and other caesars against other disciples of mine. And this too will truly be the power of darkness. For whatever my disciples endure and whatever they say, they will not endure by their own strength or say of

295. Cf. John 19 : 10–11.   296. John 12 : 35.   297. Cf. Luke 23 : 34.
298. Matt. 15 : 14.

themselves, but conquering through my strength they will win their souls by their patience,[299] and it is my Father's spirit that will speak in them.[300] So too those who persecute and kill them will neither do nor speak anything of themselves. Rather, the prince of darkness who is already coming and who has no power over me[301] will instill his poison in the breasts of these tyrants and tormentors and will demonstrate and exercise his strength through them for the brief time allowed him. Hence my comrades-in-arms will be struggling not against flesh and blood but against princes and powers, against the rulers of the darkness of this world, against the spiritual forces of evil in high places.[302] Thus Nero is yet to be born, in whom the prince of darkness will kill Peter and to him will add Paul, who does not yet have that name and is still displaying his hatred of me. Through the prince of darkness other caesars and their governors will rise up against other disciples of my flock.

But although the nations have raged and the people devised vain things, although the kings of the earth have risen up and the princes gathered together against the Lord and against His Christ, striving to break their chains and to cast off that most sweet yoke which a loving God, through His pastors, places upon their stubborn necks, then He who dwells in the heavens will laugh at them and the Lord will deride them. He sits not on a curule throne like earthly princes, raised up a few feet above the earth, but rather He rises above the setting of the sun,[303] He sits above the cherubim,[304] the heavens are His throne, the earth is the footstool beneath His feet,[305] His name is the Lord.[306] He is the king of kings and the lord of lords,[307] a terrible king who daunts the hearts of princes.[308] This king will speak to them in His anger,

299. Luke 21 : 19.   300. Matt. 10 : 20.   301. John 14 : 30.
302. Eph. 6 : 12.   303. Ps. 67 : 5 (AV, 68 : 4).
304. Ps. 98 : 1 (AV, 99 : 1). Cf. Ps. 79 : 2 (AV, 80 : 1).   305. Isa. 66 : 1.
306. Ps. 67 : 5 (AV, 68 : 4).   307. 1 Tim. 6 : 15.
308. Ps. 75 : 12–13 (AV, 76 : 11–12).

and in His rage He will throw them into confusion.[309] He will establish His Christ, the son whom He has today begotten, as king on His holy mountain of Sion,[310] a mountain which will not be shaken.[311] He will cast all His enemies down before Him like a footstool under His feet.[312] Those who tried to break His chains and cast off His yoke, He will rule against their will with a rod of iron, and He will shatter them like a potter's vessel.[313] Against them and their instigator, the prince of darkness, my disciples will be strengthened in the Lord.

And putting on the armor of God, their loins girt with truth, wearing the breastplate of justice, shod in preparation to preach the gospel of peace, taking up in all things the shield of faith and putting on the helmet of salvation and the sword of the spirit, which is the word of God,[314] they shall be clothed with power from on high.[315] And they will stand against the snares of the devil,[316] that is, against the soft speeches he will place on the lips of their persecutors to cajole them into leaving the way of truth. The open assaults of Satan they will also resist on the evil day:[317] compassed about by the shield of faith,[318] pouring forth tears in their prayers and shedding their blood in the agony of their suffering, they shall extinguish all the fiery darts hurled against them by the underlings of that monster of evil, Satan.[319] Thus, when they have taken up their cross to follow me,[320] when they have conquered the prince of darkness, the devil, when they have trod under foot the earthly minions of Satan, then finally, riding aloft on a triumphal chariot, the martyrs will enter into heaven in a magnificent and marvelous procession.

309. Ps. 2 : 5.   310. Ps. 2 : 6–7.
311. Ps. 124 : 1 (AV, 125 : 1). Cf. Ps. 92 : 1 (AV, 93 : 1) and 95 : 10 (AV, 96 : 10).
312. Ps. 109 : 1 (AV, 110 : 1). Cf. 1 Cor. 15 : 25, Heb. 1 : 13 and 10 : 13.
313. Ps. 2 : 3, 9.   314. Eph. 6 : 10–17.   315. Luke 24 : 49.
316. Eph. 6 : 11.   317. Eph. 6 : 13.
318. Cf. Ps. 90 : 5 (AV, 91 : 4) and Eph. 6 : 16.   319. Eph. 6 : 16.
320. Matt. 10 : 38 and 16 : 24, Mark 8 : 34.

But you who now give vent to your malice against me, and also that corrupt generation to come which will imitate your malice, that brood of vipers[321] which will assail my disciples with impenitent malice similar to yours, all of you, to your everlasting infamy, will be thrust down into the dark fires of hell. But in the meantime you are permitted to demonstrate and exercise your power. Still, lest you should take too much pride in it, remember that it must shortly come to an end. For the span of time allotted to your wanton arrogance is not endless but has been shortened to the span of a brief hour for the sake of the elect, that they might not be tried beyond their strength.[322]

And so this hour of yours and this power of darkness are not long-lasting and enduring but quite as brief as the present moment to which they are limited, an instant of time always caught between a past that is gone and a future that has not arrived. Therefore, lest you should lose any of this hour of yours which is so short, proceed immediately to use it for your own evil purposes. Since you seek to destroy me, be quick about it,[323] arrest me without delay, but let these men go their way.

The flight of the disciples

"Then all the disciples abandoned Him and fled."[324]

From this passage it is easy to see how difficult and arduous a virtue patience is. For many can bring themselves to face certain death bravely provided they can strike back at their assailants and give vent to their feelings by inflicting wounds on those who attack them. But to suffer without any comfort from revenge, to meet death with a patience that not only refrains from striking back but also takes blows without returning so much as an angry

321. Cf. Matt. 3 : 7, 12 : 34, and 23 : 33, Luke 3 : 7.
322. Matt. 24 : 22, Mark 13 : 20, 1 Cor. 10 : 13.   323. John 13 : 27.
324. Matt. 26 : 56, Mark 14 : 50.

word, that, I assure you, is such a lofty peak of heroic virtue that
even the apostles were not yet strong enough to scale it. Remembering that grand promise of theirs that they would die together
with Him rather than desert Him,[325] even they held out at least to
the point of professing themselves ready to die providing that
they had the chance to die fighting. And in deed as well as word
Peter gave concrete evidence of this willingness by striking
Malchus. But when our Savior denied them permission to fight
and withheld the power to defend themselves, "they all abandoned Him and fled."

I have sometimes asked myself this question: when Christ left
off praying and returned to the apostles only to find them sleeping, did He go to both groups or only to those He had brought
farther along and placed nearest to Him? But when I consider
these words of the evangelist, "All of them abandoned Him and
fled," I no longer have any doubt that it was all of them who fell
asleep. While they should have been staying awake and praying
that they might not enter into temptation (as Christ so often told
them to do), instead they were sleeping and thus gave the tempter
an opportunity to weaken their wills with thoughtless drowsiness
and make them far more inclined to fight or flee than to bear all
with patience. And this was the reason that they all abandoned
Him and fled. And thus that saying of Christ was fulfilled, "This
night you will all be scandalized because of me,"[326] and also that
prediction of the prophet[327]

"But a certain young man was following Him, having only a
linen cloth wrapped about his naked body, and throwing it off, he
fled from them naked."[328]

---

325. Matt. 26 : 35.   326. Matt. 26 : 31.
327. More almost surely intended the blank space he left after "prophet" to be
filled with Christ's quotation (Matt. 26 : 31) of Zech. 13 : 7: "I will strike the shepherd and the sheep of the flock will be scattered."
328. Mark 14 : 51.

Just who this young man was has never been determined with
certainty. Some think he was the James who was called the
brother of the Lord and was distinguished by the epithet "the
just." Others assert that he was the evangelist John, who always
had a special place in our Lord's heart and who must have been
still quite young, since he lived for so many years after Christ's
death. For, according to Jerome, he died in the sixty-eighth year
after our Lord's passion.[329] But there are also some ancient writers
who say that this young man was not one of the apostles at all but
one of the servants in the household where Christ had celebrated
the Passover that night. And certainly I myself find this opinion
easier to accept. Apart from the fact that I find it unlikely for an
apostle to be wearing nothing but a linen cloth, and even that so
loosely fastened that it could be quickly thrown off, I am inclined
to this opinion first of all by the sequence of historical events and
then by the very words of the account.

Now, among those who think the young man was one of the
apostles, the preponderance of opinion is for John. But this seems
to me unlikely because of John's own words: "But Simon Peter
was following Jesus and so was another disciple. Now that disciple was known to the high priest, and he entered the courtyard of
the high priest together with Jesus. But Peter was standing outside at the gate. So the other disciple, who was known to the high
priest, went out and spoke to the portress, and brought Peter
in."[330] Writers who assert that it was the blessed evangelist who
followed Christ and fled when He was taken prisoner are faced
with a slight hitch in their argument—namely, the fact that he
threw off the linen cloth and fled naked. For this seems to conflict
with what follows—namely, that John entered the courtyard of
the high priest, that he brought Peter in (for everyone agrees that

---

329. *Adversus Jovinianum* 1, 26 (*PL 23,* 247) and *Liber de viris illustribus* 9 (*PL 23,*
625–26).
330. John 18 : 15–16.

the disciple who did this was the evangelist), that he followed Christ all the way to the place of the crucifixion, and that he stood near the cross with Christ's most beloved mother (two pure virgins standing together), and that when Christ commended her to him he accepted her as his own mother from that day on.[331]

Now there can be no doubt that at all these times and in all these places John was wearing clothes. For he was a disciple of Christ, not of the cynic sect;[332] and therefore, though he had enough good sense not to avoid nakedness when circumstances required it or necessity demanded it, nevertheless I hardly think his virgin modesty would have allowed him to go out in public naked, for everyone to see, with no good reason at all. This difficulty they try to explain away by saying that he went somewhere else in the meantime and put on other clothes—a point I will not dispute, but it hardly seems likely to me, especially when I see in this passage that he continuously followed after Christ with Peter and that he entered the residence of Annas, the father-in-law of the high priest, together with Jesus.

Furthermore, another consideration that strongly persuades me to side with those who think that the young man was not one of the apostles but one of the servants of the inn is the sort of connection Mark makes between the apostles who ran away and the young man who stayed behind. "Then the disciples abandoned Him and all of them ran away. But a certain young man was following Him." Notice, he says not that some ran away but "all of them" and that the person who (unlike them) stayed behind and followed Christ was not any one of the apostles (for all of them had already run away) but rather a "certain" young man, that is, it would seem, an unknown young man, whose name Mark either did not know or thought it not worthwhile to report.

---

331. John 19 : 25–27.
332. Shamelessness, including public indecency, was recommended and practiced by some cynic philosophers.

Here, then, is how I would imagine it. This young man, who had previously been excited by Christ's fame and who now saw Him in person as he was bringing in food to Christ and His disciples reclining at table, was touched by a secret breath of the Spirit and felt the moving force of charity. Then, impelled to pursue a life of true devotion, he followed Christ when He left after dinner and continued to follow Him, at a little distance, perhaps, from the apostles but still with them. And he sat down and got up again together with them until finally, when the mob came, he lost himself in the crowd. Furthermore, when all the apostles had escaped in terror from the hands of the sluggish soldiers, this young man dared to remain behind, with all the more confidence because he knew that no one as yet was aware of the love he felt for Christ. But how hard it is to disguise the love we feel for someone! Although this young man had mingled with that crowd of people who hated Christ, still he betrayed himself by his gait and his bearing, making it clear to everyone that he pursued Christ (now deserted by the others) not as a persecutor but as a devoted follower. And so, when they finally noticed that the rest of Christ's band had fled and saw that this one had stayed behind and still dared to follow Christ, they quickly seized him.

This act of theirs convinces me that they also intended to seize all the apostles but were so taken by surprise that they lost their chance, and thus that prophetic command of Christ, "Let these men go their way," was indeed fulfilled. Christ did not intend this command to be limited to the apostles, whom He had chosen (though it was meant to apply principally to them), but He also wished to extend the riches of His kindness even more abundantly by making the command apply also to this young man, who, without being summoned, had followed Him of his own accord and had slipped into the holy band of His apostles. And in this way Christ displayed His own secret power more clearly and at the same time exposed the weakness of the crowd more fully, because not only did they lose through negligence the eleven apostles, whose escape distressed them very much, but also they could not even detain this one young man whom they had already seized and who was (one may conjecture) completely walled in by their ranks: for "they seized him and he threw off the linen cloth and fled from them naked." Moreover, I have not the slightest doubt that this young man, who followed Christ that night and could not be torn away from Him until the last possible moment, after all the apostles had fled—and even then it took manhandling and rough force—later took the first opportunity to return to Christ's flock and that even now he lives with Christ in everlasting glory in heaven, where I hope and pray that we will one day live with him. Then he himself will tell us who he was, and we will get a most pleasant and full account of many other details of what happened that night which are not contained in scripture.

In the meantime, in order to make our heavenward journey safer and easier, it will be of no small use for us to gather wholesome spiritual counsels from the flight of the disciples before they were captured and from the escape of this young man after he was captured: these counsels will be the provisions, as it were, for us to carry with us on the journey. The ancient fathers of the church warn us not to be so sure of our strength as to place ourselves willingly and needlessly in danger of falling into sin. But if someone should happen to find himself in a situation where he recognizes an imminent danger that he will be driven by force to offend God, he ought to do what the apostles did—avoid capture by fleeing. I do not say this to suggest that the apostles' flight was praiseworthy, on the grounds that Christ, in His mercy (though He is indeed merciful) had permitted them to do so because of their weakness. Far from praising it, He had foretold it that very night as [an] occasion of sin for them. But if we feel that our character is not strong enough, let us all imitate this flight of theirs insofar as we can, without sinning, flee the danger of falling into sin. For otherwise, if a person runs away when God commands him to stand and face the danger confidently, either for his own salvation or for that of those whom he sees have been entrusted to his care, then he is acting foolishly indeed, unless he does it out of concern for this present life—no, even then he acts foolishly. For what could be more stupid than to choose a brief time of misery over an eternity of happiness?

But if he does it because of the future life, with the idea that if he does not run away he may be forced to offend God, he compounds not only his folly but also his crime. For to desert one's post is itself a very serious crime, and if one adds to it the enormous gravity of despair, it is quite as serious as going over to the enemy's side. What worse offense could be imagined than to despair of God's help and by running away to hand over to the enemy the battle station which God had assigned you to guard? Furthermore, what greater madness could be conceived than to seek to avoid the possible sin that may happen if you stay, by committing the certain sin of running away? But when flight entails no offense against God, certainly the safer plan is to make haste to escape rather than to delay so long as to be captured and thus fall into the danger of committing a terrible sin. For it is easy and (where allowable) safe to run away in time, but it is difficult and dangerous to fight.

On the other hand, the example of this young man shows us what sort of person can afford to hold his ground longer with less danger and can easily escape from the hands of his captors if he should happen to be taken. For, although this young man stayed behind after all the others and followed Christ so long that they laid hands on him and held him, nevertheless, because he was not dressed in various garments but wore only a simple linen cloth— and even that not sewn together or buttoned on, but thrown carelessly over his naked body in such a way that he could easily shake it off—this young man suddenly threw off the cloth, leaving it there in the hands of his captors, and fled from them naked—

taking the kernel, as it were, and leaving them holding the shell.[333] What is the figurative meaning of this? What else but this: just as a potbellied man, slowed down by his fat paunch,[334] or a man who goes around wearing a heavy load of clothes, is hardly in a condition to run fast, so too the man who is hemmed in by a belt full of money bags is hardly able to escape when troubles suddenly descend on him and put him in a bind. Neither will a man run very fast or very far if his clothing, however light it may be, is so tightly laced and knotted that he cannot breathe freely. For a man who is wearing a lot of clothing but can get rid of it quickly will find it easier to escape than a man who is wearing only a little but has it tied around his neck so tightly that he has to carry it with him wherever he runs. One sees rich men—less often, it is true, than I would like—but still, thank God, one sometimes sees exceedingly rich men who would rather lose everything they have than keep anything at all by offending God through sin. These men have many clothes, but they are not tightly confined by them, so that when they need to run away from danger, they escape easily by throwing off their clothes. On the other hand we see people—and far more of them than I would wish—who happen to have only light garments and quite skimpy outfits and yet have so welded their affections to those poor riches[335] of theirs that you could sooner strip skin from flesh than separate them from their goods. Such a person had better get going while there is still time. For once someone gets hold of his clothes, he will sooner die than leave his linen cloth behind. In summary, then, we learn from the example of this young man that we should always be prepared for troubles that arise suddenly, dangers that strike without warning and might make it necessary for us to run away; to be prepared, we ought not to be so loaded

333. Plautus, *Captivi,* 655.   334. Cf. Juvenal, 3, 107.
335. Cf. Horace, *Odes,* 3, 16, 28 and Ovid, *Metamorphoses,* 3, 466.

with various garments, or so buttoned up in even one, that in an emergency we are unable to throw away our linen cloth and escape naked.

Now anyone who is willing to devote a little more attention to this deed of the young man can see that it offers us another teaching, even more forceful than the first. For the body is, as it were, the garment of the soul. The soul puts on the body when it comes into the world and takes off the body when it leaves the world at death. Hence, just as the clothes are worth much less than the body, so too the body is far less precious than the soul. Thus, to give away the soul to buy the body is the same kind of raving lunacy as to prefer the loss of the body to the loss of a cloak. Concerning the body, Christ did indeed say, "Is not the body worth more than its clothing?"[336] But concerning the soul He was far more emphatic: "What does it profit you if you gain the whole world but suffer the loss of your soul? or what will a man give in exchange for his soul?[337] But I say to you, my friends, do not be afraid of those who kill the body, and after that have nothing more that they can do. But I will show you the one to be afraid of. Fear Him who, after He has killed, has the power to cast into hell. Yes, I say to you, fear Him."[338] Thus, the example of this young man warns us about what sort of clothing for our souls our bodies ought to be when we are faced with such trials: they should not be obese from debauchery and flabby from dissolute living but thin like the linen cloth, with the fat worked off by fasting; and then we should not be so strongly attached to them that we cannot willingly cast them off when God's cause demands it. This is the lesson which that young man teaches us; when he was in the clutches of wicked men, he preferred to leave his linen cloth behind and flee from them naked rather than be forced to do or say anything which might impugn the honor of Christ.

336. Matt. 6 : 25.   337. Matt. 16 : 26.   338. Luke 12 : 4–5.

In a similar way, another young man who lived long before this one, the holy and innocent patriarch Joseph, left to posterity a notable example, teaching that one should flee from the danger of unchaste defilement no less than if it were an attempted murder. Because he had a handsome face and was a fine figure of a man, the wife of Potiphar, in whose house he was the chief servant, cast her eyes on him and fell passionately in love with him. She was so carried away by the raving madness of her desire that she not only offered herself freely and shamelessly to the young man by her glances and words, enticing him to overcome his aversion, but also, when he refused, she went so far as to clutch his garment in her hands and presented the shameful spectacle of a woman wooing a man by force. But Joseph, who would rather have died than commit such a horrible sin and who also knew how dangerous it is to engage the embattled forces of Venus at close quarters and that against them the surest victory is flight, Joseph, I say, left his cloak in the hands of the adulteress and escaped by dashing out of doors.[339]

But, as I was saying, to avoid falling into grave sin we must throw off not merely a cloak or gown or shirt or any other such garment of the body but even the garment of the soul, the body itself. For if we strive to save the body by sin, we destroy it and we also lose the soul. But if we patiently endure the loss of the body for the love of God, then, just as the snake sloughs off its old skin (called, I think, its "senecta") by rubbing it against thorns and thistles, and, leaving it behind in the thick hedges, comes forth young and shining, so too those of us who follow Christ's advice and become wise as serpents[340] will leave behind on earth our old bodies, rubbed off like a snake's old skin among the thorns of tribulation suffered for the love of God, and will quickly be carried up to heaven, shining and young and never more to feel the effects of old age.

339. Gen. 39 : 6–12.   340. Matt. 10 : 16.

The capture of Christ

"Then they came up and laid hands on Jesus. The cohort and the tribune and the servants of the Jews seized Jesus and holding Him fast they bound Him and took Him first to Annas. For he was the father-in-law of Caiaphas. But it was Caiaphas who had advised the Jews that it is expedient that one man die for the people.[341] And all the priests, scribes, pharisees, and elders gathered together."[342]

Exactly when they first laid hands on Jesus is a point on which the experts disagree. Among the interpreters of the gospel accounts, which agree on the fact but vary in their way of presenting it (for one anticipates, another goes back to pick up a detail omitted earlier), some commentators follow one opinion, others another, though none of them impugn the historical truth of the accounts or deny that an opinion differing from their own may be the correct one. For Matthew and Mark relate the events in such an order as to allow the conjecture that they laid hands on Jesus immediately after Judas' kiss. And this is the opinion adopted not only by many celebrated doctors of the church but also approved by that remarkable man John Gerson, who follows it in presenting the sequence of events in his work entitled *Monotessaron* (the work which I have generally followed in enumerating the events of the passion in this discussion).

But in this one place I have departed from him and followed those interpreters (and they, too, are celebrated authorities) who are persuaded by very probable inferences from the accounts of Luke and John to adopt the opinion that only after Judas had given his kiss and returned to the cohort and the Jews, after Christ had thrown down the cohort merely by speaking to them, after the ear of the high priest's servant had been cut off and restored, after the other apostles had been forbidden to fight and Peter (who had already begun to fight) had been rebuked, after

341. John 18 : 12–14.   342. Matt. 26 : 57, Mark 14 : 53.

Christ had once more addressed the Jewish magistrates who were present at that time and had announced that they now had permission to do what they had not been able to do before—to take Him captive—after all the apostles had escaped by running away, after the young man who had been seized but could not be held had saved himself by his active and eager acceptance of nakedness, only then, after all these events, did they lay hands on Jesus.[343]

343. In the Valencia manuscript, this phrase is followed by seven entirely blank leaves, after which appears an independent composition by More, a catena of scriptural passages interspersed with some reflections on martyrdom (see *CW 14*, 627–91 and notes).

Instructions *and* Prayers

A godly instruction,[1] written by Sir Thomas More Knight, within a while after he was prisoner in the Tower of London in the year of our Lord 1534.

Bear no malice nor evil will to no man living. For either the man is good or nought.[2] If he be good, and I hate him, then am I nought.

If he be nought, either he shall amend and die good, and go to God, or abide[3] nought, and die nought, and go to the devil. And then let me remember that if he shall be saved, he shall not fail (if I be saved too, as I trust to be) to love me very heartily, and I shall then in likewise love him.

And why should I now then hate one for this while[4] which shall hereafter love me for evermore, and why should I be now, then, enemy to him with whom I shall in time coming be coupled in eternal friendship? And on the other side, if he shall continue nought and be damned, then is there so outrageous eternal sorrow towards[5] him that I may well think myself a deadly cruel wretch if I would not now rather pity his pain than malign his person. If one would say that we may well with good conscience wish an evil man harm, lest he should do harm to such other folk as are innocent and good, I will not now dispute upon that point, for that root hath mo[6] branches to be well weighed and considered than I can now conveniently write (having none other pen than a coal). But verily thus will I say, that I will give counsel to every good friend of mine, but if[7] he be put in such a room[8] as to punish an evil man lieth in his charge by reason of his office, else leave the desire of punishing unto God and unto such other folk as are so grounded in charity, and so fast cleave to God, that no

1. lesson.   2. wicked.   3. remain.   4. period of time.
5. facing.   6. more.   7. *but if:* unless.   8. position.

secret, shrewd,[9] cruel affection,[10] under the cloak of a just and a virtuous zeal, can creep in and undermine them. But let us that are no better than men of a mean[11] sort ever pray for such merciful amendment in other folk as our own conscience showeth us that we have need in ourself.

A godly meditation, written by Sir Thomas More Knight while he was prisoner in the Tower of London in the year of our Lord 1534.[1]

Give me Thy grace, good Lord,
To set the world at nought;[2]

To set my mind fast[3] upon Thee,
And not to hang upon the blast[4]
 of men's mouths;

To be content to be solitary;
Not to long for worldly company;

Little and little utterly to cast off the world,
And rid my mind of all the business[5] thereof;

Not to long to hear of any worldly things,
But that the hearing of worldly fantasies[6] may
 be to me displeasant;[7]

9. malicious.   10. inclination.   11. inferior.
1. This heading is from the 1557 *English Works,* but the text of the prayer given here is taken directly from More's handwritten version in the margins of a book of hours he had with him in the Tower (*Thomas More's Prayer Book,* ed. Louis Martz and Richard Sylvester, London and New Haven, 1969, xxxvii–xxxviii, 3–21).
2. *set . . . nought:* have no esteem for the world.   3. firmly.   4. utterance.
5. activity.   6. delusions.   7. disagreeable.

Gladly to be thinking of God,
Piteously to call for His help;

To lean unto the comfort of God,
Busily to labor to love Him;

To know mine own vility[8] and wretchedness,
To humble and meeken myself under the
   mighty hand of God;

To bewail my sins passed;
For the purging of them patiently to
   suffer adversity;

Gladly to bear my purgatory here;
To be joyful of tribulations;

To walk the narrow way that leadeth to life,
To bear the cross with Christ;

To have the last thing[9] in remembrance,
To have ever afore[10] mine eye my death that is
   ever at hand;

To make death no stranger to me,
To foresee and consider the everlasting fire of hell;

To pray for pardon before the judge come,
To have continually in mind the passion that Christ
   suffered for me;

---

8. baseness.   9. *last thing:* last judgment.   10. before.

For His benefits uncessantly[11] to give Him thanks,
To buy[12] the time again that I before have lost;

To abstain from vain confabulations,[13]
To eschew light[14] foolish mirth and gladness;

Recreations[15] not necessary—to cut off;
Of worldly substance, friends, liberty, life and all,
    to set the loss at right nought[16] for the
        winning[17] of Christ:

To think my most[18] enemies my best friends;
For the brethren of Joseph could never have done
    him so much good with their love and favor as
        they did him with their malice and
           hatred.

These minds[19] are more to be desired of every man
    than all the treasure of all the princes and kings,
        Christian and heathen, were it gathered and
           laid together all upon one heap.

---

11. continually.   12. redeem.   13. conversations.   14. frivolous.
15. pleasurable employments.   16. *right nought:* absolutely nothing.
17. gaining.   18. greatest.   19. attitudes.

A devout prayer, made by Sir Thomas More Knight
after he was condemned to die, and before he was
put to death, who was condemned the Thursday,
the first day of July, in the year of our Lord God
1535, and in the twenty-seventh year of the reign of
King Henry the Eight, and was beheaded at the
Tower Hill at London the Tuesday following.[1]

Pater noster, Ave maria, Credo.[2]

O holy Trinity, the Father, the Son, and the Holy Ghost—three
egal[3] and coeternal persons, and one almighty God—have mercy
on me, vile, abject, abominable, sinful wretch, meekly knowledg-
ing[4] before Thine high majesty my long-continued sinful life,
even from my very childhead[5] hitherto.

In my childhead in this point and that point, etc.[6]

After my childhead in this point and that point, etc., and so
forth by every age.

Now, good gracious Lord, as Thou givest me Thy grace to
knowledge them, so give me Thy grace, not in only word but in
heart also, with very sorrowful contrition to repent them and
utterly to forsake them. And forgive me those sins also in which
by mine own default,[7] through evil affections[8] and evil custom,
my reason is with sensuality so blinded that I cannot discern them
for sin. And illumine, good Lord, mine heart, and give me Thy
grace to know them and to knowledge them, and forgive me my

1. The prayer is both More's personal expression and a devotion intended for use
by others.
2. This rubric indicates one should say the Our Father, Hail Mary, and the Creed.
3. equal.   4. confessing.   5. childhood.
6. Here and in the next sentence, one should think of one's own sins.
7. misdeed.   8. feelings.

sins negligently forgotten, and bring them to my mind with grace to be purely confessed of them.

Glorious God, give me from henceforth the grace, with little respect unto the world, so to set and fix firmly mine heart upon Thee that I may say with Thy blessed apostle Saint Paul, *Mundus mihi crucifixus est, et ego mundo. Mihi vivere Christus est et mori lucrum. Cupio dissolvi et esse cum Christo.*[9]

Give me the grace to amend my life and to have an eye to mine end without grudge of death,[10] which to them that die in Thee (good Lord) is the gate of a wealthy[11] life.

Almighty God, *Doce me facere voluntatem tuam. Fac me currere in odore unguentorum tuorum. Apprehende manum meam dexteram, et deduc me in via recta propter inimicos meos. Trahe me post te. In chamo et freno maxillas meas constringe, cum non approximo ad te.*[12]

O glorious God, all sinful fear, all sinful sorrow and pensiveness, all sinful hope, all sinful mirth and gladness take from me. And on the tother[13] side, concerning such fear, such sorrow, such heaviness,[14] such comfort, consolation, and gladness as shall be profitable for my soul, *Fac mecum secundum magnam bonitatem tuam Domine.*[15]

Good Lord, give me the grace in all my fear and agony to have recourse to that great fear and wonderful agony that Thou my sweet Savior hadst at the Mount of Olivet before Thy most bitter

9. Gal. 6 : 14 and Phil. 1 : 21–23. "The world is crucified to me, and I to the world. For to me to live is Christ and to die is gain. I wish to be dissolved and be with Christ."

10. *grudge of death:* reluctance to die.   11. possessing well-being.

12. Ps. 142 : 10 (*AV,* 143 : 10), Cant. 1 : 3, Ps. 72 : 24 (*AV,* 73 : 23), Ps. 26 : 11 (*AV,* 27: 11), Ps. 31 : 9 (*AV,* 32 : 9). "Teach me to do your will. Make me run in the scent of your unguents. Take my right hand, and lead me in the right path because of my enemies. Draw me after you. With a muzzle and bridle restrain my jaws when I do not draw near to you."

13. other.   14. grief.

15. Cf. Ps. 118 : 124 (*AV,* 119 : 124). "Deal with me according to your great goodness, O Lord."

passion, and in the meditation thereof to conceive ghostly[16] comfort and consolation profitable for my soul.

Almighty God, take from me all vainglorious minds,[17] all appetites of mine own praise, all envy, covetise,[18] gluttony, sloth and lechery, all wrathful affections, all appetite of revenging, all desire or delight of other folks' harm, all pleasure in provoking any person to wrath and anger, all delight of exprobration[19] or insultation[20] against any person in their affliction and calamity.

And give me, good Lord, an humble, lowly, quiet, peaceable, patient, charitable, kind, tender, and pitiful mind, with all my works, and all my words, and all my thoughts to have a taste of Thy holy blessed Spirit.

Give me, good Lord, a full faith, a firm hope, and a fervent charity, a love to Thee, good Lord, incomparable[21] above the love to myself, and that I love nothing to Thy displeasure, but everything in an order to[22] Thee.

Give me, good Lord, a longing to be with Thee, not for the avoiding of the calamities of this wretched world, nor so much for the avoiding of the pains of purgatory, nor of the pains of hell neither, nor so much for the attaining of the joys of heaven, in respect of mine own commodity,[23] as even for a very[24] love to Thee.

And bear me, good Lord, Thy love and favor, which thing my love to Thee-ward[25] (were it never so great) could not but of Thy great goodness deserve.

And pardon me, good Lord, that I am so bold to ask so high petitions, being so vile a sinful wretch and so unworthy to attain the lowest. But yet, good Lord, such they be as I am bounden[26] to wish, and should be nearer the effectual desire of them if my manifold sins were not the let.[27] From which, O glorious Trinity,

16. spiritual.　　17. attitudes.　　18. covetousness.　　19. reproaching.
20. insult.　　21. incomparably.　　22. *in . . . to:* for the sake of.
23. benefit.　　24. genuine.　　25. *to Thee-ward:* toward Thee.
26. obliged.　　27. hindrance.

vouchsafe of Thy goodness to wash me with that blessed blood that issued out of Thy tender body (O sweet Savior Christ) in the divers torments of Thy most bitter passion.

Take from me, good Lord, this lukewarm fashion, or rather key-cold[28] manner, of meditation, and this dullness in praying unto Thee. And give me warmth, delight, and quickness[29] in thinking upon Thee, and give me Thy grace to long for Thine holy sacraments, and specially to rejoice in the presence of Thy very blessed body, sweet Savior Christ, in the holy sacrament of the altar, and duly to thank Thee for Thy gracious visitation therewith, and at that high memorial, with tender compassion to remember and consider Thy most bitter passion.

Make us all, good Lord, virtually[30] participant of that holy sacrament this day, and every day make us all lively[31] members, sweet Savior Christ, of Thine holy mystical body, Thy Catholic Church.

Dignare Domine die isto sine peccato nos custodire.[32]
Miserere nostri Domine, miserere nostri.[33]
Fiat misericordia tua Domine super nos, quemadmodum speravimus in te.[34]
In te Domine speravi, non confundar in aeternum.[35]
Ora pro nobis, sancta Dei genetrix, ut digni efficiamur promissionibus Christi.[36]

---

28. apathetic.   29. vitality.   30. with spiritual effect.   31. living.
32. "Deign, O Lord, on that day to preserve us without sin."
33. Ps. 122 : 3 (AV, 123 : 3). "Have Mercy upon us, O Lord, have mercy upon us."
34. Ps. 32 : 22 (AV, 33 : 22). "Let your mercy, O Lord, be upon us, just as we have hoped in you."
35. Ps. 30 : 2 (AV, 31 : 1). "In you, O Lord, have I hoped, let me not be confounded forever."
36. "Pray for us, holy mother of God, that we may be made worthy of the promises of Christ" (from the prayer *Salve regina*).

Pro amicis.[37]

Almighty God, have mercy on N.[38] and N., etc., with special meditation and consideration of every friend, as godly affection and occasion requireth.

Pro inimicis.[39]

Almighty God, have mercy on N. and N., etc., and on all that bear me evil will, and would me harm; and their faults and mine together, by such easy tender merciful means as Thine infinite wisdom best can devise, vouchsafe to amend and redress, and make us saved souls in heaven together, where we may ever live and love together with Thee and Thy blessed saints. O glorious Trinity, for the bitter passion of our sweet Savior Christ, Amen.

Lord, give me patience in tribulation, and grace in everything to conform my will to Thine, that I may truly say: *Fiat voluntas tua, sicut in caelo, et in terra.*[40]

The things, good Lord, that I pray for, give me the grace to labor for. Amen.

37. "For friends."
38. The liturgical abbreviation for the Latin *nomen* ("name"), providing for one to add names appropriate to one's own prayer.
39. "For enemies."
40. Matt. 6 : 10. "Thy will be done on earth, as it is in heaven."

Last Letters

To Margaret Roper

For the first time in English history, an Act of Parliament was passed to regulate the succession to the throne, to prevent interference as "in times past" by the pope. The Act of Succession states that the marriage with Catherine is "adjudged to be against the laws of Almighty God, and also accepted, reputed and taken of no value nor effect." The marriage with Anne "we your said subjects—do firmly accept, approve and ratify for good, and consonant to the laws of Almighty God. . . . No man, of what estate, degree or condition soever he be, hath power to dispense with God's laws. . . . All the issue had and procreate, or hereafter to be had and procreate, between your Highness and your said most dear and entirely beloved wife Queen Anne shall be your lawful children, and be inheritable, and inherit according to the course of inheritance and laws of this realm, the imperial crown of the same." No loyal Catholic could conscientiously swear to these statements.

The traitor's death was to be the penalty for any who "maliciously give occasion by writing, print, deed or act" to disturb the King or the crown, or to derogate from the lawful matrimony between the King and the said Queen Anne. Loss of goods and imprisonment for life were the penalties for misprision of treason, incurred if any persons "by any words, without writing, or any exterior deed or act, maliciously and obstinately shall publish, divulge or utter any thing or things to the peril of your Highness, or to the slander or prejudice of the said matrimony."

All persons "shall make a corporal oath . . . that they shall truly, firmly and constantly, without fraud or guile, observe, fulfill, maintain, defend and keep, to their cunning, wit, and uttermost of their powers, the whole effects and contents of this present act." Those who refuse the oath are guilty of misprision of treason.

The Act does not, however, contain the oath. Letters patent contained the form and appointed the commission. The commissioners added to the oath a formula "abjuring any foreign potentate," and the clergy thus had to renounce the pope. More was called upon so to abjure, though "they sent for no more temporal men." We do not know the form of the oath offered to More. In the following November a second Act of Succession was passed and the oath offered to More and Fisher was "reputed the very oath intended by the Act of Succession," and its form was included in the new act.

<Tower of London
c. 17 April 1534>

Sir Thomas More, upon warning[1] given him, came before the King's Commissioners[2] at the Archbishop of Canterbury's place[3] at Lambeth (the Monday the thirteenth day of April in the year of our Lord 1534, and in the latter end of the twenty-fifth year of the reign of King Henry the Eighth), where he refused the oath then offered unto him. And thereupon was he delivered to the Abbot of Westminster[4] to be kept as a prisoner, with whom he remained till Friday following, and then was sent prisoner to the Tower of London. And shortly after his coming thither he wrote a letter and sent unto his eldest daughter Mistress Margaret Roper, the copy whereof here followeth.

When I was before the Lords of Lambeth, I was the first that was called in, albeit Master Doctor the Vicar of Croydon[5] was

1. summons.
2. Archbishop Cranmer; Sir Thomas Audley, Chancellor; Thomas Duke of Norfolk, Treasurer; and the Duke of Suffolk were commissioned to receive the oath to the Act of Succession.
3. palace.
4. William Benson, born at Boston in Lincolnshire, B.D. Cambridge 1521, D.D. 1528, became Abbot of Westminster 1533. In 1540 he surrendered the Abbey to the King, and became the first Dean of the new Cathedral.
5. Rowland Phillips (c. 1468?–1538) M.A. Oxford, Warden of Merton College

come before me, and divers others. After the cause of my sending for, declared unto me (whereof I somewhat marveled in my mind, considering that they sent for no more temporal men[6] but me), I desired the sight of the oath, which they showed me under the great seal.[7] Then desired I the sight of the Act of the Succession, which was delivered me in a printed roll. After which read secretly by myself, and the oath considered with the act, I showed unto them that my purpose was not to put any fault either in the act or any man that made it, or in the oath or any man that sware it, nor to condemn the conscience of any other man. But as for myself in good faith my conscience so moved me in the matter that though I would not deny to swear to the succession, yet unto the oath that there was offered me I could not swear, without the iubarding[8] of my soul to perpetual damnation. And that if they doubted whether I did refuse the oath only for the grudge[9] of my conscience, or for any other fantasy,[10] I was ready therein to satisfy them by mine oath. Which if they trusted not, what should they be the better to give me any oath? And if they trusted that I would therein swear true, then trusted I that of their goodness they would not move[11] me to swear the oath that they offered me, perceiving that for to swear it was against my conscience.

1521–25, D. D. 1522, was collated to Croydon by Archbishop Morton in 1497, and held many other preferments. He was often in a difficult situation during the religious changes under Henry VIII. In 1531 he had confessed and been pardoned for "all offenses against the Crown and the Statute of Provisors." He was taken prisoner in the autumn of 1533, but was released and in March 1534 heard the sermons at Court, and in April was licensed to dispute with Hugh Latimer. More's letter shows that he took the Oath to the Succession, and in 1535 he labored "to bring the Carthusians into obedience to the King as head of this Church." In July 1537 he appeared before Cranmer but we have no information about his trial. In May 1538 he resigned the living of Croydon and received a pension "on account of his great age." 6. laymen.
7. The Act of Succession did not give the oath, but letters patent contained its form.
8. jeopardizing, imperiling. 9. uneasiness. 10. caprice.
11. urge, impel.

Unto this my Lord Chancellor[12] said that they all were sorry[13] to hear me say thus, and see me thus refuse the oath. And they said all that on their faith I was the very first that ever refused it; which would cause the King's Highness to conceive great suspicion of me and great indignation toward me. And therewith they showed me the roll, and let me see the names of the lords and the commons which had sworn, and subscribed their names already.[14] Which notwithstanding when they saw that I refused to swear the same myself, not blaming[15] any other man that had sworn, I was in conclusion commanded to go down into the garden, and thereupon I tarried in the old burned chamber,[16] that looketh into the garden and would not go down because of the heat. In that time saw I Master Doctor Latimer[17] come into the garden, and there walked he with divers other doctors and chaplains of my Lord of Canterbury, and very merry I saw him, for he laughed, and took one or twain about the neck so handsomely, that if they had been women, I would have went[18] he had been waxen[19] wanton. After that came Master Doctor Wilson[20] forth

12. Sir Thomas Audley.   13. distressed.   14. signed as consenting parties. 15. censuring.   16. audience room.
17. Hugh Latimer (1492?–1555), Protestant martyr under Queen Mary, B.A. Cambridge 1510, M.A. 1514, B.D. 1524, was ordained priest at Lincoln 1515. He was suspected of Lutheran tendencies as early as 1525. He was summoned before Convocation for heresy in 1532 because of his views on pilgrimages, purgatory, invocations to saints, and power of the keys, and was excommunicated. He recanted but was allowed to make his submission on lesser charges, agreeing that "no man ought to preach who has been forbidden by the bishops," and that "consecrations, sanctifications and benedictions in the church are laudable and useful." Stokesley, Bishop of London, pronounced absolution from heretical pravity, "at the special request of our lord the King." By 1534, he was appointed to preach before the King on all the Wednesdays in Lent, but was warned by Archbishop Cranmer to avoid controversy. He was made royal chaplain and in August 1535 was chosen Bishop of Worcester, to replace the Italian Ghinucci.
18. weened, supposed.   19. become.
20. Dr. Nicholas Wilson, B.A. Cambridge (Christ's College) 1508/9, D.D. 1533, was chaplain and confessor to the King, held church preferments, and in 1533 was Master of Michaelhouse, Cambridge. In Convocation he was in the minority which thought that the Pope could dispense for the marriage of Henry with his brother's widow. After two years' imprisonment in the Tower, he took the oath to the Suc-

from the lords and was with two gentlemen brought by me, and gentlemanly²¹ sent straight unto the Tower. What time my Lord of Rochester was called in before them, that cannot I tell. But at night I heard that he had been before them, but where he remained that night, and so forth till he was sent hither, I never heard. I heard also that Master Vicar of Croydon, and all the remnant²² of the priests of London that were sent for, were sworn, and that they had such favor at the council's hand that they were not lingered²³ nor made to dance any long attendance to their travail²⁴ and cost, as suitors were sometimes wont to be, but were sped apace²⁵ to their great comfort so far forth that Master Vicar of Croydon, either for gladness or for dryness, or else that it might be seen (*quod ille notus erat pontifici*)²⁶ went to my Lord's buttery bar²⁷ and called for drink, and drank (*valde familiariter*).²⁸

When they had played their pageant²⁹ and were gone out of the place, then was I called in again. And then was it declared unto me what a number had sworn, even since I went inside, gladly, without any sticking.³⁰ Wherein I laid no blame in no man, but for my own self answered as before. Now as well before as then, they somewhat laid unto me for obstinacy, that where as before, sith³¹ I refused to swear, I would not declare any special part of that oath that grudged³² my conscience, and open the cause wherefore. For thereunto I had said to them, that I feared lest the King's Highness would as they said take displeasure enough

---

cession and was released. He was preferred to the deanery of Wimborne in the diocese of Salisbury and held it until its dissolution in 1547. From June 1540 for some months he was again in the Tower "for having maintained the Pope's side." Released in 1541, he received further preferment, including a prebend at St. Paul's. He was appointed, with bishops and other doctors, to examine the New Testament in the English Bibles, as "many things needed reformation." He died in 1548.
21. as befits a gentleman.   22. remaining number.
23. caused to linger.   24. trouble.   25. expedited.
26. that he was known to the archbishop.
27. A board or ledge on the top of the buttery hatch, the half-door over which provisions are served.
28. very familiarly.   29. empty show.   30. hesitation.   31. since.
32. murmured against.

toward me for the only[33] refusal of the oath. And that if I should open and disclose the causes why, I should therewith but further exasperate his Highness, which I would in no wise do, but rather would I abide all the danger and harm that might come toward me, than give his Highness any occasion of further displeasure than the offering of the oath unto me of pure necessity constrained me. Howbeit when they divers times imputed this to me for stubbornness and obstinacy that I would neither swear the oath nor yet declare the causes why, I declined[34] thus far toward them that rather than I would be accounted for obstinate,[35] I would upon the King's gracious license[36] or rather his such commandment had[37] as might be my sufficient warrant[38] that my declaration[39] should not offend his Highness, nor put me in the danger of any of his statutes, I would be content to declare the causes in writing; and over[40] that to give an oath in the beginning, that if I might find those causes by any man in such wise answered as I might think mine own conscience satisfied, I would after that with all mine heart swear the principal oath, too.

To this I was answered that though the King would give[41] me license under his letters patent,[42] yet would it not serve against the statute. Whereto I said that yet if I had them, I would stand unto the trust of his honor at my peril for the remnant. But yet it thinketh me,[43] lo, that if I may not declare the causes without peril, then to leave them undeclared is no obstinacy.

My Lord of Canterbury taking hold upon that that I said,[44] that I condemned not the conscience of them that sware, said unto me that it appeared well that I did not take it for a very sure thing and a certain that I might not lawfully swear it, but rather as a thing

33. only for the refusal.   34. gave in.   35. be considered obstinate.
36. permission.   37. rather having such commandment.   38. safeguard.
39. exposition.   40. beyond.   41. that even if the King should give.
42. open letters to put an agreement on record.   43. I think.
44. what I had said.

uncertain and doubtful. But then (said my Lord) you know for a certainty and a thing without doubt that you be bounden to obey your sovereign lord your King. And therefore are ye bounden to leave off the doubt of your unsure conscience in refusing the oath, and take the sure way in obeying of your prince, and swear it. Now all was it so[45] that in mine own mind methought myself not concluded,[46] yet this argument seemed me[47] suddenly so subtle and namely with such authority coming out of so noble[48] a prelate's mouth, that I could again answer nothing thereto but only that I thought myself I might not well do so, because that in my conscience this was one of the cases in which I was bounden that I should not obey my prince, sith that whatsoever other folk thought in the matter (whose conscience and learning I would not condemn nor take upon me to judge), yet in my conscience the truth seemed on the other side. Wherein I had not informed my conscience neither suddenly nor slightly but by long leisure and diligent search for the matter. And of truth if that reason may conclude,[49] then have we a ready way to avoid all perplexities. For in whatsoever matters the doctors stand in great doubt, the King's commandment given upon whither side he list[50] soyleth[51] all the doubts.

Then said my Lord of Westminster to me that howsoever the matter seemed unto mine own mind, I had cause to fear that mine own mind was erroneous when I see the great council[52] of the realm determine of my mind the contrary,[53] and that therefore I ought to change my conscience. To that I answered that if there were no mo[54] but myself upon my side and the whole Parliament upon the other, I would be sore afraid to lean to mine own mind

45. Even though I agreed to the extent.
46. that I thought myself (as a layman) not included.   47. to me.
48. notable.   49. truly if reason may conclude.
50. on whichever side is pleasing to him.   51. resolves.   52. Parliament.
53. determine contrary to my mind.   54. more.

only against so many. But on the other side, if it so be that in some things for which I refuse the oath, I have (as I think I have) upon my part as great a council and a greater too, I am not then bounden to change my conscience, and confirm[55] it to the council of one realm, against the general council of Christendom. Upon this Master Secretary[56] (as he that tenderly favoreth me), said and sware a great oath that he had lever[57] that his own only son[58] (which is of truth a goodly young gentleman, and shall I trust come to much worship) had lost his head than that I should thus have refused the oath. For surely the King's Highness would now conceive a great suspicion against me, and think that the matter of the nun of Canterbury was all contrived[59] by my drift.[60] To which I said that the contrary was true and well known, and whatsoever should mishap[61] me, it lay not in my power to help it without peril of my soul. Then did my Lord Chancellor repeat before me my refusal unto Master Secretary, as to him that was going unto the King's Grace. And in the rehearsing, his Lordship repeated again that I denied not but was content to swear to the succession. Whereunto I said that as for that point, I would be content, so that I might see[62] my oath in that point so framed[63] in such a manner as might stand with my conscience.

Then said my Lord: "Marry,[64] Master Secretary mark that too, that he will not swear that neither but under some certain manner." "Verily, no, my Lord," quoth I, "but that I will see it made in such wise first, as I shall myself see, that I shall neither be forsworn[65] nor swear against my conscience. Surely as to swear to the succession I see no peril, but I thought and think it reason that to mine own oath I look well myself, and be of counsel also in the

---

55. conform.   56. Thomas Cromwell.   57. liefer, rather.
58. Gregory Cromwell was just of age. He seems hardly to have deserved More's tribute.
59. devised.   60. controlling influence.   61. happen unfortunately to.
62. if I might see.   63. composed.   64. Interjection: Mary.
65. perjured.

fashion,[66] and never intended to swear for a pece,[67] and set my
hand to the whole oath. Howbeit (as help me God),[68] as touching
the whole oath, I never withdrew any man from it, nor never
advised any to refuse it, nor never put, nor will, any scruple in any
man's head, but leave every man to his own conscience. And
methinketh[69] in good faith that so were it good reason[70] that every
man should leave me to mine."

To Margaret Roper

Tower of London
<April–May? 1534>

A letter written with a coal[1] by Sir Thomas More to his daughter
Mistress Margaret Roper, within a while after he was prisoner in
the Tower.

MINE OWN GOOD DAUGHTER.

Our Lord be thanked, I am in good health of body, and in good
quiet of mind; and of worldly things I no more desire than I have. I
beseech him make you all merry in the hope of heaven. And such
things as I somewhat longed to talk with you all, concerning the
world to come, our Lord put them into your minds, as I trust he
doth, and better, too, by his Holy Spirit, who bless you and preserve
you all. Written with a coal by your tender loving father, who in his
poor prayers forgetteth none of you all, nor your babes, nor your
nurses, nor your good husbands, nor your good husbands' shrewd[2]
wives, nor your father's shrewd wife neither, nor our other friends.
And thus fare you heartily well for lack of paper.

THOMAS MORE, Knight

66. and have counsel in the way.   67. piece, part.   68. so God help me.
69. I think.   70. it would be good reason.   1. charcoal used for writing.
2. clever.

Our Lord keep me continually true, faithful and plain,[3] to the contrary whereof I beseech him heartily never to suffer me to live. For as for long life (as I have often told thee, Meg) I neither look for, nor long for, but am well content to go, if God call me hence tomorrow. And I thank our Lord I know no person living that I would had one philip[4] for my sake, of which mind[5] I am more glad than of all the world beside.

Recommend me to[6] your shrewd Will and mine other sons,[7] and to John Harris my friend, and yourself knoweth to whom else, and to my shrewd wife above all, and God preserve you all, and make and keep you his servants all.

To Margaret Roper

Tower of London
<May? 1534>

Within a while after Sir Thomas More was in prison in the Tower, his daughter Mistress Margaret Roper wrote and sent unto him a letter,[1] wherein she seemed somewhat to labor to persuade him to take the oath (though she nothing so thought) to win thereby credence[2] with Master Thomas Cromwell, that she might the rather get liberty to have free resort[3] unto her father (which she only[4] had for the most time of his imprisonment) unto which letter her father wrote an answer, the copy whereof here followeth.

---

3. straightforward.   4. A smart stroke with the nail joint of the finger.
5. state of mind.   6. commend me to the favor of.
7. William Roper, William Daunce, Giles Heron, John More.
1. Margaret Roper's letter is not extant.   2. confidence, trust.   3. access.
4. she alone.

OUR LORD BLESS YOU ALL.

If I had not been, my dearly beloved daughter, at a firm and fast[5] point (I trust in God's great mercy), this good great while before, your lamentable[6] letter had not a little abashed me,[7] surely far above all other things, of which I hear divers times not a few terrible toward me. But surely they all touched me never so near, nor were so grievous[8] unto me, as to see you, my well-beloved child, in such vehement[9] piteous manner labor to persuade unto me that thing wherein I have of pure necessity for respect unto mine own soul so often given you so precise answer before. Wherein as touching the points of your letter, I can make none answer, for I doubt not but you well remember that the matters which move my conscience (without declaration whereof I can nothing touch the points) I have sundry times showed you that I will disclose them to no man. And therefore daughter Margaret, I can in this thing no further, but like as you labor[10] me again to follow your mind, to desire and pray you both again to leave off such labor, and with my former answers to hold yourself content.

A deadly grief unto me, and much more deadly than to hear of mine own death (for the fear thereof, I thank our Lord, the fear of hell, the hope of heaven and the passion of Christ daily more and more assuage) is that I perceive my good son your husband, and you my good daughter, and my good wife, and mine other good children and innocent friends, in great displeasure and danger of great harm thereby. The let[11] whereof, while it lieth not in my hand, I can no further but commit all unto God. (*Nam in manu Dei*) saith the scripture (*cor regis est, et sicut diuisiones aquarum quocunque voluerit, impellit illud*),[12] whose high goodness I most

5. steadfast.   6. distressing.   7. destroyed my self-confidence.
8. intense, severe.   9. passionate.   10. urge.
11. hindrance, stoppage.
12. Prov. 21 : 1. ("The King's heart is in the hand of the Lord, as the rivers of water: he turneth it whithersoever he will." *King James Version*; hereafter, *KJV*)

humbly beseech to incline the noble heart of the King's Highness to the tender[13] favor of you all, and to favor me no better than God and myself know that my faithful heart toward him and my daily prayer for him, do deserve. For surely if his Highness might inwardly see my true mind such as God knoweth it is, I would (I trust) soon assuage[14] his high displeasure. Which while I can in this world never in such wise show but that his Grace may be persuaded to believe the contrary of me, I can no further go, but put all in the hands of him, for fear of whose displeasure for the safeguard of my soul stirred by mine own conscience (without insectation[15] or reproach laying to any other man's) I suffer and endure this trouble. Out of which I beseech him to bring me, when his will shall be, into his endless bliss of heaven, and in the meanwhile, give me grace and you both in all our agonies and troubles, devoutly to resort prostrate unto the remembrance of that bitter agony, which our Saviour suffered before his passion at the Mount.[16] And if we diligently so do, I verily trust we shall find therein great comfort and consolation. And thus my dear daughter the blessed spirit of Christ for his tender mercy govern and guide you all, to his pleasure and your weal[17] and comforts both body and soul.

Your tender loving father,

Thomas More, Knight[18]

13. gentle.   14. soften, appease.   15. pursuing with words, railing.
16. St. Matt. 26 : 36–46.   17. well-being.
18. Margaret answered this letter, telling her father that the family found comfort in "the experience we have had of your life past and godly conversation." She desired "above all worldly things to be in John Wood's stead to do you some service." John à Wood was More's servant, who attended him in the Tower. He saved More's works written during his imprisonment.

To All His Friends

Roper tells us that Margaret's visit was permitted when More "had remained in the Tower a little more than a month." Their conversation began "after the seven psalms and litany said."

In August, Alice Alington, More's stepdaughter, wrote Margaret Roper that the Chancellor had "come to take a course at a buck in our park," and gave her the opportunity to speak for her father. Sir Thomas Audley reminded her that he had helped in the affair of the Nun, but now "marveled that my father is so obstinate in his own conceit, as that everybody went forth withal save only the blind Bishop and he." He callously refused help, putting Lady Alington off with the telling of two of Aesop's fables. Margaret shared the letter with her father when she next visited him. The reply to her stepsister is a repetition of the dialogue with her father. It is so characteristic of More that when it was printed, after More's and Margaret's deaths, the remaining members of the family circle could not tell whether the writer was More himself, or Margaret.

Tower of London
<1534>

Within a while after Sir Thomas More had been in prison in the Tower, his daughter Mistress Margaret Roper obtained license of the King, that she might resort unto her father in the Tower, which she did. And thereupon he wrote with a coal[1] a letter to all his friends, whereof the copy followeth.

TO ALL MY LOVING FRIENDS.

For as much as being in prison I cannot tell what need I may have, or what necessity I may hap to stand in, I heartily beseech

---

1. charcoal used for writing.

you all, that if my well beloved daughter Margaret Roper (which only of all my friends hath by the King's gracious favor license to resort to me) do anything desire of any of you, of such things as I shall hap to need, that it may like you no less to regard and ten-der[2] it, than if I moved it unto you and required it of you person-ally present myself. And I beseech you all to pray for me, and I shall pray for you.

Your faithful lover and poor bedeman,[3]

THOMAS MORE, Knight, prisoner

To Dr. Nicholas Wilson

Tower of London

1534

A letter written and sent by Sir T. More to Master Doctor Nicholas Wilson[1] (then both prisoners in the Tower of London) in the year of our Lord God 1534, and in the twenty-sixth year of the reign of King Henry the Eighth.

Our Lord be your comfort and whereas I perceive by sundry means that you have promised to swear the oath, I beseech our Lord give you thereof good luck. I never gave any man counsel to the contrary in my days nor never used any ways to put any scru-ple in other folks' conscience concerning the matter. And whereas I perceive that you would gladly know what I intend to do, you wot[2] well that I told you when we were both abroad that I would therein neither know your mind nor no man's else, nor you nor no man else should therein know mine, for I would be no part

---

2. attend to.   3. One who prays for another.
1. For Dr. Wilson see above, letter to Margaret Roper, intro., p. 134.   2. know.

taker[3] with no man nor of truth never I will, but leaving every other man to their own conscience myself will with good grace follow mine. For against mine own to swear were peril of my damnation and what mine own shall be tomorrow myself cannot be sure and whether I shall have finally the grace to do according to mine own conscience or not hangeth in God's goodness and not in mine, to whom I beseech you heartily remember me in your devout prayers and I shall and daily do remember you in mine, such as they be, and as long as my poor short life shall last, any thing that I have, your part shall be therein.

To Dr. Nicholas Wilson

Tower of London
1534

Another letter written and sent by Sir Thomas More to Master Doctor Wilson (then both prisoners in the Tower) in the year of our Lord 1534, and in the twenty-sixth year of the reign of King Henry the Eighth.

MASTER WILSON IN MY RIGHT HEARTY WISE I RECOMMEND[1]
ME TO YOU.

And very sorry am I to see you, beside the trouble that you be in by this imprisonment with loss of liberty, goods, revenues of your livelihood and comfort of your friends' company, fallen also into such agony and vexation of mind through doubts falling in your mind that diversely[2] to and fro toss and trouble your conscience to your great heaviness of heart as I (to no little grief of mine own mind for your sake) perceive. And so much am I for

3. partisan.   1. commend.   2. in diverse ways.

you, good Master Doctor, the more sorry for that it lieth not in me to give you such kind of comfort as meseemeth[3] you somewhat desire and look for at mine hand.

For whereas you would somewhat hear of my mind in your doubts, I am a man at this day very little meet[4] therefor. For this you know well, good Master Doctor, that at such time as the matter came in such manner in question as mine opinion was asked therein amongst other and yet you made privy thereunto before me, you remember well that at that time you and I many things talked together thereof. And by all the time after by which I did at the King's gracious commandment both seek out and read and commen[5] with all such as I knew made privy to the matter to perceive what I might therein upon both sides and by indifferent[6] weighing of everything as near as my poor wit and learning would serve to see to which side my conscience could incline, and as my own mind should give me so to make his Highness report which way myself should hap to think therein. For other commandment had I never of his Grace in good faith, saving that this knot[7] his Highness added thereto that I should therein look first unto God and after God unto him, which word was also the first lesson that his Grace gave me what time I came first into his noble service and neither a more indifferent commandment nor a more gracious lesson could there in my mind never King give his counselor or any his other[8] servant.

But as I began to tell you by all this long time,[9] I cannot now tell how many years, of all those that I talked with of the matter and with whom I most conferred[10] those places of Scripture and of the old holy Doctors that touched either the one side or the other, with the councils and laws on either side, that speak thereof also, the most, as I trow[11] you wot[12] well, was yourself. For with no man communed I so much and so often thereof as with you,

3. it seems to me.   4. suitable.   5. confer, discuss.   6. impartial.
7. bond, obligation.   8. any other servant of his.   9. in all this long time.
10. compared.   11. think.   12. know.

both for your substantial learning and for your mature judgment,
and for that[13] I well perceived ever in you that no man had or
lightly could have a more faithful respect unto the King's honor
and surety[14] both of body and soul than I ever saw that you had.

And yet among many other things which I well liked in you,
one specially was that I well perceived in the thing that the King's
Grace did put you in trust with,[15] your substantial[16] secret manner. For where I had heard (I wot not now of whom) that you had
written his Highness a book of that matter from Paris before, yet
in all those years of our long acquaintance and often talking and
reasoning upon the thing, I never heard you so much as make
once any mention of that book. But else (except there were any
other things in that book that you peradventure[17] thought not on)
I suppose that all that ever came to your mind, that might in the
matter make for the one side or the other comprised[18] either in
the Scripture or in the old ancient Doctors, I verily think in my
mind that you did communicate with[19] me and I likewise with
you and at the least wise I remember well that of those points
which you call now newly to your remembrance there was none
at this time forgotten.

I remember well also by your often[20] conference[21] in the matter
that by all the time in which I studied about it, you and I were in
every point both twain[22] of one opinion and remember well that
the laws and councils and the words of Saint Augustine *De civitate Dei* and the epistle of Saint Ambrose *Ad paternum* and the
epistle of Saint Basil translated out of Greek and the writing of
Saint Gregory[23] you and I read together and over that the places
of the Scripture self[24] both in Leviticus[25] and in the Deuteronomy

13. because.   14. security.   15. in which the King's Grace trusted you.
16. essentially.   17. possibly.   18. comprehended.   19. impart to.
20. frequent.   21. action of taking counsel.   22. two.
23. For references on the opinions of the Fathers, consult the *Catholic Encyclopae-
dia,* "Divorce."
24. itself.   25. Levit. 20 : 21.

and in the Gospel[26] and in Saint Paul's epistles[27] and over[28] this in that other place of Saint Augustine that you remember now and beside that other places of his, wherein he properly toucheth[29] the matter expressly with the words of Saint Jerome and of Saint Chrysostom too, and I cannot now remember of how many more. But I verily think that on your part, and I am very sure that on my part, albeit that it had been peradventure over long to show and read with you every man's book that I read by myself, whereto the parties peradventure that trusted me therewith gave me no leave to show their books further as you peradventure used the like manner with me; yet in good faith as it was of reason my part in that case to do, you and I having both one commandment indifferently[30] to consider the matter, everything of Scripture and of the Doctors I faithfully communed with you and as I suppose verily so did you with me too, so that of me, good Master Doctor, though I had all the points as ripe in mind now as I had then and had still all the books about me that I then had, and were as willing to meddle[31] in the matter as any man could be, yet could you now no new thing hear of me, more than you have, I wyn,[32] heard often before, nor I wyn I of you neither.

But now standeth it with me in far other case. For afterward when I had signified unto the King's Highness mine own poor opinion in the matter which his Highness very graciously took in good part and that I saw further progress in the matter wherein to do his Grace service to his pleasure I could not, and anything meddle[33] against his pleasure I would not, I determined utterly with myself to discharge[34] my mind of any farther studying or musing[35] of the matter and thereupon I sent home again such books as I had saving that some I burned by the consent of the owner that was minded[36] as myself was no more to meddle of[37]

26. Deut. 25 : 5, St. Mark 10, St. Matt. 19.   27. 1 Cor. 7, 1 Tim. 5 : 14.
28. besides.   29. considers.   30. impartially.   31. concern myself.
32. ween, suppose.   33. contend.   34. disburden.   35. pondering.
36. disposed.   37. engage in.

the matter, and therefore now good Master Doctor I could not be sufficient and able to reason those points again though I were minded thereto sith[38] many things are out of my mind which I never purpose to look for again nor though I would were never like to find again while I live. Besides this, all that ever I looked for was, you wot well, concerning two or three questions to be pondered and weighed by the study of Scripture and the interpreters of the same, save for somewhat that hath been touched in the same by the canon[39] laws of the Church.

But then were there at that time in the matter other things more, divers faults found in the bull[40] of the dispensation,[41] by which the King's Council learned in the spiritual law reckoned the bull vicious, partly for untrue suggestion, partly by reason of unsufficient suggestion.[42] Now concerning those points I never meddled. For I neither understand the Doctors of the law nor well can turn their books. And many things have there since in this great matter grown in question wherein I neither am sufficiently learned in the law nor full informed of the fact and therefore I am not he that either murmur or grudge, make assertions, hold opinions or keep dispicions[43] in the matter, but like the King's true, poor, humble subject daily pray for the preservation of his Grace, and the Queen's Grace and their noble issue and of all the realm, without harm doing or intending, I thank our Lord, unto any man living.

Finally as touching the oath, the causes for which I refused it, no man wotteth[44] what they be for they be secret in mine own

38. since.
39. Church laws from councils and decrees of the popes.
40. Pope's edict, with leaden *bulla* or seal.
41. Ecclesiastical license to do what is otherwise forbidden by canon law.
42. Henry took the position that the dispensation could not allow the marriage with a brother's widow, if that first marriage had really been consummated. But before the trial Catherine showed Cardinal Campeggio the copy of a brief of Pope Julius II which dispensed for the marriage, though considering that the marriage with Arthur had been consummated. This, in any case, Catherine denied.
43. disputations.   44. knows.

conscience, some other peradventure, than those that other men would ween,[45] and such as I never disclosed unto any man yet nor never intend to do while I live. Finally as I said unto you, before the oath offered unto us when we met in London at adventure[46] I would be no part taker[47] in the matter but for mine own self follow mine own conscience, for which myself must make answer unto God, and shall leave every other man to his own, so say to you still and I dare say further that no more never intended you neither.[48] Many things every man learned[49] wotteth well there are, in which every man is at liberty without peril of damnation to think which way him list[50] till the one part be determined for necessary to be believed by a general council[51] and I am not he that take upon me to define or determine of what kind or nature everything is that the oath containeth, nor am so bold or presumptuous to blame or dispraise the conscience of other men, their truth nor their learning neither, nor I meddle with no man but of myself, nor of no man's conscience else will I meddle but of mine own. And in mine own conscience I cry God mercy, I find of mine own life, matters enough to think on.

I have lived, methinks,[52] a long life and now neither I look nor I long to live much longer. I have since I came in the Tower looked once or twice to have given up my ghost[53] ere[54] this and in good faith mine heart waxed[55] the lighter with hope thereof. Yet forget I not that I have a long reckoning and a great to give account of,[56] but I put my trust in God and in the merits of his bitter passion, and I beseech him give me and keep me the mind to long to be out of this world and to be with him. For I can never but trust that who so long to be with him shall be welcome to him and on the other side my mind giveth me verily that any that ever

---

45. suppose.　　46. by chance.　　47. partisan.
48. neither did you intend more.　　49. learned man.　　50. he is inclined.
51. Determined by a general council as necessary belief.　　52. it seems to me.
53. to have died.　　54. before.　　55. grew.　　56. i.e., to God.

shall come to him shall full heartily wish to be with him or[57] ever he shall come at[58] him. And I beseech him heartily to set your heart at such rest and quiet as may be to his pleasure and eternal weal[59] of your soul and so I verily trust that he shortly shall and shall also if it be his pleasure incline the King's noble heart to be gracious and favorable to you and me both, sith we be both twain of true faithful mind unto him, whether we be in this matter of one mind both,[60] or of diverse. *Sicut diuisiones aquarum, ita cor regis in manu Domini, quocunque voluerit, inclinabit illud.*[61] And if the pleasure of God be on any of us both otherwise to dispose,[62] I need to give you no counsel nor advice.

But for myself I most humbly beseech him to give me the grace in such wise patiently to conform my mind unto his high pleasure therein, that after the troublous storm of this my tempestuous time his great mercy may conduct me into the sure haven of the joyful bliss of heaven, and after at his further pleasure (if I have any)[63] all mine enemies too, for there shall we love together well enough and I thank our Lord for my part so do I here too. Be not angry now though I pray not like for you; you be sure enough I would my friends fare no worse than they, nor yet they, so help me God, no worse than myself.

For our Lord's sake, good Master Wilson, pray for me for I pray for you daily and sometime when I would be sorry but if I thought you were asleep. Comfort yourself, good Master Doctor, with remembering God's great mercy and the King's accustomed goodness, and by my troth I think that all his Grace's Council favoreth you in their hearts. I cannot judge in my mind any one of them so evil as to be of the mind that you should do otherwise than well. And for conclusion in God is all. *Spes non confundit.*[64] I

57. before.   58. to.   59. happiness.   60. both of one mind.
61. Proverbs 21 : 1. (See translation, note 12, above, p. 141.)
62. To dispose otherwise for either of us.
63. This clause should follow *enemies*.
64. Rom. 5 : 5. ("Hope maketh not ashamed." *KJV*)

pray you pardon my scribbling for I cannot always so well endure to write as I might sometime. And I pray you when ye see time convenient at your pleasure, send me this rude bill again. *Quia quanquam nihil inest mali, tamen propter ministrum nolim rescire.*[65]

To Margaret Roper

Margaret wrote sympathetically of More's being "shut up again" more closely in the Tower. He had been allowed to hear Mass in one of the chapels and to be in the garden with Dame Alice More and Margaret.

Tower of London

1534

A letter written and sent by Sir Thomas More to his daughter Mistress Roper answering her letter here next before.

THE HOLY SPIRIT OF GOD BE WITH YOU.

If I would with my writing (mine own good daughter) declare how much pleasure and comfort your daughterly loving letters were unto me, a peck of coals would not suffice to make me the pens. And other pens have I (good Margaret) none here: and therefore can I write you no long process,[1] nor dare adventure,[2] good daughter, to write often.

The cause of my close keeping[3] again did of likelihood grow of my negligent[4] and very plain true word which you remember. And verily where as my mind gave me (as I told you in the gar-

---

65. "Because, although there is nothing evil (disloyal or treasonous) in it, yet on account of the servant I would not wish them to discover it." George Golde, the Lieutenant's servant, carried letters for prisoners. More wished to keep letters to prove their harmlessness, but Golde said there was no better keeper than the fire and burned them.

1. narrative.   2. try.   3. strict confinement.   4. careless.

den) that some such thing were likely to happen, so doth my mind alway give me that some folk yet ween[5] that I was not so poor as it appeared in the search, and that it may therefore happen that yet eftsoon[6] ofter than once, some new sudden searches may hap to be made in every house of ours as narrowly as is possible. Which thing if ever it so should hap can make but game[7] to us that know the truth of my poverty but if they find out my wife's gay girdle and her golden beads. Howbeit I verily believe in good faith that the King's Grace of his benign pity will take nothing from her.

I thought and yet think that it may be that I was shut up again upon some new causeless suspicion, grown peradventure[8] upon some secret sinister information, whereby some folk haply[9] thought that there should be found out against me some other greater things. But I thank our Lord whensoever this conjecture hath fallen in my mind, the clearness of my conscience hath made my heart hop for joy. For one thing am I very sure of hitherto, and trust in God's mercy to be while I live, that as often I have said unto you, I shall for anything toward my prince never take great harm, but if I take great wrong, in the sight of God, I say, howsoever it shall seem in the sight of men. For to the world, wrong may seem right sometime by false conjecturing, some-times by false witnesses, as that good Lord said unto you, which is I dare say my very good lord in his mind, and said it of very good will. Before the world also, my refusing of this oath is accounted an heinous[10] offense, and my religious fear[11] toward God is called obstinacy toward my Prince. But my Lords of the Council before whom I refused it might well perceive by the heaviness of my heart appearing well more ways than one unto them that all sturdy stubbornness whereof obstinacy groweth was very far

5. think.   6. again.   7. sport.   8. perhaps.   9. by chance.
10. criminal.   11. mingled feeling of dread and reverence.

from my mind. For the clearer proof whereof, sith[12] they seemed
to take for one argument of obstinacy in me that refusing of the
oath, I would not declare the causes why, I offered with a full
heart, that albeit I rather would endure all the pain and peril of
the statute than by declaring of the causes, give any occasion of
exasperation unto my most dread Sovereign Lord and Prince, yet
rather than his Highness should for not disclosing the causes
account me for stubborn and obstinate, I would upon such his
gracious license and commandment as should discharge me of his
displeasure and peril of any statute declare those points that let-
ted[13] my poor conscience to receive that oath; and would over that
be sworn before, that if I should after the causes disclosed and
declared find them so answered as my conscience should think
itself satisfied, I would thereupon swear the oath that I there
refused. To this, Master Secretary answered me that though the
King's Grace gave me such a license, yet it could not discharge me
against[14] the statutes in saying anything that were by them upon
heinous[15] pains prohibited. In this good warning he showed himself my special tender friend.

   And now you see well, Margaret, that it is no obstinacy to leave
the causes undeclared, while I could not declare them without
peril. But now is it accounted great obstinacy that I refuse the
oath, whatsoever my causes be, considering that of so many wiser
and better men none sticked[16] thereat. And Master Secretary of a
great zeal that he bare unto me sware there before them a great
oath that for the displeasure that he thought the King's Highness
would bear me, and the suspicion that his Grace would conceive
of me, which would now think in his mind that all the Nun's
business was wrought and devised by me, he had liefer[17] than I
should have refused the oath that his own only son (which is a
goodly young gentleman of whom our Lord send him much joy)

12. since.   13. prevented.   14. exempt me from.   15. severe.
16. scrupled.   17. rather.

had had his head stricken off. This word Margaret, as it was a marvelous declaration of Master Secretary's great good mind and favor toward me, so was it an heavy hearing to me that the King's Grace, my most dread Sovereign Lord, were likely to conceive such high suspicion of me and bear such grievous indignation toward me, for the thing which without the danger and peril of my poor soul lay not in my hand to help, nor doth.

Now have I heard since that some say that this obstinate manner of mine in still refusing the oath shall peradventure force and drive the King's Grace to make a further law for me. I cannot let[18] such a law to be made. But I am very sure that if I died by such a law, I should die for that point innocent afore[19] God. And albeit (good daughter) that I think our Lord that hath the hearts of Kings in his hand would never suffer of his high goodness, so gracious a Prince, and so many honorable men, and so many good men as be in the Parliament to make such an unlawful law, as that should be it is so mishapped,[20] yet lest I note that point unthought upon, but many times more than one revolved and cast in my mind before my coming hither, both that peril and all other that might put my body in peril of death by the refusing of this oath. In devising whereupon, albeit (mine own good daughter) that I found myself (I cry God mercy) very sensual[21] and my flesh much more shrinking from pain and from death than methought it the part of a faithful Christian man, in such a case as my conscience gave me, that in the saving of my body should stand the loss of my soul, yet I thank our Lord, that in that conflict the Spirit had in conclusion the mastery, and reason with help of faith finally concluded that for to be put to death wrongfully for doing well (as I am very sure I do, in refusing to swear against mine own conscience, being such as I am not upon peril of my soul bounden[22] to

18. prevent.   19. before.   20. unfortunately happened.
21. depending on the senses only and not on the intellect or spirit.'
22. bound.

change whether my death should come without law, or by color[23] of a law) it is a case in which a man may leese[24] his head and yet have none harm, but instead of harm inestimable good at the hand of God.

And I thank our Lord (Megge) since I am come hither I set by[25] death every day less than other. For though a man leese of his years in this world, it is more than manifold recompensed by coming the sooner to heaven. And though it be a pain to die while a man is in health, yet see I very few that in sickness die with ease. And finally, very sure am I that whensoever the time shall come that may hap to come, God wot[26] how soon, in which I should lie sick in my death bed by nature, I shall then think that God had done much for me, if he had suffered me to die before by the color of such a law. And therefore my reason showeth me (Margaret) that it were great folly for me to be sorry to come to that death, which I would after wish that I had died. Beside that, that a man may hap with less thank of God and more adventure[27] of his soul to die as violently and as painfully by many other chances as by enemies or thieves. And therefore mine own good daughter I assure you (thanks be to God) the thinking of any such albeit it hath grieved[28] me ere[29] this, yet at this day grieveth me nothing. And yet I know well for all this mine own frailty, and that Saint Peter which feared it much less than I, fell in such fear soon after that at the word of a simple girl he forsook and forswore[30] our Saviour.[31] And therefore am I not (Megge) so mad[32] as to warrant[33] myself to stand. But I shall pray, and I pray thee mine own good daughter to pray with me, that it may please God that hath given me this mind, to give me the grace to keep it.

And thus have I mine own good daughter disclosed unto you

23. under the pretext.   24. lose.   25. esteem.   26. knows.
27. peril.   28. troubled.   29. before.   30. denied on oath.
31. Matt. 26 : 69–75.   32. unwise.   33. pledge.

the very secret bottom of my mind, referring the order thereof only to the goodness of God, and that so fully that I assure you Margaret on my faith I never have prayed God to bring me hence nor deliver me from death, but referring all thing whole unto his only pleasure, as to him that seeth better what is best for me than myself doth. Nor never longed I since I came hither to set my foot in mine own house, for any desire of or pleasure of my house, but gladly would I sometime somewhat talk with my friends, and specially my wife and you that pertain to my charge. But sith that God otherwise disposeth,[34] I commit all wholly to his goodness and take daily great comfort in that I perceive that you live together so charitably and so quietly; I beseech our Lord continue it. And thus, mine own good daughter, putting you finally in remembrance that albeit if the necessity so should require, I thank our Lord in this quiet and comfort is mine heart at this day, and I trust in God's goodness so shall have grace to continue, yet (as I said before) I verily trust that God shall so inspire and govern the King's heart that he shall not suffer his noble heart and courage to requite my true faithful heart and service with such extreme unlawful and uncharitable dealing, only for the displeasure that I cannot think so as others do. But his true subject will I live and die, and truly pray for him will I, both here and in the other world too.

And thus mine own good daughter have me recommended to my good bedfellow and all my children, men, women and all, with all your babes and your nurses and all the maids and all the servants, and all our kin, and all our other friends abroad. And I beseech our Lord to save them all and keep them. And I pray you all pray for me, and I shall pray for you all. And take no thought for me whatsoever you shall hap to hear, but be merry in God.

34. ordains.

To Margaret Roper

Tower of London
1534

Another letter written and sent by Sir Thomas More (in the year of our Lord, 1534 and in the twenty-sixth year of King Henry the Eighth) to his daughter Mistress Roper, answering a letter[1] which she wrote and sent unto him.

THE HOLY SPIRIT OF GOD BE WITH YOU.

Your daughterly loving letter, my dearly beloved child, was and is, I faithfully assure you, much more inward comfort unto me than my pen can well express you, for divers things that I marked therein but of all things most especially, for that God of his high goodness giveth you the grace to consider the incomparable difference between the wretched estate of this present life and the wealthy state of the life to come, for them that die in God, and to pray God in such a good Christian fashion that it may please him (it doth me good here to rehearse your own words) "of his tender pity so firmly to rest our love in him, with little regard of this world, and so to flee sin and embrace virtue, that we may say with Saint Paul, *Mihi viuere Christus est et mori luchrum.* And this, *Cupio dissolui et esse cum Christo.*"[2] I beseech our Lord, my dearly beloved daughter, that wholesome prayer that he hath put in your mind, it may like him to give your father the grace daily to remember and pray, and yourself as you have written it even so daily devoutly to kneel and pray it. For surely if God give us that, he giveth us and will give us therewith all that ever we can well

1. Margaret's letter is lost.
2. Phil. 1 : 21, 23. ("For to me to live is Christ, and to die is gain . . . having a desire to depart, and to be with Christ.")

wish. And therefore good Marget, when you pray it, pray it for us both, and I shall on my part the like, in such manner as it shall like our Lord to give me, poor wretch,[3] the grace, that likewise as in this wretched world I have been very glad of your company and you of mine, and yet would if it might be (as natural charity bindeth the father and the child) so we may rejoice and enjoy each other's company, with our other kinsfolk, allies,[4] and friends everlastingly in the glorious bliss of heaven, and in the meantime with good counsel and prayer each help other thitherward.

And where you write these words of yourself, "But good father, I wretch am far, far, farthest of all other from such point of perfection, our Lord send me the grace to amend my life, and continually to have an eye to mine end, without grudge[5] of death, which to them that die in God, is the gate of a wealthy life to which God of his infinite mercy bring us all. Amen. Good Father strength[6] my frailty with your devout prayers." The father of heaven mote[7] strenght thy frailty, my good daughter and the frailty of thy frail father too. And let us not doubt but he so will, if we will not be slack[8] in calling upon him therefor. Of my poor prayers, such as they be, ye may be bold to reckon. For Christian charity and natural love and your very daughterly dealing (*funiculo triplici,* as saith the Scripture, *difficile rumpitur*)[9] both bind me and strain me thereto. And of yours I put as little doubt.

That you fear your own frailty Marget, nothing misliketh me.[10] God give us both twain[11] the grace to despair of our own self, and whole[12] to depend and hang upon the hope and strength of God. The blessed apostle Saint Paul found such lack of strength in himself that in his own temptation he was fain thrice to call and cry out unto God, to take that temptation from him.

3. one sunk in deep distress.   4. relatives by marriage.   5. fear.
6. strengthen.   7. must.   8. remiss.
9. Eccles. 4 : 12. ("... a threefold cord is not quickly broken." *KJV*)
10. I do not disapprove.   11. two.   12. wholly.

And yet sped he not of his prayer,[13] in the manner that he required. For God of his high wisdom, seeing that it was (as himself saith) necessary for him to keep him from pride that else he might peradventure[14] have fallen in, would not at his thrice praying, by and by[15] take it from him, but suffered him to be panged[16] in the pain and fear thereof, giving him yet at the last this comfort against his fear of falling (*Sufficit tibi gratia mea*).[17] By which words it well seemeth that the temptation was so strong (whatsoever kind of temptation it was) that he was very feared[18] of falling, through the feebleness of resisting that he began to feel in himself. Wherefore for his comfort God answered (*Sufficit tibi gratia mea*) putting him in surety, that were he of himself never so feeble and faint, nor never so likely to fall, yet the grace of God was sufficient to keep him up and make him stand. And our Lord said further (*Virtus in infirmitate proficitur*).[19] The more weak that man is, the more is the strength of God in his safeguard declared. And so Saint Paul saith (*Omnia possum in eo qui me confortat*).[20]

Surely Megge a fainter heart than thy frail father hath, canst you not have. And yet I verily trust in the great mercy of God, that he shall of his goodness so stay[21] me with his holy hand that he shall not finally suffer me to fall wretchedly from his favor. And the like trust (dear daughter) in his high goodness I verily conceive of you. And so much the more, in that there is neither of us both, but that if we call his benefits to mind and give him oft thanks for them, we may find tokens[22] many, to give us good hope for all our manifold offenses toward him, that his great mercy, when we will heartily call therefor, shall not be withdrawn from us. And verily, my dear daughter, in this is my great comfort, that

13. attained he not his prayer.   14. possibly.   15. straightway.
16. affected.   17. 2 Cor. 12 : 7–10. ("My grace is sufficient for Thee." *KJV*)
18. afraid.   19. 2 Cor. 12:9. ("... my strength is made perfect in weakness." *KJV*)
20. Phil. 4 : 13. ("I can do all things through Christ which strengtheneth me." *KJV*)
21. support.   22. signs of divine power.

albeit I am of nature so shrinking from pain that I am almost afeard of a fillip,[23] yet in all the agonies that I have had, whereof before my coming hither (as I have showed you ere[24] this) I have had neither small nor few, with heavy fearful heart, forecasting[25] all such perils and painful deaths, as by any manner of possibility might after fall unto me, and in such thought lain long restless and waking, while my wife had weened[26] I had slept, yet in any such fear and heavy pensiveness[27] (I thank the mighty mercy of God) I never in my mind intended to consent that I would for the enduring of the uttermost do any such thing as I should in mine own conscience (for with other men's I am not a man meet[28] to take upon me to meddle) think to be to myself, such as should damnably cast me in the displeasure of God. And this is the least point that any man may with his salvation come to, as far as I can see, and is bounden if he see peril to examine his conscience surely by learning and by good counsel and be sure that his conscience be such as it may stand with his salvation, or else reform it. And if the matter be such as both the parties may stand with salvation, then on whither[29] side his conscience fall, he is safe enough before God. But that mine own may stand with my own salvation, thereof I thank our Lord I am very sure. I beseech our Lord bring all parts[30] to his bliss.

It is now, my good daughter, late. And therefore thus I commend you to the holy Trinity, to guide you, comfort you and direct you with his Holy Spirit, and all yours and my wife with all my children and all our other friends.

THOMAS MORE, Knight

23. afraid of a small tap with the finger.   24. before.
25. imagining beforehand.   26. thought.   27. melancholy.
28. fit.   29. whichever.   30. sides in the contention.

To Master Leder

Tower of London
Saturday
16 January 1534/5

.A letter written by Sir Thomas More to one Master Leder,[1] a virtuous priest, the sixteenth day of January in the year of our Lord 1534 after the computation[2] of the Church of England, and in the twenty-sixth year of the reign of King Henry the Eighth.

The tale that is reported, albeit I cannot but thank you though you would it were true, yet I thank God it is a very vanity. I trust in the great goodness of God, that he shall never suffer it to be true. If my mind had been obstinate indeed I would not let[3] for any rebuke or worldly shame plainly to confess the truth. For I purpose not to depend upon the fame of the world. But I thank our Lord that the thing that I do is not for obstinacy but for the salvation of my soul, because I cannot induce mine own mind otherwise to think than I do concerning the oath.

As for other men's consciences, I will be no judge of, nor I never advised any man neither to swear nor to refuse, but as for mine own self if ever I should mishap[4] to receive the oath (which I trust our Lord shall never suffer me), ye may reckon sure that it were expressed and extorted by duresse[5] and hard handling.[6] For as for all the goods of this world, I thank our Lord I set not much more by than I do by dust.[7] And I trust both that they will use no violent forcible ways, and also that if they would, God would of his grace and the rather a great deal through good folks' prayers give me strength to stand. *Fidelis Deus* (saith Saint Paul) *qui non patitur vos*

1. Master Leder seems not otherwise known.   2. reckoning.   3. refrain.
4. have the misfortune.   5. compulsion.
6. More feared that he would be put to the torture.
7. esteem them as worth no more than I do esteem dust.

tentari supra id quod potestis ferre, sed dat cum tentatione prouentum vt possitis sustinere.[8] For this I am very sure, that if ever I should swear it, I should swear deadly against mine own conscience. For I am very sure in my mind that I shall never be able to change mine own conscience to the contrary; as for other men's, I will not meddle of.

It hath been showed me that I am reckoned willful and obstinate because that since my coming hither I have not written unto the King's Highness and by mine own writing made some suit unto his Grace. But in good faith I do not forbear it of an obstinacy, but rather of a lowly mind and a reverent, because that I see nothing that I could write but that I fear me sore[9] that his Grace were likely rather to take displeasure with me for it than otherwise, while his Grace believeth me not that my conscience is the cause but rather obstinate willfulness. But surely that my let[10] is but my conscience, that knoweth God to whose order I commit the whole matter. *In cuius manu corda regum sunt.*[11] I beseech our Lord that all may prove as true faithful subjects to the King that have sworn as I am in my mind very sure that they be, which have refused to swear.

In haste, the Saturday the sixteenth day of January by the hand of your beadsman,[12]

THOMAS MORE, Knight and prisoner

To Margaret Roper

More wrote, "fearing lest she, being (as he thought) with child, should take some harm."

On April 20 John Houghton; Augustine Webster; Robert Lawrence; the priors of the Charterhouses of London, Beauvale and Axholme; and Dr. Richard Reynolds of the Bridgettine monastery of

8. 1 Cor. 10 : 13. ("... but God is faithful, who will not suffer you to be tempted above that ye are able; ..." *KJV*)   9. I am greatly afraid.   10. hindrance.
11. Prov. 21 : 1. ("In whose hand are the hearts of kings.")
12. One who prays for another.

Syon were arrested and were brought to trial on the 28th for denying
that the King was Supreme Head of the English Church. They
urged that the obedience to the Pope was "to the salvation of man
of necessity, and that this superiority of the Pope was a sure truth
and manifest of the law of God, and instituted by Christ as necessary
to the conservation of the spiritual unity of the mystical body of
Christ."

Tower of London

2 or 3 May 1535

A letter written and sent by Sir Thomas More to his daughter Mistress Roper, written the second or third day of May, in the year of
our Lord 1535 and in the twenty-seventh year of the reign of King
Henry the Eighth.

OUR LORD BLESS YOU.

MY DEARLY BELOVED DAUGHTER.

I doubt not but by the reason of the Councilors resorting
hither, in this time (in which our Lord be their comfort) these
fathers of the Charterhouse and Master Reynolds of Syon that be
now judged to death for treason (whose matters and causes I
know not) may hap to put you in trouble and fear of mind concerning me being here prisoner, specially for that it is not unlikely
but that you have heard that I was brought also before the Council here myself. I have thought it necessary to advertise[1] you of the
very truth, to the end that you neither conceive more hope than
the matter giveth, lest upon other turn[2] it might aggrieve your
heaviness, nor more grief and fear than the matter giveth of, on
the other side. Wherefore shortly ye shall understand that on Friday the last day of April in the afternoon, Master Lieutenant[3]

---

1. inform.   2. change.
3. Sir Edmund Walsingham, an old friend, who felt himself "bounden ... to
make him good cheer," but could not "without the King's indignation."

came in here unto me and showed me that Master Secretary[4] would speak with me. Whereupon I shifted my gown and went out with Master Lieutenant into the gallery to him. Where I met many, some known and some unknown, in the way. And in conclusion coming into the chamber where his Mastership sat with Master Attorney,[5] Master Solicitor,[6] Master Bedill,[7] and Master Doctor Tregonwell,[8] I was offered to sit with them, which in no wise I would.

Whereupon Master Secretary showed unto me that he doubted not but that I had by such friends as hither had resorted to me seen the new statutes made at the last sitting of the Parliament. Whereunto I answered: "Yea verily. Howbeit for as much as being here, I have no conversation with any people, I thought it little need for me to bestow much time upon them, and therefore I redelivered the book shortly and the effect of the statutes I never marked nor studied to put in remembrance." Then he asked me whether I had not read the first statute of them, of the King being Head of the Church. Whereunto I answered, "Yes." Then his Mastership declared unto me that sith[9] it was now by act of Parliament ordained that his Highness and his heirs be, and ever right have been, and perpetually should be Supreme Head in yerth[10] of the Church of England under Christ, the King's pleasure was that those of his Council there assembled should demand mine opinion, and what my mind was therein. Whereunto I answered that in good faith I had well trusted that the King's

4. Cromwell.
5. Sir Christopher Hales, Attorney General since 1525.
6. Richard Rich was newly appointed as Solicitor General. He was an able lawyer, but treacherous and cruel. In his *Life of Sir Thomas More* (q.v.) Roper shows how More proved Rich's perjury in evidence against himself.
7. Thomas Bedill (d. 1537), Clerk of the Privy Council, had been engaged in affairs connected with the divorce case. He was now obtaining oaths to the Royal Supremacy.
8. Sir John Tregonwell (d. 1565), now principal judge of the Court of Admiralty, had been proctor for the King in the divorce case.
9. since. 10. on earth.

Highness would never have commanded any such question to be demanded of me, considering that I ever from the beginning well and truly from time to time declared my mind unto his Highness, and since that time I had (I said) unto your Mastership Master Secretary also, both by mouth and by writing. And now I have in good faith discharged my mind of all such matters, and neither will dispute King's titles nor Pope's, but the King's true faithful subject I am and will be, and daily I pray for him and for all his, and for you all that are of his honorable Council, and for all the realm, and otherwise than thus I never intend to meddle.

Whereunto Master Secretary answered that he thought this manner[11] answer should not satisfy nor content the King's Highness, but that his Grace would exact a more full answer. And his Mastership added thereunto that the King's Highness was a prince not of rigor but of mercy and pity, and though that he had found obstinacy at some time in any of his subjects, yet when he should find them at another time confyrmable[12] and submit themself, his Grace would show mercy. And that concerning myself, his Highness would be glad to see me take such confyrmable ways, as I might be abroad in the world again among other men as I have been before.

Whereunto I shortly (after the inward affection[13] of my mind) answered for a very truth that I would never meddle in the world again, to have the world given me. And to the remnant[14] of the matter I answered in effect as before, showing that I had fully determined with myself neither to study nor meddle with any matter of this world, but that my whole study should be upon the passion of Christ and mine own passage out of this world.

Upon this I was commanded to go forth for a while, and after called in again. At which time Master Secretary said unto me that though I was prisoner and condemned to perpetual prison, yet I was not thereby discharged of mine obedience and allegiance unto the King's Highness. And thereupon demanded me whether

11. kind of.   12. comfortable.   13. feeling.   14. remainder.

that I thought that the King's Grace might exact of me such things as are contained in the statutes and upon like pains[15] as he might of other men. Whereto I answered that I would not say the contrary. Whereto he said that likewise as the King's Highness would be gracious to them that he found comfortable, so his Grace would follow the course of his laws toward such as he shall find obstinate. And his Mastership said further that my demeanor[16] in that matter was of a thing that of likelihood made now other men so stiff[17] therein as they be.

Whereto I answered, that I give no man occasion to hold any point one or other, nor never gave any man advice or counsel therein one way or other. And for conclusion I could no further go, whatsoever pain should come thereof. I am, quoth I, the King's true faithful subject and daily bedesman[18] and pray for his Highness and all his and all the realm. I do nobody harm, I say none harm, I think none harm, but wish everybody good. And if this be not enough to keep a man alive in good faith I long not to live. And I am dying already, and have since I came here, been divers times in the case[19] that I thought to die within one hour, and I thank our Lord I was never sorry for it, but rather sorry when I saw the pang[20] past. And therefore my poor body is at the King's pleasure—would God my death might do him good.

After this Master Secretary said, "Well ye find no fault in that statute, find you any in any of the other statutes after?" Whereto I answered, "Sir, whatsoever thing should seem to me other than good, in any of the statutes or in that statute either, I would not declare what fault I found, nor speak thereof." Whereunto finally his mastership said full gently that of anything that I had spoken, there should none advantage be taken, and whether he said further that there be none to be taken, I am not well remembered.[21]

15. punishment.   16. conduct.   17. obstinate.
18. one who prays for another.   19. condition.
20. brief, keen spasm of pain.   21. do not remember.

But he said that report should be made unto the King's Highness, and his gracious pleasure known.

Whereupon I was delivered[22] again to Master Lieutenant, which was then called in, and so was I by Master Lieutenant brought again into my chamber, and here am I yet in such case as I was, neither better nor worse. That that shall follow lieth in the hand of God, whom I beseech to put in the King's Grace's mind that thing that may be to his high pleasure, and in mine, to mind only the weal[23] of my soul, with little regard of my body.

And you with all yours, and my wife and all my children and all our other friends both bodily and ghostly[24] heartily well to fare. And I pray you and all them pray for me, and take no thought whatsoever shall happen me. For I verily trust in the goodness of God, seem it never so evil to this world, it shall indeed in another world be for the best.

Your loving father,

THOMAS MORE, Knight[25]

To Margaret Roper

The Commission of the King's Council were now Archbishop Cranmer; Sir Thomas Audley; Charles Brandon, Duke of Suffolk; Thomas Boleyn, Earl of Wiltshire and Ormonde, the Lord Privy Seal; and Thomas Cromwell, the King's principal Secretary.

*   *   *

22. handed over.   23. good.   24. spiritually.
25. On 4 May, Margaret was allowed to visit her father again, and together they saw the monks start on their martyrs' journey to Tyburn, to be hanged as traitors. The authorities had probably thought Margaret would move her father by her distress at this sight. More said, "Lo, dost thou not see, Meg, that these blessed fathers be now as cheerfully going to their deaths as bridegrooms to their marriage?"

<Tower of London
3 June 1535>

Another letter written and sent by Sir Thomas More to his daughter Mistress Roper, written in the year of our Lord 1535, and in the
twenty-seventh year of the reign of King Henry the Eighth.

OUR LORD BLESS YOU AND ALL YOURS.

Forasmuch, dearly beloved daughter, as it is likely that you
either have heard or shortly shall hear that the Council was here
this day, and that I was before them, I have thought it necessary to
send you word how the matter standeth. And verily to be short I
perceive little difference between this time and the last, for as far
as I can see the whole purpose is either to drive me to say precisely
the one way, or else precisely the other.

Here sat my Lord of Canterbury, my Lord Chancellor, my
Lord of Suffolk, my Lord of Wiltshire, and Master Secretary.
And after my coming, Master Secretary made rehearsal[1] in what
wise he had reported unto the King's Highness, what had been
said by his Grace's Council to me, and what had been answered
by me to them at mine other being before them last. Which thing
his Mastership rehearsed in good faith very well, as I knowl-
edged[2] and confessed and heartily thanked him therefor. Whereupon he added thereunto that the King's Highness was nothing
content nor satisfied with mine answer, but thought that by my
demeanor[3] I had been occasion[4] of much grudge[5] and harm in the
realm, and that I had an obstinate mind and an evil toward him
and that my duty was, being his subject, and so he had sent them
now in his name upon my allegiance to command me, to make a
plain and terminate[6] answer whether I thought the statute lawful
or not and that I should either knowledge and confess it lawful

1. related.   2. acknowledged.   3. conduct.   4. cause.
5. injurious influence.   6. final.

that his Highness should be Supreme Head of the Church of England or else to utter plainly my malignity.[7]

Whereto I answered that I had no maliginity and therefore I could none utter. And as to the matter I could none other answer make than I had before made, which answer his Mastership had there rehearsed. Very heavy[8] I was that the King's Highness should have any such opinion of me. Howbeit if there were one that had informed his Highness many evil things of me that were untrue, to which his Highness for the time gave credence,[9] I would be very sorry that he should have that opinion of me the space of one day. Howbeit if I were sure that other should come on the morrow by whom his Grace should know the truth of mine innocency, I should in the meanwhile comfort myself with consideration of that. And in like wise now though it be great heaviness[10] to me that his Highness have such opinion of me for the while, yet have I no remedy to help it, but only to comfort myself with this consideration that I know very well that the time shall come, when God shall declare my truth toward his Grace before him and all the world. And whereas it might haply[11] seem to be but small cause of comfort because I might take harm here first in the meanwhile, I thanked God that my case was such in this matter through the clearness of mine own conscience that though I might have pain I could not have harm, for a man may in such case leese[12] his head and have no harm. For I was very sure that I had no corrupt[13] affection, but that I had always from the beginning truly used myself to looking first upon God and next upon the King according to the lesson that his Highness taught me at my first coming to his noble service, the most virtuous lesson that ever prince taught his servant; whose Highness to have of me such opinion is my great heaviness, but I have no mean[14] as I said to help it, but only comfort myself in the

7. deep-rooted ill will.   8. weighed down with sorrow.
9. accepted as true.   10. sorrow.   11. perhaps.   12. lose.
13. evil.   14. means, opportunity.

meantime with the hope of that joyful day in which my truth towards him shall well be known. And in this matter further I could not go nor other answer thereto I could not make.

To this it was said by my Lord Chancellor and Master Secretary both that the King might by his laws compel me to make a plain answer thereto, either the one way or the other.

Whereunto I answered I would not dispute[15] the King's authority, what his Highness might do in such case, but I said that verily under correction it seemed to me somewhat hard. For if it so were that my conscience gave me against the statutes (wherein how my mind giveth me I make no declaration), then I nothing doing nor nothing saying against the statute, it were a very hard thing to compel me to say either precisely with it against my conscience to the loss of my soul, or precisely against it to the destruction of my body.

To this Master Secretary said that I had ere this when I was Chancellor examined heretics and thieves and other malefactors and gave me a great praise above my deserving in that behalf. And he said that I then, as he thought and at the leastwise Bishops did use to examine heretics, whether they believed the Pope to be head of the Church and used to compel them to make a precise answer thereto. And why should not then the King, sith[16] it is a law made here that his Grace is Head of the Church, here compel men to answer precisely to the law here as they did then concerning the Pope.

I answered and said that I protested that I intended not to defend any part or stand in contention,[17] but I said there was a difference between those two cases because that at that time as well here as elsewhere through the corps[18] of Christendom the Pope's power was recognized for an undoubted thing which seemeth not like a thing agreed in this realm and the contrary taken for truth in other realms, whereunto Master Secretary answered that they were as well burned for the denying of that as they be beheaded

---

15. contest.   16. since.   17. strife, dispute.   18. body.

for denying of this, and therefore as good reason to compel them to make precise answer to the one as to the other.

Whereto I answered that sith in this case a man is not by a law of one realm so bound in his conscience, where there is a law of the whole corps of Christendom to the contrary in matter touching belief, as he is by a law of the whole corps though there hap to be made in some place a law local[19] to the contrary, the reasonableness or the unreasonableness in binding a man to precise answer standeth not in the respect or difference between heading[20] or burning, but because of the difference in charge of conscience, the difference standeth between heading and hell.

Much was there answered unto this both by Master Secretary and my Lord Chancellor over[21] long to rehearse. And in conclusion they offered me an oath by which I should be sworn to make true answer to such things as should be asked me on the King's behalf, concerning the King's own person.

Whereto I answered that verily I never purposed to swear any book oath[22] more while I lived. Then they said that was very obstinate if I would refuse that, for every man doth it in the Star Chamber[23] and everywhere. I said that was true but I had not so little foresight but that I might well conjecture what should be part of my interrogatory[24] and as good it was to refuse it at the first, as afterward.

Whereto my Lord Chancellor answered that he thought I guessed truth, for I should see them and so they were showed me and they were but twain.[25] The first whether I had seen the statute. The other whether I believed that it were a lawful made interrogatory[26] or not. Whereupon I refused the oath and said

19. local law.   20. beheading.   21. too.
22. oath of special solemnity, on a book (the Bible).
23. judicial sittings of the King's Council, meeting in the Star Chamber at Westminster, usually for criminal jurisdiction.
24. questioning, interrogation.   25. two.
26. question formally put to an accused person; the 1557 *Works* print "statute."

further by mouth that the first I had before confessed, and to the second I would make none answer.

Which was the end of the communication and I was thereupon sent away. In the communication before it was said that it was marveled that I stack[27] so much in my conscience while at the uttermost I was not sure therein. Whereto I said that I was very sure that mine own conscience so informed as it is by such diligence as I have so long taken therein may stand with mine own salvation. I meddle not with the conscience of them that think otherwise, every man *suo domino stat et cadit*.[28] I am no man's judge. It was also said unto me that if I had as lief[29] be out of the world as in it, as I had there said, why did I not speak even out plain against the statute. It appeared well I was not content to die though I said so. Whereto I answered as the truth is, that I have not been a man of such holy living as I might be bold to offer myself to death, lest God for my presumption might suffer me to fall, and therefore I put not myself forward, but draw back. Howbeit if God draw me to it himself, then trust I in his great mercy, that he shall not fail to give me grace and strength.

In conclusion Master Secretary said that he liked me this day much worse than he did the last time, for then he said he pitied me much and now he thought that I meant not well, but God and I know both that I mean well and so I pray God do by me.[30]

I pray you be you and mine other friends of good cheer whatsoever fall of me,[31] and take no thought for me but pray for me as I do and shall do for you and all them.

Your tender loving father,

THOMAS MORE, Kg.

27. persisted.
28. Rom. 14 : 4. ("to his own master he standeth or falleth." *KJV*)
29. if I were as willing to.   30. deal with me.   31. fall to my lot.

To Antonio Bonvisi

Bonvisi had sent More a warm camlet gown (of the hair of the Angora goat) and gifts of wine and meat.

Bonvisi himself suffered later as a loyal Catholic. He fled from England in 1544. His house (and also Clement's) was seized in 1550, and he was specially excepted from the pardon of the Parliament of 1553. He recovered his property under Queen Mary and when he died in 1558 left it to his nephew. He was buried in Louvain.

Tower of London

1535

Sir Thomas More a little before he was arraigned and condemned (in the year of our Lord 1535, and in the twenty-seventh year of the reign of King Henry the Eighth), being shut up so close in prison in the Tower that he had no pen nor ink, wrote with a coal[1] a pistle[2] in Latin to Master Anthony Bonvisi (merchant of Luke[3] and then dwelling in London), his old and dear friend, and sent it unto him, the copy whereof here followeth. [Latin text follows in *1557*.]

The translation into English of the Latin pistle next before.

GOOD MASTER BONVISI OF ALL FRIENDS MOST FRIENDLIEST, AND TO ME WORTHILY DEARLIEST BELOVED, I HEARTILY GREET YOU.

Sith[4] my mind doth give me (and yet may chance falsely but yet so it doth) that I shall not have long liberty to write unto you, I determined therefore while I may to declare unto you by this little epistle of mine how much I am comforted with the sweetness of your friendship, in this decay of my fortune.

For afore[5] (right Worshipful[6] Sir) although I always delighted marvelously in this your love towards me, yet when I consider in

1. charcoal pencil.   2. an epistle.   3. Lucca, in northern Italy.
4. since.   5. before.   6. distinguished.

my mind that I have been now almost this forty years not a guest, but a continual nursling[7] in Master Bonvisi's house, and in the mean season[8] have not showed myself in requiting you again, a friend, but a barren lover only, my shamefastness[9] verily made that that sincere sweetness, which otherwise I received of the revolving[10] of your friendship, somewhat waxed[11] sourish, by reason of a certain rustical[12] shame as neglecting of my duty toward you. But now I comfort myself with this, that I never had the occasion[13] to do you pleasure. For such was always your great wealth that there was nothing left in which I might be unto you beneficial. I therefore (knowing that I have not been unthankful to you by omitting my duty toward you but for lack of occasion and opportunity, and seeing moreover all hope of recompense taken away, you so to persevere in love toward me, binding me more and more to you, yea rather so to run forward still, and as it were with a certain indefatigable course to go forth, that few men so fawn upon their fortunate friends, as you favor, love, foster and honor me, now overthrown, abjected,[14] afflicted, and condemned to prison) cleanse myself both from this bitterness (such as it is) of mine old shamefastness and also repose myself in the sweetness of this marvelous friendship of yours.

And this faithful prosperity of this amity and friendship of yours towards me (I wot[15] not how) seemeth in a manner to counterpoise[16] this unfortunate shipwreck of mine, and saving the indignation of my Prince, of me no less loved than feared, else as concerning all other things, doth almost more than counterpoise. For all those are to be accounted amongst the mischances of fortune. But if I should reckon the possession of so constant friendship (which no storms of adversity hath taken away, but rather hath fortified and strengthed[17]) amongst the brittle[18] gifts of fortune, then

---

7. object of a nurse's care.   8. meanwhile.   9. ashamedness.
10. turning.   11. became.   12. unmannerly.   13. opportunity.
14. cast down.   15. know.   16. balance, compensate for.
17. strengthened.   18. fragile.

were I mad.[19] For the felicity of so faithful and constant friendship in
the storms of fortune (which is seldom seen) is doubtless a high and a
noble gift proceeding of a certain singular[20] benignity of God. And
indeed as concerning myself, I cannnot otherwise take it nor reckon
it, but that it was ordained by the great mercy of God, that you, good
Master Bonvisi, amongst my poor friends, such a man as you are and
so great a friend, should be long afore provided that should by your
consolation assuage[21] and relieve a great part of these troubles and
griefs of mine, which the hugeness[22] of fortune hath hastily brought
upon me. I therefore my dear friend and of all mortal men to me
most dearest do (which now only[23] I am able to do) earnestly pray to
Almighty God, which hath provided you for me, that sith he hath
given you such a debtor as shall never be able to pay you, that it may
please him of his benignity to requite this bountifulness of yours,
which you every day thus plenteously[24] pour upon me. And that for
his mercy sake he will bring us from this wretched[25] and stormy
world into his rest, where shall need no letters, where no wall shall
dissever[26] us, where no porter shall keep us from talking together,
but that we may have the fruition[27] of the eternal joy with God the
Father, and with his only begotten Son our Redeemer Jesu Christ,
with the holy spirit of them both, the Holy Ghost proceeding from
them both. And in the mean season, Almighty God grant both you
and me, good Master Bonvisi, and all mortal men everywhere, to set
at naught all the riches of this world, with all the glory of it, and the
pleasure of this life also, for the love and desire of that joy. Thus of all
friends most trusty, and to me most dearly beloved, and as I was
wont to call you the apple of mine eye, right heartily fare ye well.
And Jesus Christ keep safe and sound and in good health, all your
family, which be of like affection toward me as their master is.

Thomas More: I should in vain put to it, yours, for thereof can

19. unwise.   20. unique.   21. soften.   22. heavy weight.
23. is the only thing that.   24. abundantly.   25. miserable.
26. separate.   27. possession.

you not be ignorant, since you have bought it with so many benefits. Nor now I am not such a one that it forceth[28] whose I am.

To Margaret Roper

Tower of London
5 July 1535

Sir Thomas More was beheaded at the Tower hill in London on
Tuesday the sixth day of July in the year of our Lord 1535, and in
the twenty-seventh year of the reign of King Henry the Eighth.
And on the day next before, being Monday and the fifth day of
July, he wrote with a coal[1] a letter to his daughter Mistress Roper,
and sent it to her (which was the last thing that ever he wrote).
The copy whereof here followeth.

Our Lord bless you good daughter and your good husband and
your little boy and all yours and all my children and all my godchil-
dren and all our friends. Recommend[2] me when you may to my
good daughter Cecilye, whom I beseech our Lord to comfort, and I
send her my blessing and to all her children and pray her to pray
for me. I send her an handekercher[3] and God comfort my good son
her husband. My good daughter Daunce hath the picture in parch-
ment that you delivered me from my Lady Coniers; her name is on
the back side. Show her that I heartily pray her that you may send it
in my name again for a token from me to pray for me.

I like special[4] well Dorothy Coly,[5] I pray you be good unto her. I

28. matters.   1. charcoal   pencil.   2. commend.   3. handkerchief.
4. specially.
5. Margaret Roper's maid. Margaret sent her to the Tower every day during
More's imprisonment, often with gifts. She married John Harris, More's secretary.
Together they preserved many of More's letters and took them to the Low Coun-
tries in their exile.

would wit[6] whether this be she that you wrote me of. If not I pray you be good to the other as you may in her affliction and to my good daughter Joan Aleyn[7] to give her I pray you some kind answer, for she sued[8] hither to me this day to pray you be good to her.

I cumber[9] you good Margaret much, but I would be sorry, if it should be any longer than tomorrow, for it is Saint Thomas even, and the utas of Saint Peter[10] and therefore tomorrow long I to go to God, it were a day very meet[11] and convenient for me. I never liked your manner toward me better than when[12] you kissed me last for I love when daughterly love and dear charity hath no leisure to look to worldly courtesy.

Fare well my dear child and pray for me, and I shall for you and all your friends that we may merrily meet in heaven. I thank you for your great cost.[13]

I send now unto my good daughter Clement[14] her algorism stone[15] and I send her and my good son and all hers God's blessing and mine.

I pray you at time convenient recommend me to my good son John More. I liked well his natural fashion.[16] Our Lord bless him and his good wife my loving daughter,[17] to whom I pray him be good, as he hath great cause, and that if the land of mine come to his hand, he break not my will concerning his sister Daunce. And our Lord bless Thomas and Austen[18] and all that they shall have.

6. know.
7. Another of Margaret Roper's maids. She had been educated in More's "School" and so is called "daughter."
8. appealed.   9. trouble.
10. The eve of the translation of the relics of St. Thomas of Canterbury (Becket), kept in England on 7 July. Octave of the feast of St. Peter, 29 June.
11. fitting.
12. When she embraced her father on Tower Wharf, on his return from Westminster Hall after conviction and sentence.
13. expenditure of labor.   14. Margaret Gyge, now wife of John Clement.
15. Probably a slate.
16. John More had knelt on Tower Wharf and asked his father's blessing.
17. Anne Cresacre, once More's ward.
18. The children of John More and Anne Cresacre.

THE LIFE OF
SIR THOMAS MORE

by William Roper

Forasmuch as Sir Thomas More, Knight, sometime Lord Chancellor of England, a man of singular virtue and of a clear, unspotted conscience, as witnesseth Erasmus, more pure and white than the whitest snow, and of such an angelical wit as England (he saith) never had the like before, nor never shall again, universally, as well in the laws of our own realm, a study in effect able to occupy the whole life of a man, as in all other sciences[1] right well studied, was in his days accompted[2] a man worthy perpetual famous memory:

I, William Roper, though most unworthy, his son-in-law by marriage of his eldest daughter,[3] knowing—at this day—no one man living that of him and of his doings understood so much as myself, for that I was continually resident in his house by the space of sixteen years and more,[4] thought it therefore my part to set forth such matters touching his life as I could at this present call to remembrance.

Among which things, very many notable things (not meet[5] to have been forgotten) through negligence and long continuance of time are slipped out of my mind. Yet to the intent the same should not all utterly perish, I have at the desire of divers worshipful friends of mine, though very far from the grace and worthiness of

1. branches of knowledge.   2. accounted.
3. Margaret, More's favorite daughter, married Roper on July 2, 1521.
4. Since More was executed in July 1535, Roper must therefore have entered his service in the year 1518. He was then about twenty years old.   5. fit, proper.

them, nevertheless as far forth as my mean wit, memory, and knowledge would serve me, declared so much thereof as in my poor judgment seemed worthy to be remembered.

This Sir Thomas More, after he had been brought up in the Latin tongue at Saint Anthony's[6] in London, was by his father's[7] procurement received into the house of the right reverend, wise, and learned prelate, Cardinal Morton.[8] Where, though he was young of years, yet would he at Christmas-tide suddenly sometimes step in among the players, and never studying for the matter, make a part of his own there presently among them, which made the lookers-on more sport than all the players beside. In whose wit and towardness the Cardinal much delighting would often say of him unto the nobles that divers times dined with him, "This child here waiting at the table, whosoever shall live to see it, will prove a marvellous man."

Whereupon for his better furtherance in learning, he placed him at Oxford, where when he was both in the Greek and Latin tongue sufficiently instructed, he was then for the study of the law of the realm put to an Inn of Chancery called New Inn, where for his time he very well prospered, and from thence was admitted to Lincoln's Inn, with very small allowance, continuing there his study until he was made and accompted a worthy utter[9] barrister. After this, to his great commendation, he read for a good space a public lecture of Saint Augustine, *De Civitate Dei,* in the Church of Saint Lawrence in the old Jewry, whereunto there resorted Doctor Grocyn,[10] an excellent cunning man, and all the chief learned of the City of London. Then was he made Reader of Furnival's Inn,[11] so remaining by the space of three years and more.

---

6. A free school associated with the Hospital of St. Anthony.
7. Judge John More (1451?–1530).
8. Lord Chancellor of England (1487–1500). More entered the Cardinal's household in 1490.   9. fully qualified.
10. Vicar of St. Lawrence, and one of the most learned men of his time.
11. An Inn of Chancery attached to Lincoln's Inn. *Reader:* i.e. a lecturer on law.

After which time he gave himself to devotion and prayer in the Charterhouse of London,[12] religiously living there without vow[13] about four years, until he resorted to the house of one Master Colt, a gentleman of Essex, that had oft invited him thither, having three daughters, whose honest conversation[14] and virtuous education provoked him there specially to set his affection. And albeit his mind most served him to the second daughter, for that he thought her the fairest and best favored, yet when he considered that it would be both great grief and some shame also to the eldest to see her younger sister in marriage preferred before her, he then of a certain pity framed his fancy towards her, and soon after married her[15]—neverthemore discontinuing his study of the law at Lincoln's Inn, but applying still the same, until he was called to the bench, and had read[16] there twice, which is as often as ordinarily any judge of the law doth read.

Before which time he had placed himself and his wife at Bucklersbury in London, where he had by her three daughters and one son, in virtue and learning brought up from their youth, whom he would often exhort to take virtue and learning for their meat, and play for their sauce.

Who, ere ever he had been reader in Court,[17] was in the latter time of King Henry the Seventh made a burgess of the Parliament, wherein there were by the King demanded (as I have heard reported) about three-fifteenths[18] for the marriage of his eldest daughter, that then should be the Scottish queen; at the last debating whereof he made such arguments and reasons there against,

---

12. A Carthusian monastery.
13. *Religiously . . . vow:* i.e., he never took orders but did participate regularly in the religious life of the community.   14. behavior.
15. More's marriage to Jane Colt took place in, or shortly before, January 1505. She died in 1511. More remarried almost immediately, this time a widow, Alice Middleton, the "Dame Alice" of the biography.
16. given a series of lectures.   17. Inn of Court.
18. A personal property tax amounting to three-fifteenths of the value of the property.

that the King's demands thereby were clean overthrown. So that one of the King's privy chamber, named Master Tyler, being present thereat, brought word to the King out of the Parliament House that a beardless boy had disappointed all his purpose. Whereupon the King, conceiving great indignation towards him, could not be satisfied until he had some way revenged it. And forasmuch as he, nothing having, nothing could lose, his grace devised a causeless quarrel against his father, keeping him in the Tower until he had made him pay to him an hundred pounds fine.

Shortly hereupon it fortuned[19] that this Sir Thomas More, coming in a suit to Doctor Foxe, Bishop of Winchester, one of the King's privy council, the Bishop called him aside and pretending great favor towards him, promised him that if he would be ruled by him he would not fail into the King's favor again to restore him, meaning, as it was after conjectured, to cause him thereby to confess his offense against the King, whereby his highness might with the better color[20] have occasion to revenge his displeasure against him.

But when he came from the Bishop, he fell in communication with one Master Whitford, his familiar friend, then chaplain to that Bishop, and after a Father of Sion,[21] and showed him what the Bishop had said unto him, desiring to have his advice therein, who for the Passion of God prayed him in no wise to follow his counsel. "For my lord, my master," quoth he, "to serve the King's turn, will not stick to agree to his own father's death." So Sir Thomas More returned to the Bishop no more. And had not the King soon after died,[22] he was determined to have gone over the sea, thinking that, being in the King's indignation, he could not live in England without great danger.

19. chanced.   20. appearance of right.
21. Bridgettine monastery of Sion in Middlesex.
22. Henry VII died in April 1509.

After this he was made one of the undersheriffs²³ of London, by which office and his learning together (as I have heard him say), he gained without grief not so little as four hundred pounds by the year, sith there was at that time in none of the prince's courts of the laws of this realm any matter of importance in controversy wherein he was not with the one part of counsel. Of whom, for his learning, wisdom, knowledge, and experience, men had such estimation that, before he came to the service of King Henry the Eighth, at the suit and instance of the English merchants, he was by the King's consent made twice ambassador in certain great causes between them and the merchants of the Steel-yard.²⁴ Whose wise and discreet dealing therein, to his high commendation, coming to the King's understanding, provoked his highness to cause Cardinal Wolsey, then Lord Chancellor, to procure him to his service.

And albeit the Cardinal, according to the King's request, earnestly travailed²⁵ with him therefore—among many other his persuasions alleging unto him how dear his service must needs be unto his majesty, which could not, with his honor, with less than he should yearly lose thereby seem to recompense him—yet he, loath to change his estate, made such means to the King by the Cardinal to the contrary²⁶ that his grace for that time was well satisfied.

Now happened there after this a great ship of his that then was Pope to arrive at Southampton, which the King claiming for a forfeiture, the Pope's ambassador, by suit unto his grace, obtained that he might for his master the Pope have counsel learned in the laws of this realm, and the matter in his own presence (being him-

---

23. Important executive officials responsible to the High Sheriff. Their duties included the supervision of prisoners, the execution of writs, and the imposition of death sentences.   24. Hanseatic League colony in London.   25. labored.
26. *by the . . . contrary:* i.e., the Cardinal conveyed to the King More's reluctance to enter the royal service.

self a singular civilian)[27] in some public place to be openly heard and discussed.

At which time there could none of our law be found so meet to be of counsel with this ambassador as Sir Thomas More, who could report to the ambassador in Latin all the reasons and arguments by the learned counsel on both sides alleged. Upon this, the counsellors of either part,[28] in presence of the Lord Chancellor and the other judges, in the Star Chamber[29] had audience accordingly. Where Sir Thomas More not only declared to the ambassador the whole effect of all their opinions, but also in defense of the Pope's side argued so learnedly himself that both was the foresaid forfeiture to the Pope restored, and himself among all the hearers, for his upright and commendable demeanor therein so greatly renowned, that for no entreaty would the King from thenceforth be induced any longer to forbear[30] his service. At whose first entry thereunto, he made him Master of the Requests,[31] having then no better room[32] void, and within a month after, knight and one of his privy council.

And so from time to time was he by the prince advanced, continuing in his singular favor and trusty service twenty years and above—a good part whereof used the King upon holidays, when he had done his own devotions, to send for him into his traverse,[33] and there sometime in matters of astronomy, geometry, divinity, and such other faculties, and sometimes of his worldly affairs, to sit and confer with him. And other whiles would he in the night have him up into his leads,[34] there for to consider with him

27. one especially well-versed in civil law, in this case the Pope's ambassador.
28. both parties.
29. A famous court with jurisdiction chiefly, though not exclusively, over criminal cases. It was presided over by the King's Council. Abolished in 1641.
30. dispense with.
31. i.e., Judge in the Court of Requests, sometimes called the "Poor Man's Court." The appointment was made in late 1517.   32. office.
33. a screened-off apartment.   34. lead roof.

the diversities, courses, motions, and operations of the stars and planets.

And because he was of a pleasant disposition, it pleased the King and Queen after the council had supped, at the time of their supper, for their pleasure commonly to call for him to be merry with them. Whom when he perceived so much in his talk to delight that he could not once in a month get leave to go home to his wife and children, whose company he most desired, and to be absent from the court two days together but that he should be thither sent for again—he, much misliking this restraint of his liberty, began thereupon somewhat to dissemble his nature, and so by little and little from his former accustomed mirth to disuse[35] himself, that he was of them from thenceforth at such seasons no more so ordinarily sent for.

Then died one Master Weston, Treasurer of the Exchequer, whose office after his death the King, of his own offer, without any asking, freely gave unto Sir Thomas More.[36]

In the fourteenth year of his grace's reign was there a Parliament holden,[37] whereof Sir Thomas More was chosen Speaker. Who, being very loath to take that room upon him, made an oration (not now extant) to the King's highness for his discharge[38] thereof. Whereunto when the King would not consent, he spake unto his grace in the form following:

Sith I perceive, most redoubted Sovereign, that it standeth not with your high pleasure to reform[39] this election and cause it to be changed, but have by the mouth of the most reverend father in God, the legate, your highness's Chancel-

35. disengage.
36. A mistake on Roper's part. In May 1521 More was made Under-Treasurer, not Treasurer, of the Exchequer. Furthermore, his predecessor was not Weston but Sir John Cutte.   37. In April 1523.
38. relief from that obligation (to be Speaker).   39. revoke.

lor, thereunto given your most royal assent, and have of your benignity determined—far above that I may bear—to enable me, and for this office to repute me meet,[40] rather than you should seem to impute unto your Commons that they had unmeetly chosen, I am therefore, and always shall be, ready obediently to conform myself to the accomplishment of your high commandment—in my most humble wise beseeching your most noble majesty that I may with your grace's favor, before I farther enter thereunto, make mine humble intercession unto your highness for two lowly petitions: the one privately concerning myself, the other the whole assembly of your Common House.

For myself, gracious Sovereign, that if it mishap me[41] in anything hereafter that is on the behalf of your Commons in your high presence to be declared, to mistake my message, and in the lack of good utterance, by my misrehearsal[42] to pervert or impair their prudent instructions, it may then like your most noble majesty, of your abundant grace, with the eye of your accustomed pity, to pardon my simpleness—giving me leave to repair again to the Common House and there to confer with them, and to take their substantial advice what thing and in what wise I shall on their behalf utter and speak before your noble grace, to the intent their prudent devices and affairs be not by my simpleness and folly hindered or impaired. Which thing, if it should so mishap, as it were well likely to mishap in me, if your gracious benignity relieved not my oversight, it could not fail to be during my life a perpetual grudge[43] and heaviness to my heart. The help and remedy whereof, in manner aforesaid remembered, is, most gracious Sovereign, my first lowly suit and humble petition unto your most noble grace.

40. *repute me meet:* declare me qualified.　　41. *if . . . me:* if it is my bad luck.
42. misrepresentation.　　43. uneasiness.

Mine other humble request, most excellent prince, is this: forasmuch as there be of your Commons, here by your high commandment assembled for your Parliament, a great number which are after the accustomed manner appointed in the Common House to treat and advise of the common affairs among themselves apart; and albeit, most dear liege-lord, that according to your prudent advice, by your honorable writs everywhere declared, there hath been as due diligence used in sending up to your highness's Court of Parliament the most discreet persons out of every quarter that men could esteem meet thereunto—whereby it is not to be doubted but that there is a very substantial assembly of right wise and politick persons; yet, most victorious prince, sith among so many wise men neither is every man wise alike, nor among so many men, like well-witted, every man like well-spoken. And it often happeneth that, likewise, as much folly is uttered with painted, polished speech; so many boisterous and rude in language see deep indeed, and give right substantial counsel.

And sith also in matters of great importance, the mind is often so occupied in the matter that a man rather studieth what to say than how, by reason whereof the wisest man and the best spoken in a whole country fortuneth among,[44] while his mind is fervent in the matter, somewhat to speak in such wise as he would afterward wish to have been uttered otherwise, and yet no worse will had when he spake it than he hath when he would so gladly change it; therefore, most gracious Sovereign, considering that in your high Court of Parliament is nothing entreated[45] but matter of weight and importance concerning your realm and your own royal estate, it could not fail to let[46] and put to silence from the giving of their advice and counsel many of your discreet Com-

44. now and then.   45. treated.   46. hinder.

mons, to the great hindrance of the common affairs, except that every of your Commons were utterly discharged[47] of all doubt and fear how anything that it should happen them to speak should happen of your highness to be taken.[48] And in this point, though your well known and proved benignity putteth every man in right good hope, yet such is the weight of the matter, such is the reverend[49] dread[50] that the timorous hearts of your natural subjects conceive toward your high majesty, our most redoubted King and undoubted Sovereign, that they cannot in this point find themselves satisfied, except your gracious bounty therein declared put away the scruple of their timorous minds, and animate and encourage them, and put them out of doubt.

It may therefore like your most abundant grace, our most benign and godly King, to give all your Commons here assembled your most gracious license and pardon, freely, without doubt of your dreadful displeasure, every man to discharge his conscience, and boldly in every thing incident among us to declare his advice. And whatsoever happen any man to say that it may like your noble majesty, of your inestimable goodness, to take all in good part, interpreting every man's words, how uncunningly[51] soever they be couched, to proceed yet of good zeal towards the profit of your realm and honor of your royal person, the prosperous estate and preservation whereof, most excellent Sovereign, is the thing which we all, your most humble loving subjects, according to the most bounden duty of our natural allegiance, most highly desire and pray for.

At this Parliament Cardinal Wolsey found himself much grieved with the burgesses thereof, for that nothing was so soon

47. relieved.	48. interpreted.	49. reverenced.	50. fear.
51. unskillfully.

THE LIFE OF SIR THOMAS MORE [189

done or spoken therein but that it was immediately blown abroad in every alehouse. It fortuned at that Parliament a very great subsidy[52] to be demanded, which the Cardinal fearing would not pass the Common House, determined for the furtherance thereof to be personally present there. Before whose coming, after long debating there, whether it were better but with a few of his lords (as the most opinion of the house was) or with his whole train royally to receive him there amongst them—"Masters," quoth Sir Thomas More, "forasmuch as my Lord Cardinal lately, ye wot well, laid to our charge the lightness[53] of our tongues for things uttered out of this house, it shall not in my mind be amiss with all his pomp to receive him, with his maces, his pillars, his pole-axes, his crosses, his hat, and Great Seal, too—to the intent, if he find the like fault with us hereafter, we may be the bolder from ourselves to lay the blame on those that his grace bringeth hither with him." Whereunto the house wholly agreeing, he was received accordingly.

Where, after that he had in a solemn oration by many reasons proved how necessary it was the demand there moved to be granted, and further showed that less would not serve to maintain the prince's purpose, he—seeing the company sitting still silent, and thereunto nothing answering and contrary to his expectation showing in themselves towards his requests no towardness of inclination,[54] said unto them:

"Masters, you have many wise and learned men among you, and since I am from the King's own person sent hither unto you for the preservation of yourselves and all the realm, I think it meet you give me some reasonable answer."

Whereat every man holding his peace, then began he to speak to one Master Marney, after Lord Marney: "How say you," quoth

52. money granted by Parliament to the Crown to meet specific needs.
53. looseness.
54. *towardness of inclination:* readiness to accede (to Wolsey's requests).

he, "Master Marney?" Who making him no answer neither, he severally asked the same question of divers others accompted the wisest of the company.

To whom, when none of them all would give so much as one word, being before agreed, as the custom was, by their speaker to make answer—"Masters," quoth the Cardinal, "unless it be the manner of your house, as of likelihood it is, by the mouth of your speaker, whom you have chosen for trusty and wise, as indeed he is, in such cases to utter your minds, here is without doubt a marvellous obstinate silence."

And thereupon he required answer of Master Speaker. Who first reverently upon his knees excusing the silence of the house, abashed at the presence of so noble a personage, able to amaze[55] the wisest and best learned in a realm, and after by many probable arguments proving that for them to make answer was it neither expedient nor agreeable with the ancient liberty of the house, in conclusion for himself showed that though they had all with their voices trusted him, yet except every one of them could put into his one head all their several wits,[56] he alone in so weighty a matter was unmeet[57] to make his grace answer.

Whereupon the Cardinal, displeased with Sir Thomas More, that had not in this Parliament in all things satisfied his desire, suddenly arose and departed.

And after the Parliament ended, in his gallery at Whitehall in Westminster, uttered unto him his griefs, saying: "Would to God you had been at Rome, Master More, when I made you Speaker!"

"Your grace not offended, so would I too, my lord," quoth he. And to wind such quarrels out of the Cardinal's head, he began to talk of that gallery and said: "I like this gallery of yours, my lord, much better than your gallery at Hampton Court." Wherewith so wisely brake he off the Cardinal's displeasant talk that the Cardinal at that present (as it seemed) wist[58] not what more to say to

55. confound.   56. minds.   57. unqualified.   58. knew.

him. But for revengement of his displeasure counselled the King
to send him ambassador into Spain, commending to his highness
his wisdom, learning, and meetness for that voyage; and, the difficulty of the cause considered, none was there, he said, so well
able to serve his grace therein.

Which, when the King had broken to Sir Thomas More, and
that he had declared unto his grace how unfit a journey it was for
him, the nature of the country and disposition of his complexion[59]
so disagreeing together, that he should never be likely to do his
grace acceptable service there, knowing right well that if his grace
sent him thither, he should send him to his grave. But showing
himself nevertheless ready, according to his duty (all were it with
the loss of his life), to fulfill his grace's pleasure in that behalf.

The King, allowing well[60] his answer, said unto him: "It is not
our meaning, Master More, to do you hurt, but to do you good
would we be glad. We will therefore for this purpose devise upon
some other, and employ your service otherwise." And such entire
favor did the King bear him that he made him Chancellor of the
Duchy of Lancaster upon the death of Sir Richard Wingfield,[61]
who had that office before.

And for the pleasure he took in his company would his grace
suddenly sometimes come home to his house at Chelsea to be
merry with him. Whither on a time, unlooked for, he came to
dinner to him; and after dinner, in a fair garden of his, walked
with him by the space of an hour, holding his arm about his neck.

As soon as his grace was gone, I, rejoicing thereat, told Sir
Thomas More how happy he was, whom the King had so familiarly entertained, as I never had seen him to do to any other
except Cardinal Wolsey, whom I saw his grace once walk with,

59. More apparently felt that the Spanish climate might fatally affect his constitution ("complexion").   60. *allowing well:* accepting as satisfactory.
61. Interestingly enough, shortly after he arrived in Spain, Sir Richard (who
replaced More on the mission) was taken ill in Toledo and died there in July 1525.
More succeeded him as Chancellor of the Duchy in the same year.

arm in arm. "I thank our Lord, son," quoth he, "I find his grace my very good lord indeed; and I believe he doth as singularly favor me as any subject within this realm. Howbeit, son Roper, I may tell thee I have no cause to be proud thereof, for if my head could win him a castle in France (for then was there war between us) it should not fail to go."

This Sir Thomas More, among all other his virtues, was of such meekness that, if it had fortuned him with any learned men resorting to him from Oxford, Cambridge, or elsewhere, as there did divers,[62] some for desire of his acquaintance, some for the famous report of his wisdom and learning, and some for suits of[63] the universities, to have entered into argument (wherein few were comparable unto him) and so far to have discoursed with them therein that he might perceive they could not, without some inconvenience, hold out much further disputation with him, then lest he should discomfort them—as he that sought not his own glory but rather would seem conquered than to discourage students in their studies, ever showing himself more desirous to learn than to teach—would he by some witty device courteously break off into some other matter and give over.

Of whom for his wisdom and learning had the King such an opinion that at such time as he attended upon his highness, taking his progress[64] either to Oxford or Cambridge, where he was received with very eloquent orations, his grace would always assign him, as one that was prompt and ready therein, *ex tempore* to make answer thereunto. Whose manner was, whensoever he had occasion either here or beyond the sea to be in any university, not only to be present at the readings and disputations there commonly used, but also learnedly to dispute among them himself. Who being Chancellor of the Duchy was made ambassador

62. on sundry occasions.   63. *suits of:* petitions from.
64. formal state journey.

twice, joined in commission with Cardinal Wolsey—once to the Emperor Charles into Flanders, the other time to the French King into France.

Not long after this, the Water-bailly of London,[65] sometime his servant, hearing (where he had been at dinner) certain merchants liberally[66] to rail against his old master, waxed so discontented therewith that he hastily came to him and told him what he had heard. "And were I, sir," quoth he, "in such favor and authority with my prince as you are, such men surely should not be suffered so villainously and falsely to misreport and slander me. Wherefore I would wish you to call them before you, and to their shame for their lewd[67] malice to punish them."

Who, smiling upon him, said: "Why, Master Water-bailly, would you have me punish those by whom I receive more benefit than by you all that be my friends? Let them, a God's name, speak as lewdly as they list of me and shoot never so many arrows at me. As long as they do not hit me, what am I the worse? But if they should once hit me, then would it indeed not a little trouble me. Howbeit I trust, by God's help, there shall none of them all once be able to touch me. I have more cause, I assure thee, Master Water-bailly, to pity them than to be angry with them." Such fruitful communication had he oft-times with his familiar friends.

So on a time, walking with me along the Thames-side at Chelsea,[68] in talking of other things he said unto me: "Now would to our Lord, son Roper, upon condition that three things were well established in Christendom, I were put in a sack and here presently cast into the Thames."

65. An important official, one of four attendants upon the Lord Mayor of London.   66. unrestrainedly.   67. villainous.
68. The site of More's beloved country estate. In his day Chelsea was about ten miles up the Thames River from the City of London. All contemporary authors who allude in any detail to the estate rhapsodize over its idyllic setting and character.

"What great things be those, sir," quoth I, "that should move you so to wish?"

"Wouldst thou know what they be, son Roper?" quoth he.

"Yea, marry, with good will, sir, if it please you," quoth I.

"In faith, son, they be these," said he. "The first is that where the most part of Christian princes be at mortal war, they were all at an universal peace. The second, that where the Church of Christ is at this present sore afflicted with many errors and heresies, it were settled in a perfect uniformity of religion. The third, that where the King's matter of his marriage is now come in question, it were to the glory of God and quietness of all parts brought to a good conclusion." Whereby, as I could gather, he judged that otherwise it would be a disturbance to a great part of Christendom.

Thus did it by his doings throughout the whole course of his life appear that all his travail and pains, without respect of earthly commodities[69] either to himself or any of his, were only upon the service of God, the prince, and the realm, wholly bestowed and employed. Whom I heard in his later time to say that he never asked the King for himself the value of one penny.

As Sir Thomas More's custom was daily, if he were at home, besides his private prayers, with his children to say the Seven Psalms, Litany and Suffrages following, so was his guise[70] nightly before he went to bed, with his wife, children, and household, to go to his chapel and there upon his knees ordinarily to say certain psalms and collects[71] with them. And because he was desirous for godly purposes sometime to be solitary, and sequester himself from worldly company, a good distance from his mansion house builded he a place called the New Building, wherein there was a chapel, a library, and a gallery. In which, as his use was upon other days to occupy himself in prayer and study together, so

69. benefits or profits.   70. custom.   71. short prayers.

on the Friday there usually continued he from morning to evening, spending his time only in devout prayers and spiritual exercises.

And to provoke[72] his wife and children to the desire of heavenly things, he would sometimes use these words unto them:

"It is now no mastery[73] for you children to go to heaven, for everybody giveth you good counsel, everybody giveth you good example—you see virtue rewarded and vice punished. So that you are carried up to heaven even by the chins. But if you live the time that no man will give you good counsel, nor no man will give you good example, when you shall see virtue punished and vice rewarded, if you will then stand fast and firmly stick to God, upon pain of my life, though you be but half good, God will allow you for whole good."

If his wife or any of his children had been diseased or troubled, he would say unto them: "We may not look at our pleasure to go to heaven in featherbeds. It is not the way, for our Lord himself went thither with great pain and by many tribulations, which was the path wherein he walked thither. For the servant may not look to be in better case than his master."

And as he would in this sort persuade them to take their troubles patiently, so would he in like sort teach them to withstand the devil and his temptations valiantly, saying:

"Whosoever will mark the devil and his temptations shall find him therein much like to an ape. For, like as an ape, not well looked unto, will be busy and bold to do shrewd turns[74] and contrariwise, being spied, will suddenly leap backward and adventure no farther, so the devil finding a man idle, slothful, and without resistance ready to receive his temptations, waxeth so hardy that he will not fail still to continue with him until to his purpose he have thoroughly brought him. But, on the other side,

72. stimulate.   73. achievement.   74. *shrewd turns:* harmful tricks.

if he see a man with diligence[75] persevere to prevent and withstand his temptations, he waxeth so weary that in conclusion he
utterly forsaketh him. For as the devil of disposition is a spirit of
so high a pride that he cannot abide to be mocked, so is he of
nature so envious that he feareth any more to assault him, lest he
should thereby not only catch a foul[76] fall himself but also minister to the man more matter of merit."

Thus delighted he evermore not only in virtuous exercises to
be occupied himself, but also to exhort his wife, children, and
household to embrace and follow the same.

To whom for his notable virtue and godliness, God showed, as it
seemed, a manifest miraculous token of his special favor towards
him, at such time as my wife, as many other that year were, was
sick of the sweating sickness.[77] Who, lying in so great extremity of
that disease as by no invention or devices that physicians in such
cases commonly use (of whom she had divers both expert,[78] wise,
and well-learned, then continually about her) she could be kept
from sleep. So that both physicians and all other there despaired of
her recovery and gave her over.

Her father, as he that most entirely tendered[79] her, being in no
small heaviness for her, by prayer at God's hand sought to get her
remedy. Whereupon going up, after his usual manner, into his
foresaid New Building, there in his chapel, upon his knees, with
tears most devoutly besought almighty God that it would like
His goodness, unto whom nothing was impossible, if it were His
blessed will, at his mediation to vouchsafe graciously to hear his
humble petition. Where incontinent[80] came into his mind that a
clyster[81] should be the only way to help her. Which, when he told

75. *a man with diligence:* i.e., the diligent, wary man.   76. ignominious.
77. A terrible epidemic disease, which swept England periodically during the fif-
teenth and sixteenth centuries and later; characterized by heavy sweating and a
general debility. The incidence of death was extremely high.
78. experienced.   79. loved.   80. all of a sudden.   81. enema.

the physicians, they by and by[82] confessed that, if there were any hope of health, that was the very best help indeed, much marvelling of themselves that they had not before remembered it.

Then was it immediately ministered unto her sleeping, which she could by no means have been brought unto waking. And albeit after that she was thereby thoroughly awaked, God's marks,[83] an evident undoubted token of death plainly appeared upon her, yet she, contrary to all their expectations, was as it was thought by her father's fervent prayer miraculously recovered, and at length again to perfect health restored. Whom, if it had pleased God at that time to have taken to His mercy, her father said he would never have meddled with worldly matters after.

Now while Sir Thomas More was Chancellor of the Duchy, the See of Rome chanced to be void, which was cause of much trouble. For Cardinal Wolsey, a man very ambitious and desirous (as good hope and likelihood he had) to aspire unto that dignity, perceiving himself of his expectation disappointed, by means of the Emperor Charles[84] so highly commending one Cardinal Adrian,[85] sometime his schoolmaster, to the cardinals of Rome, in the time of their election, for his virtue and worthiness, that thereupon was he chosen Pope. Who from Spain where he was then resident, coming on foot to Rome, before his entry into the city, did put off his hosen and shoes, barefoot and barelegged passing through the streets towards his palace with such humbleness that all the people had him in great reverence—Cardinal Wolsey, I say, waxed so wood[86] therewith that he studied to invent all ways of revengement of his grief against the Emperor; which, as it was the beginning of a lamentable tragedy, so some

---

82. *by and by:* immediately.　　　83. visible marks of the plague.
84. Charles V, 1500–1558. He became Emperor of the Holy Roman Empire in June 1519.　　　85. Adrian VI, 1459–1523. He was elected Pope in January 1522.
86. *waxed so wood:* became so angry.

part of it as not impertinent to my present purpose I reckoned requisite here to put in remembrance.

This Cardinal, therefore, not ignorant of the King's inconstant and mutable disposition, soon inclined to withdraw his devotion from his own most noble, virtuous, and lawful wife, Queen Catherine—aunt to the Emperor—upon every light[87] occasion. And upon other,[88] to her in nobility, wisdom, virtue, favor, and beauty far incomparable, to fix his affection, meaning to make this his so light[89] disposition an instrument to bring about his ungodly intent, devised to allure the King, then already (contrary to his mind, nothing less looking for) falling in love with the Lady Anne Boleyn, to cast fantasy[90] to one of the French King's sisters. Which thing, because of the enmity and war that was at that time between the French King and the Emperor—whom for the cause afore remembered he mortally maligned—he was very desirous to procure. And for the better achieving thereof, requested Longland,[91] Bishop of Lincoln, and ghostly father to the King, to put a scruple into his grace's head, that it was not lawful for him to marry his brother's wife.

Which the King, not sorry to hear of, opened it first to Sir Thomas More, whose counsel he required therein, showing him certain places of scripture that somewhat seemed to serve his appetite.[92] Which when he had perused and thereupon, as one that had never professed the study of divinity, himself excused to be unmeet many ways to meddle with such matters, the King, not satisfied with this answer, so sore still pressed upon him therefore, that in conclusion he condescended[93] to his grace's motion.[94] And further, forasmuch as the case was of such importance as needed great advisement and deliberation, he besought his grace of suffi-

87. trivial.　　88. another.　　89. wanton.　　90. *cast fantasy:* take a fancy.
91. John Longland, Bishop of Lincoln from 1520 to 1547, confessor to the King, and a close friend of Cardinal Wolsey.　　92. willful purpose.
93. assented.　　94. proposal.

cient respite advisedly to consider of it. Wherewith the King, well-contented, said unto him that Tunstal and Clerk,[95] Bishops of Durham and Bath, with other learned of his privy council, should also be dealers therein.

So Sir Thomas More departing conferred[96] those places of scripture with expositions of divers of the old holy doctors. And at his coming to the court, in talking with his grace of the afore-said matter, he said: "To be plain with your grace, neither my Lord of Durham nor my Lord of Bath, though I know them both to be wise, virtuous, learned, and honorable prelates, nor myself, with the rest of your council, being all your grace's own servants, for your manifold benefits daily bestowed on us so most bounden to you, be in my judgment meet counsellors for your grace herein. But if your grace mind to understand the truth, such counsellors may you have devised, as neither for respect of their own worldly commodity[97] nor for fear of your princely authority, will be inclined to deceive you." To whom he named then Saint Jerome, Saint Augustine, and divers other old holy doctors, both Greeks and Latins, and, moreover, showed him what authorities he had gathered out of them. Which, although the King (as disagreeable with his desire) did not very well like of, yet were they by Sir Thomas More who, in all his communication with the King in that matter, had always most discreetly behaved himself, so wisely tempered, that he both presently took them in good part and oft-times had thereof conference with him again.

After this were there certain questions among his council pro-poned,[98] whether the King needed in this case to have any scruple at all; and if he had what way were best to be taken to deliver him of it. The most part of whom were of opinion that there was good cause of scruple and that, for discharging of it, suit were meet to

---

95. Cuthbert Tunstal was Bishop of London from 1522 to 1530. In the summer of 1529 he and More were appointed joint ambassadors to go to Cambrai. See below, p. 201. John Clerk was Bishop of Bath from 1523 to 1541.   96. compared. 97. convenience, profit.   98. proposed.

be made to the See of Rome, where the King hoped by liberality[99] to obtain his purpose. Wherein, as it after appeared, he was far deceived.

Then was there for the trial and examination of this matrimony procured from Rome a commission, in which Cardinal Campeggio[100] and Cardinal Wolsey were joined commissioners. Who, for the determination thereof, sat at the Blackfriars in London, where a libel[101] was put in for the annulling of the said matrimony, alleging the marriage between the King and Queen to be unlawful. And for proof of the marriage to be lawful was there brought in a dispensation, in which after divers disputations thereon holden, there appeared an imperfection which, by an instrument[102] or brief, upon search found in the Treasury of Spain and sent to the commissioners into England, was supplied. And so should judgment have been given by the Pope accordingly—had not the King, upon intelligence thereof, before the same judgment, appealed to the next general council. After whose appellation,[103] the Cardinal upon that matter sat no longer.

It fortuned before the matter of the said matrimony brought in question when, I, in talk with Sir Thomas More, of a certain joy commended unto him the happy estate of this realm that had so catholic a prince that no heretic durst show his face, so virtuous and learned a clergy, so grave and sound a nobility, and so loving, obedient subjects all in one faith agreeing together, "Truth, it is indeed, son Roper," quoth he, and in commending all degrees and estates of the same went far beyond me. "And yet, son Roper, I pray God," said he, "that some of us, as high as we seem to sit

---

99. either "by a generous interpretation," or "through gift-giving on his own (the King's) part."
100. Lorenzo Campeggio (1464–1539), distinguished Italian Cardinal. Arriving in London on October 9, 1528, he represented the Pope in the divorce proceedings. The Pope at this time was Clement VII, who had succeeded Adrian VI after his death in 1523.   101. plea.
102. An instrument was a formal legal document; a brief, a short, compendious papal letter.   103. action of appeal.

upon the mountains treading heretics under our feet like ants, live not in the day that we gladly would wish to be at a league and composition with them to let them have their churches quietly to themselves, so that they would be content to let us have ours quietly to ourselves."

After that I had told him many considerations why he had no cause so to say—"Well," said he, "I pray God, son Roper, some of us live not till that day," showing me no reason why he should put any doubt therein. To whom I said, "by my troth, sir, it is very desperately[104] spoken." That vile term, I cry God mercy, did I give him. Who by these words perceiving me in a fume[105] said merrily unto me: "Well, well, son Roper, it shall not be so, it shall not be so." Whom, in sixteen years and more, being in house conversant[106] with him, I could never perceive as much as once in a fume.

But now to return again where I left. After the supplying of the imperfections of the dispensation sent, as is before rehearsed, to the commissioners into England, the King taking the matter for ended and then meaning no farther to proceed in that matter, assigned the Bishop of Durham and Sir Thomas More to go ambassadors to Cambrai,[107] a place neither imperial nor French, to treat[108] a peace between the Emperor, the French King, and him. In the concluding whereof, Sir Thomas More so worthily handled himself, procuring in our league far more benefits unto this realm than at that time by the King or his Council was thought possible to be compassed,[109] that for his good service in that voyage, the King, when he after made him Lord Chancellor, caused the Duke of Norfolk openly to declare unto the people (as you shall hear hereafter more at large) how much all England was bound unto him.

104. despairingly.   105. fit of irritation.   106. intimately dwelling.
107. a town in the north of France. The Treaty of Cambrai was signed in 1529.
108. negotiate.   109. achieved.

Now upon the coming home of the Bishop of Durham and Sir Thomas More from Cambrai, the King was as earnest in persuading Sir Thomas More to agree unto the matter of his marriage as before, by many and divers ways provoking[110] him thereunto. For the which cause, as it was thought, he the rather[111] soon after made him Lord Chancellor.

And further declaring unto him that, though at his going over sea to Cambrai, he was in utter despair thereof, yet he had conceived since some good hope to compass it.[112] For albeit his marriage being against the positive laws of the Church and the written laws of God was holpen[113] by the dispensation, yet was there another thing found out of late, he said, whereby his marriage appeared to be so directly against the law of nature, that it could in no wise by the Church be dispensable—as Doctor Stokesley,[114] whom he had then preferred to be Bishop of London and in that case chiefly credited, was able to instruct him—with whom he prayed him in that point to confer. But, for all his conference with him, he saw nothing of such force as could induce him to change his opinion therein. Which notwithstanding, the Bishop showed himself in his report of him to the King's highness so good and favorable that he said he found him in his grace's cause very toward[115] and desirous to find some good matter wherewith he might truly serve his grace to his contentation.

This Bishop Stokesley, being by the Cardinal not long before in the Star Chamber openly put to rebuke and awarded to the Fleet,[116] not brooking this contumelious usage, and thinking that forasmuch as the Cardinal, for lack of such forwardness in setting forth the King's divorce as his grace looked for, was out of his highness's favor, he had now a good occasion offered him to

110. urging.   111. *the rather:* all the more quickly.
112. i.e., to secure More's agreement to the divorce proceedings.
113. helped, promoted.
114. John Stokesley was made Bishop of London in 1530.
115. favorably inclined.   116. *awarded . . . Fleet:* sentenced to Fleet Prison.

revenge his quarrel against him, further to incense the King's displeasure towards him, busily travailed to invent some colorable[117] device for the King's furtherance in that behalf. Which, as before is mentioned, he to his grace revealed, hoping thereby to bring the King to the better liking of himself, and the more misliking of the Cardinal; whom his highness therefore soon after of his[118] office displaced, and to Sir Thomas More, the rather to move him to incline to his side, the same in his stead committed.[119]

Who, between the Dukes of Norfolk and Suffolk being brought through Westminster Hall to his place in the Chancery, the Duke of Norfolk in audience of all the people there assembled showed that he was from the King himself straitly charged, by special commission, there openly in presence of them all to make declaration how much all England was beholding to Sir Thomas More for his good service, and how worthy he was to have the highest room in the realm, and how dearly his grace loved and trusted him, for which—said the Duke—he had great cause to rejoice. Whereunto Sir Thomas More, among many other his humble and wise sayings not now in my memory, answered: that although he had good cause to take comfort of the highness's singular favor towards him—that he had far above his deserts so highly commended him, to whom therefore he acknowledged himself most deeply bounden—yet, nevertheless, he must for his own part needs confess that in all things by his grace alleged he had done no more than was his duty. And further disabled himself as unmeet for that room, wherein, considering how wise and honorable a prelate had lately before taken so great a fall, he had, he said, thereof no cause to rejoice.

And as they had before, on the King's behalf, charged him uprightly to minister indifferent[120] justice to the people, without

117. specious.   118. i.e., Wolsey's.
119. More was made Chancellor in October 1529.   120. impartial.

corruption or affection,[121] so did he likewise charge them again that, if they saw him at any time in any thing digress from any part of his duty in that honorable office, even as they would discharge their own duty and fidelity to God and the King, so should they not fail to disclose it to his grace, who otherwise might have just occasion to lay his fault wholly to their charge.

While he was Lord Chancellor, being at leisure (as seldom he was) one of his sons-in-law[122] on a time said merrily unto him: "When Cardinal Wolsey was Lord Chancellor, not only divers of his privy chamber, but such also as were his doorkeepers got great gain." And since he had married one of his daughters, and gave still[123] attendance upon him, he thought he might of reason look for some; where he indeed, because he was so ready himself to hear every man, poor and rich, and kept no doors shut from them, could find none, which was to him a great discourage.[124] And whereas else, some for friendship, some for kindred, and some for profit, would gladly have had his furtherance in bringing them to his presence, if he should now take anything of them, he knew, he said, he should do them great wrong. For that they might do as much for themselves as he could do for them. Which condition, although he thought in Sir Thomas More very commendable, yet to him, said he, being his son, he found it nothing profitable.

When he had told him this tale: "You say well, son," quoth he. "I do not mislike that you are of conscience so scrupulous, but many other ways be there, son, that I may both do yourself good and pleasure your friend also. For sometime may I by my word stand your friend in stead, and sometime may I by my letter help him; or if he have a cause depending[125] before me, at your request I may hear him before another. Or if his cause be not all the best,

121. bias.
122. William Daunce, who married More's daughter Elizabeth in 1525.
123. constant.　　　124. discouragement.　　　125. pending.

yet may I move the parties to fall to some reasonable end by arbitrement.[126] Howbeit this one thing, son, I assure thee on my faith, that if the parties will at my hands call for justice, then all were it my father stood on the one side and the devil on the other, his cause being good, the devil should have right." So offered he his son, as he thought, he said, as much favor as with reason he could require.

And that he would for no respect digress from justice well appeared by a plain example of another of his sons-in-law called Master Heron.[127] For when he, having a matter before him in the Chancery and presuming too much of his favor, would by him in no wise be persuaded to agree to any indifferent[128] order, then made he in conclusion a flat decree against him.

This Lord Chancellor used commonly every afternoon to sit in his open hall to the intent that, if any persons had any suit unto him, they might the more boldly come to his presence and there open their complaints before him. Whose manner was also to read every bill himself ere he would award any *sub poena,* which, bearing matter sufficient worthy a *sub poena,* would he set his hand unto, or else cancel it.

Whensoever he passed through Westminster Hall to his place in the Chancery by the court of the King's Bench, if his father, one of the judges thereof, had been sate[129] ere he came, he would go into the same court, and there reverently kneeling down in the sight of them all, duly ask his father's blessing. And if it fortuned that his father and he at readings in Lincoln's Inn met together, as they sometime did, notwithstanding his high office, he would offer in argument the preeminence to his father, though he for his

126. arbitration.
127. Giles Heron, son of Sir John Heron, Treasurer of the Chamber to Henry VIII, married More's youngest daughter, Cecily, in September 1525. He was executed at Tyburn in August 1540, for high treason, although the specific charges are nowhere documented, and there is good reason to believe that he was the victim of trumped-up accusations.   128. impartial.
129. *had been sate:* had sat down.

office's sake would refuse to take it. And for the better declaration of his natural affection towards his father, he not only while he lay on his death bed, according to his duty, oft-times with comfortable words most kindly came to visit him, but also at his departure out of the world, with tears taking him about the neck, most lovingly kissed and embraced him, commending him into the merciful hands of almighty God, and so departed from him.

And as few injunctions[130] as he granted while he was Lord Chancellor, yet were they by some of the judges of the law misliked which I, understanding, declared the same to Sir Thomas More, who answered me that they should have little cause to find fault with him therefore. And thereupon caused he one Master Crooke, chief of the six clerks, to make a docket containing the whole number and causes of all such injunctions as either in his time had already passed or at that present depended in any of the King's courts at Westminster before him.

Which done, he invited all the judges to dine with him in the council chamber at Westminster, where after dinner, when he had broken with them what complaints he had heard of his injunctions, and moreover showed them both the number and causes of everyone of them in order, so plainly that, upon full debating of those matters, they were all enforced to confess that they in like case could have done no otherwise themselves. Then offered he this unto them. That if the justices of every court—unto whom the reformation of the rigor of the law, by reason of their office, most especially appertained—would upon reasonable considerations by their own discretion, as they were as he thought in conscience bound, mitigate and reform the rigor of the law themselves, there should from thenceforth by him no more injunctions be granted. Whereunto when they refused to condescend,[131] then said he unto them: "Forasmuch as yourselves, my

130. orders to stop legal proceedings until the Court had established their equity.
131. assent.

lords, drive me to that necessity for awarding out injunctions to relieve the people's injury, you cannot hereafter any more justly blame me."

After that he said secretly unto me: "I perceive, son, why they like not so to do, for they see that they may by the verdict of the jury cast off all quarrels from themselves upon them, which they accompt[132] their chief defense. And therefore am I compelled to abide the adventure[133] of all such reports."

And as little leisure as he had to be occupied in the study of Holy Scripture and controversies upon religion and such other virtuous exercises, being in manner continually busied about the affairs of the King and the realm, yet such watch[134] and pain, in setting forth of divers profitable works in defense of the true Christian religion against heresies secretly sown abroad in the realm, assuredly sustained he,[135] that the Bishops—to whose pastoral care[136] the reformation thereof principally appertained—thinking themselves by his travail, wherein by their own confession they were not able with him to make comparison, of their duties in that behalf discharged; and considering that for all his prince's favor he was no rich man nor in yearly revenues advanced as his worthiness deserved—therefore, at a convocation among themselves and other of the clergy, they agreed together and concluded upon a sum of four or five thousand pounds at the least, to my remembrance, for his pains to recompense him. To the payment whereof every bishop, abbot, and the rest of the clergy were—after the rate of their abilities—liberal contributories, hoping this portion should be to his contentation.

Whereupon Tunstal, Bishop of Durham, Clerk, Bishop of Bath, and as far as I can call to mind, Vaysey, Bishop of Exeter,[137]

132. reckon.   133. risk.   134. vigilance.
135. *assuredly . . . he:* he maintained with such assurance.
136. spiritual jurisdiction.
137. For Tunstal and Clerk, see above, p. 199, n. 95. John Vaysey or Veysey was Bishop of Exeter from 1519 to 1551, and from 1553 to 1554.

repaired unto him, declaring how thankfully for his travails, to their discharge in God's cause bestowed, they reckoned themselves bounden to consider him. And that albeit they could not, according to his deserts so worthily as they gladly would, requite him therefore, but must reserve that only to the goodness of God, yet for a small part of recompense (in respect of his estate so unequal to his worthiness) in the name of their whole convocation they presented unto him that sum, which they desired him to take in good part.[138]

Who, forsaking[139] it, said, that like as it was no small comfort unto him that so wise and learned men so well accepted his simple doings, for which he never intended to receive reward but at the hands of God only, to whom alone was the thank thereof chiefly to be ascribed, so gave he most humble thanks to their honors all, for their so bountiful and friendly consideration.

When they for all their importune pressing upon him, that few would have went[140] he could have refused it, could by no means make him to take it, then besought they him to be content yet that they might bestow it upon his wife and children. "Not so, my lords," quoth he, "I had rather see it all cast into the Thames than I or any of mine should have thereof the worth of one penny. For though your offer, my lords, be indeed very friendly and honorable, yet set I so much by my pleasure and so little by my profit that I would not, in good faith, for so much, and much more too, have lost the rest of so many nights' sleep as was spent upon the same. And yet wish would I, for all that, upon condition that all heresies were suppressed, that all my books were burned and my labor utterly lost." Thus departing were they fain to restore unto every man his own again.

This Lord Chancellor, albeit he was to God and the world well-known of notable virtue, though not so of every man considered, yet for the avoiding of singularity would he appear none

138. *in good part:* without offense.   139. declining.   140. supposed.

otherwise than other men in his apparel and other behavior. And albeit outwardly he appeared honorable like one of his calling, yet inwardly he, no such vanities esteeming, secretly next his body wore a shirt of hair. Which my sister More,[141] a young gentlewoman, in the summer as he sat at supper singly[142] in his doublet and hose, wearing thereupon a plain shirt without ruff or collar, chancing to spy began to laugh at it. My wife, not ignorant of his manner, perceiving the same, privily told him of it. And he, being sorry that she saw it, presently amended it.

He used also sometimes to punish his body with whips, the cords knotted, which was known only to my wife, his eldest daughter, whom for her secrecy above all other he specially trusted, causing her as need required to wash the same shirt of hair.

Now shortly upon his entry into the high office of the chancellorship, the King yet eftsoons[143] again moved him to weigh and consider his great matter. Who, falling down upon his knees, humbly besought his highness to stand his gracious sovereign, as he ever since his entry into his grace's service had found him, saying there was nothing in the world had been so grievous unto his heart as to remember that he was not able, as he willingly would, with the loss of one of his limbs—for that matter anything to find whereby he could, with his conscience safely, serve his grace's contentation, as he that always bore in mind the most goodly words that his highness spake unto him at his first coming into his noble service, the most virtuous lesson that ever prince taught his servant, willing him first to look unto God, and after God to him. As in good faith he said he did, or else might his grace well accompt[144] him his most unworthy servant. To this the King answered that if he could not therein with his conscience serve him, he was content to accept his service otherwise. And using the

---

141. Anne Cresacre, wife of More's son, John.   142. simply.
143. *yet eftsoons:* soon afterwards.   144. reckon.

advice of other of his learned council, whose consciences could well enough agree therewith, would nevertheless continue his gracious favor towards him and never with that matter molest his conscience after.

But Sir Thomas More in process of time, seeing the King fully determined to proceed forth in the marriage of Queen Anne and when he with the bishops and nobles of the higher house of Parliament were, for the furtherance of that marriage, commanded by the King to go down to the Common House to show unto them both what the universities, as well of other parts beyond the seas as of Oxford and Cambridge, had done in that behalf, and their seals also testifying the same—all which matters, at the King's request, not showing of what mind himself was therein, he opened to the lower house of the Parliament. Nevertheless, doubting[145] lest further attempts after should follow which, contrary to his conscience, by reason of his office he was likely to be put unto, he made suit unto the Duke of Norfolk, his singular[146] dear friend, to be a mean[147] to the King that he might, with his grace's favor, be discharged of that chargeable room[148] of the chancellorship wherein, for certain infirmities of his body, he pretended himself unable any longer to serve.

This Duke, coming on a time to Chelsea to dine with him, fortuned to find him at the church, singing in the choir, with a surplice on his back. To whom after service as they went homeward together, arm-in-arm, the Duke said: "God body, God body, my Lord Chancellor, a parish clerk! You dishonor the King and his office."

"Nay," quoth Sir Thomas More, smiling upon the Duke: "Your grace may not think that the King, your master and mine, will with me for serving of God, his master, be offended or thereby count his office dishonored!"

145. fearing.   146. intimate.   147. *be a mean:* act as an intercessor.
148. *chargeable room:* burdensome office.

When the Duke, being thereunto often solicited, by importunate suit had at length of the King obtained for Sir Thomas More a clear discharge of his office, then at a time convenient, by his highness's appointment, repaired he to his grace to yield up unto him the Great Seal.[149] Which as his grace, with thanks and praise for his worthy service in that office, courteously at his hands received, so pleased it his highness further to say unto him that, for the service that he before had done him, in any suit which he should after have unto him that either should concern his honor (for that word it liked[150] his highness to use unto him) or that should appertain unto his profit, he should find his highness good and gracious lord unto him.

After he had thus given over the chancellorship[151] and placed all his gentlemen and yeomen with bishops and noblemen, and his eight watermen with the Lord Audeley, that in the same office succeeded him, to whom also he gave his great barge; then, calling us all that were his children unto him and asking our advice how we might now in this decay of his ability[152]—by the surrender of his office so impaired that he could not, as he was wont and gladly would, bear out the whole charge[153] of them all himself—from thenceforth be able to live and continue together, as he wished we should. When he saw us silent and in that case not ready to show our opinions to him—"Then will I," said he, "show my poor mind unto you. I have been brought up," quoth he, "at Oxford, at an Inn of Chancery, at Lincoln's Inn, and also in the King's court—and so forth from the lowest degree to the highest; and yet have I in yearly revenues at this present left me little above an hundred pounds by the year. So that now must we hereafter, if we like[154] to live together, be contented to become contributaries together. But, by my counsel, it shall not be best for

149. emblematic of the authority of the High Chancellor.   150. pleased.
151. More resigned from the Chancellorship in May 1532. Sir Thomas Audeley succeeded him and served until 1544.   152. wealth, estate.
153. expenses.   154. wish.

us to fall to the lowest fare first. We will not, therefore, descend to
Oxford fare, nor to the fare of New Inn. But we will begin with
Lincoln's Inn diet, where many right worshipful and of good
years do live full well. Which, if we find not ourselves the first
year able to maintain, then will we the next year go one step down
to New Inn fare, wherewith many an honest man is well contented. If that exceed our ability too, then will we the next year
after descend to Oxford fare, where many grave, learned, and
ancient fathers be continually conversant.[155] Which, if our power
stretch not to maintain neither, then may we yet, with bags and
wallets, go a-begging together, and hoping that for pity some
good folk will give us their charity, at every man's door to sing
Salve Regina,[156] and so still keep company and be merry together."

And whereas you have heard before, he was by the King from
a very worshipful living taken into his grace's service, with whom
in all the great and weighty causes that concerned his highness or
the realm, he consumed and spent with painful cares, travails,
and troubles as well beyond the seas as within the realm, in effect
the whole substance of his life, yet with all the gain he got thereby,
being never wasteful spender thereof, was he not able after the
resignation of his office of the Lord Chancellor, for the maintenance of himself and such as necessarily belonged unto him, sufficiently to find meat, drink, fuel, apparel, and such other necessary
charges. All the land that ever he purchased, which also he purchased before he was Lord Chancellor, was not, I am well
assured, above the value of twenty marks by the year. And after
his debts paid he had not, I know, his chain[157] excepted, in gold
and silver left him the worth of one hundred pounds.

And whereas upon the holidays during his high chancellorship
one of his gentlemen, when service at the church was done, ordi-

155. dwelling.
156. "Hail Holy Queen," a very popular medieval hymn to the Virgin.
157. The chain of gold worn about the neck was the symbol of high civic office.

narily used to come to my Lady his wife's pew and say unto her, "Madam, my lord is gone,"—the next holiday after the surrender of his office and departure of his gentlemen, *he*[158] came unto my Lady his wife's pew himself, and making a low curtsy, said unto her: "Madam, my lord is gone!"

In the time somewhat before his trouble, he would talk with his wife and children of the joys of heaven and the pains of hell, the lives of holy martyrs, of their grievous martyrdoms, of their marvellous patience, and of their passions and deaths that they suffered rather than they would offend God. And what an happy and blessed thing it was, for the love of God, to suffer loss of goods, imprisonment, loss of lands, and life also. He would further say unto them that, upon his faith, if he might perceive his wife and children would encourage him to die in a good cause, it should so comfort him that, for very joy thereof, it would make him merrily run to death. He showed unto them afore what trouble might after fall unto him. Wherewith and the like virtuous talk he had so long before his trouble encouraged them that when he after fell into the trouble indeed, his trouble to them was a great deal the less, *Quia spicula previsa minus laedunt.*[159]

Now upon this resignment of his office came Master Thomas Cromwell,[160] then in the King's high favor, to Chelsea to him with a message from the King. Wherein when they had thoroughly commoned[161] together, "Master Cromwell," quoth he, "you are now entered into the service of a most noble, wise, and liberal prince. If you will follow my poor advice, you shall, in your counsel-giving unto his grace, ever tell him what he ought to do but never what he is able to do. So shall you show yourself a true

---

158. italics added.   159. "Because anticipated spears hurt less."
160. Thomas Cromwell, 1485?–1540. From a middle-class status, Cromwell rose rapidly and with ruthless efficiency until he was appointed Secretary in 1534. He is most notorious for the part he played in the Dissolution of the Monasteries and the subsequent distribution of Church lands and valuables. Attainted for treason in 1540, he was beheaded on July 28 of the same year.
161. held familiar discourse.

faithful servant and a right worthy counsellor. For if a lion knew his own strength, hard were it for any man to rule him."

Shortly thereupon was there a commission directed to Cranmer,[162] then Archbishop of Canterbury, to determine the matter of the matrimony between the King and Queen Catherine at Saint Albans, where according to the King's mind it was thoroughly determined. Who, pretending he had no justice at the Pope's hands, from thenceforth sequestered himself from the See of Rome, and so married the Lady Anne Boleyn.[163] Which Sir Thomas More understanding, said unto me: "God give grace, son, that these matters within a while be not confirmed with oaths." I, at that time seeing no likelihood thereof, yet fearing lest for his forespeaking it would the sooner come to pass, waxed therefore for his so saying much offended with him.

It fortuned not long before the coming of Queen Anne through the streets of London from the Tower to Westminster to her coronation that he received a letter from the Bishops of Durham, Bath, and Winchester, requesting him both to keep them company from the Tower to the coronation and also to take twenty pounds that by the bearer thereof they had sent him to buy him a gown with. Which he thankfully receiving, and at home still tarrying, at their next meeting said merrily unto them:

"My lords, in the letters which you lately sent me, you required two things of me; the one whereof, sith I was so well content to grant you, the other therefore I might be the bolder to deny you. And like as the one—because I took you for no beggars and myself I knew to be no rich man—I thought I might the rather fulfill, so the other did put me in remembrance of an emperor[164]

162. Thomas Cranmer, Archbishop of Canterbury from 1533 to 1556. In both a theological and literary sense, one of the prime architects of the Reformation in England. He was burned at the stake during the reign of Queen Mary.
163. Anne and Henry VIII were secretly married about January 25, 1533. On June 1, she was crowned Queen of England.
164. Tiberius Caesar. See the story of Sejanus' daughter as related by Tacitus (Annals, VI). More's version is, of course, considerably adapted.

that had ordained a law that whosoever committed a certain offense (which I now remember not) except it were a virgin, should suffer the pains of death. Such a reverence had he to virginity. Now so it happened that the first committer of that offense was indeed a virgin, whereof the emperor hearing was in no small perplexity, as he that by some example fain would have had that law to have been put in execution. Whereupon when his council had sat long, solemnly debating this case, suddenly arose there up one of his council—a good plain man among them—and said: 'Why make you so much ado, my lords, about so small a matter? Let her first be deflowered and then after may she be devoured!'

"And so, though your lordships have in the matter of the matrimony hitherto kept yourselves pure virgins, yet take good heed, my lords, that you keep your virginity still. For some there be that by procuring[165] your lordships first at the coronation to be present, and next to preach for the setting forth of it, and finally to write books to all the world in defense thereof, are desirous to deflower you; and when they have deflowered you, then will they not fail soon after to devour you. Now, my lords," quoth he, "it lieth not in my power but that they may devour me. But God, being my good Lord, I will provide that they shall never deflower me!"

In continuance: when the King saw that he could by no manner of benefits win him to his side, then, lo, went he about by terrors and threats to drive him thereunto. The beginning of which trouble grew by occasion of a certain nun dwelling in Canterbury,[166] for her virtue and holiness among the people not a little esteemed. Unto whom, for that cause, many religious persons, doctors of

165. prevailing upon.
166. Elizabeth Barton, known as "the Holy Maid of Kent," 1506?–1534. She predicted that, if Henry VIII divorced Catherine, he would "die a villain's death." She was executed for treason at Tyburn in April 1534.

divinity and divers others of good worship[167] of the laity used to resort. Who, affirming that she had revelations from God to give the King warning of his wicked life and of the abuse of the sword and authority committed unto him by God; and understanding my Lord of Rochester, Bishop Fisher,[168] to be a man of notable virtuous living and learning, repaired to Rochester and there disclosed to him all her revelations, desiring his advice and counsel therein.

Which the Bishop perceiving might well stand with the laws of God and his Holy Church, advised her (as she before had warned and intended) to go to the King herself and to let him understand the whole circumstance thereof. Whereupon she went to the King and told him all her revelations, and so returned home again. And in short space after, she, making a voyage to the nuns of Sion, by means of one Master Reynolds,[169] a father of the same house, there fortuned concerning such secrets as had been revealed unto her—some part whereof seemed to touch the matter of the King's supremacy and marriage, which shortly thereupon followed—to enter into talk with Sir Thomas More. Who, notwithstanding he might well at that time without danger of any law—though after, as himself had prognosticated before, those matters were established by statutes and confirmed by oaths—freely and safely have talked with her therein; nevertheless, in all the communication between them, as in process[170] it appeared, had always so discreetly demeaned[171] himself that he

---

167. *of good worship:* respected members.
168. John Fisher, Bishop of Rochester from 1504 to 1534. One of the most remarkable men of his time, in terms of both achievement and integrity, he incurred the wrath of Henry VIII by refusing to subscribe to the Oath of Supremacy. He was beheaded on Tower Hill on June 22, 1535, just two weeks before More was led out to the scaffold.
169. Dr. Richard Reynolds. Executed on May 4, 1535. From a window in his Tower cell, More watches as he is conducted to his death. See below, p. 228.
170. in due time.   171. conducted.

deserved not to be blamed, but contrariwise to be commended and praised.

And had he not been one that in all his great offices and doings for the King and the realm so many years together had from all corruption of wrong-doing or bribes-taking kept himself so clear that no man was able therewith once to blemish him, or make any just quarrel against him, it would without doubt in this troublous time of the King's indignation towards him, have been deeply laid to his charge and of the King's highness most favorably accepted, as in the case of one Parnell it most manifestly appeared. Against whom, because Sir Thomas More while he was Lord Chancellor, at the suit of one Vaughan, his[172] adversary, had made a decree. This Parnell to his highness most grievously complained that Sir Thomas More, for making the same decree, had of the same Vaughan, unable for the gout to travel abroad himself, by the hands of his wife taken a fair great gilt cup for a bribe.

Who thereupon, by the King's appointment, being called before the whole council, where that matter was heinously laid to his charge, forthwith confessed that, forasmuch as that cup was long after the foresaid decree brought him for a New Year's gift, he, upon her importunate pressing upon him, therefore of courtesy refused not to receive it.

Then the Lord of Wiltshire[173]—for hatred of his religion preferrer[174] of this suit—with much rejoicing said unto the lords: "Lo, did I not tell you, my lords, that you should find this matter true?" Whereupon Sir Thomas desired their lordships that as they had courteously heard him tell the one part of his tale, so they would vouchsafe of their honors indifferently[175] to hear the other. After which obtained, he further declared unto them that, albeit he had indeed with much work received that cup, yet

172. i.e. Parnell's adversary.   173. Sir Thomas Boleyn, the father of Anne.
174. promoter.   175. impartially.

immediately thereupon he caused his butler to fill it with wine, and of that cup drank to her; and that when he had so done and she pledged him, then as freely as her husband had given it to him, even so freely gave he the same unto her again to give unto her husband for his New Year's gift. Which at his instant[176] request, though much against her will, at length yet she was fain to receive, as herself and certain other there presently before them deposed. Thus was the great mountain turned scant to[177] a little molehill.

So I remember that at another time upon a New Year's Day, there came to him one Mistress Crocker, a rich widow, for whom with no small pain he had made a decree in the Chancery against the Lord of Arundel, to present him with a pair of gloves and forty pounds in angels[178] in them for a New Year's gift. Of whom he thankfully receiving the gloves but refusing the money said unto her: "Mistress, since it were against good manners to forsake a gentlewoman's New Year's gift, I am content to take your gloves but, as for your money, I utterly refuse." So, much against her mind, enforced he her to take her gold again.

And one Master Gresham, likewise, having at the same time a cause depending[179] in the Chancery before him, sent him for a New Year's gift a fair gilted cup, the fashion whereof he very well liking, caused one of his own (though not in his fantasy of so good a fashion, yet better in value) to be brought him out of his chamber, which he willed the messenger in recompense to deliver to his master. And under other condition would he in no wise receive it.

Many things more of like effect, for the declaration of his innocency and clearness from all corruption or evil affection,[180] could I here rehearse besides; which for tediousness omitting, I refer to

---

176. urgent.　　　177. *scant to:* to barely.
178. a gold coin, whose value varied from 6s. 8d. to 10s.　　　179. pending.
180. bias.

the readers by these few before remembered examples, with their own judgments wisely to weigh and consider the same.

At the Parliament following was there put into the Lords' House a bill to attaint[181] the nun and divers other religious persons of high treason, and the Bishop of Rochester, Sir Thomas More, and certain others of misprision of treason.[182] The King presupposing of likelihood that this bill would be to Sir Thomas More so troublous and terrible that it would force him to relent and condescend[183] to his request—wherein his grace was much deceived. To which bill Sir Thomas More was a suitor personally to be received in his own defense to make answer. But the King, not liking that, assigned the Bishop of Canterbury, the Lord Chancellor, the Duke of Norfolk, and Master Cromwell, at a day and place appointed, to call Sir Thomas More before them. At which time I, thinking that I had a good opportunity, earnestly advised him to labor unto those lords for the help of his discharge[184] out of that Parliament bill. Who answered me he would.

And at his coming before them, according to their appointment, they entertained him very friendly, willing him to sit down with them, which in no wise he would. Then began the Lord Chancellor to declare unto him how many ways the King had showed his love and favor towards him, how fain he would have had him continue in his office, how glad he would have been to have heaped more benefits upon him, and finally how he could ask no worldly honor nor profit at his highness's hands that were likely to be denied him; hoping by the declaration of the King's kindness and affection towards him to provoke[185] him to recompense his grace with the like again. And unto those things that the

181. accuse.
182. *misprision of treason:* the concealment of treasonable information.
183. assent.   184. the dismissal of the charges against More.
185. induce.

Parliament, the bishops, and universities had already passed to add his consent.

To this Sir Thomas More mildly made answer, saying: "No man living is there, my lords, that would with better will do the thing that should be acceptable to the King's highness than I, which must needs confess his manifold goodness and bountiful benefits most benignly bestowed on me. Howbeit, I verily hoped that I should never have heard of this matter more, considering that I have from time to time, always from the beginning, so plainly and truly declared my mind unto his grace, which his highness to me ever seemed like a most gracious prince very well to accept, never minding (as he said) to molest me more therewith. Since which time any further thing that was able to move me to any change could I never find. And if I could, there is none in all the world that would have been gladder of it than I."

Many things more were there of like sort uttered on both sides. But in the end, when they saw they could by no manner of persuasions remove him from his former determination, then began they more terribly to touch him, telling him that the King's highness had given them in commandment, if they could by no gentleness win him, in his name with his great ingratitude to charge him—that never was there servant to his sovereign so villainous, nor subject to his prince so traitorous as he. For he by his subtle, sinister sleights most unnaturally procuring and provoking[186] him to set forth a book of *The Assertion of the Seven Sacraments*[187]— and maintenance of the Pope's authority—had caused him to his dishonor throughout all Christendom to put a sword into the Pope's hands to fight against himself.

When they had thus laid forth all the terrors they could imagine against him: "My lords," quoth he, "these terrors be arguments for children and not for me. But to answer that wherewith

186. *procuring and provoking:* prevailing upon and urging.
187. published in 1521.

you do chiefly burden me, I believe the King's highness of his honor will never lay that to my charge. For none is there that can in that point say in my excuse more than his highness himself, who right well knoweth that I never was procurer nor counsellor of his majesty thereunto; but after it was finished, by his grace's appointment and consent of the makers of the same, only a sorter-out and placer of the principal matters therein contained. Wherein when I found the Pope's authority highly advanced and with strong arguments mightily defended, I said unto his grace: 'I must put your highness in remembrance of one thing and that is this: the Pope, as your grace knoweth, is a prince as you are, and in league with all other Christian princes. It may hereafter so fall out that your grace and he may vary upon some points of the league, whereupon may grow breach of amity and war between you both. I think it best, therefore, that that place be amended and his authority more slenderly touched.'

"'Nay,' quoth his grace, 'that shall it not. We are so much bounden unto the See of Rome that we cannot do too much honor unto it.'

"Then did I further put him in remembrance of the Statute of Praemunire,[188] whereby a good part of the Pope's pastoral cure[189] here was pared away.

"To that answered his highness: 'Whatsoever impediment be to the contrary, we will set forth that authority to the uttermost. For we received from that See our crown imperial'—which till his grace with his own mouth told it me, I never heard of before. So that I trust when his grace shall be once truly informed of this and call to his gracious remembrance my doing in that behalf, his highness will never speak of it more but clear me thoroughly therein himself." And thus displeasantly departed they.

---

188. The Statute of Praemunire made it a treasonable offense to resort to the authority or jurisdiction of any foreign court, including that of the Vatican.
189. spiritual jurisdiction.

Then took Sir Thomas More his boat towards his house at Chelsea, wherein by the way he was very merry, and for that I was nothing sorry, hoping that he had got himself discharged out of the Parliament bill. When he was landed and come home, then walked we twain alone into his garden together; where I, desirous to know how he had sped, said: "I trust, sir, that all is well because you are so merry."

"It is so indeed, son Roper, I thank God," quoth he.

"Are you then put out of the Parliament bill?" said I.

"By my troth, son Roper," quoth he, "I never remembered it."

"Never remembered it, sir!" said I, "a case that toucheth your-self so near, and us all for your sake. I am sorry to hear it. For I verily trusted, when I saw you so merry, that all had been well."

Then said he: "Wilt thou know, son Roper, why I was so merry?"

"That would I gladly, sir," quoth I.

"In good faith, I rejoiced, son," quoth he, "that I had given the devil a foul fall; and that with those lords I had gone so far as, without great shame, I could never go back again."

At which words waxed I very sad; for though himself liked it well, yet liked it me but a little.

Now upon the report made by the Lord Chancellor and the other lords to the King of all their whole discourse had with Sir Thomas More, the King was so highly offended with him that he plainly told them he was fully[190] determined that the aforesaid Parliament bill should undoubtedly proceed forth against him. To whom the Lord Chancellor and the rest of the lords said that they perceived the lords of the Upper House so precisely bent to hear him, in his own defense make answer himself, that if he were not put out of the bill, it would without fail be utterly an overthrow of all. But, for all this, needs would the King have his

190. definitely.

own will therein; or else he said that at the passing thereof, he would be personally present himself.

Then the Lord Audeley and the rest seeing him so vehemently set thereupon, on their knees most humbly besought his grace to forbear the same, considering that if he should, in his own presence, receive an overthrow, it would not only encourage his subjects ever after to contemn[191] him, but also throughout all Christendom redound to his dishonor forever; adding thereunto that they mistrusted not in time against him to find some meeter matter to serve his turn better. For in this case of the nun, he was accompted,[192] they said, so innocent and clear that for his dealing therein men reckoned him far worthier of praise than reproof. Whereupon at length, through their earnest persuasion, he was content to condescend[193] to their petition.

And on the morrow after, Master Cromwell, meeting me in the Parliament House, willed me to tell my father that he was put out of the Parliament bill. But because I had appointed to dine that day in London, I sent the message by my servant to my wife to Chelsea. Whereof when she informed her father, "In faith, Meg," quoth he, *"quod differtur non aufertur."*[194]

After this, as the Duke of Norfolk and Sir Thomas More chanced to fall in familiar talk together, the Duke said unto him: "By the Mass, Master More, it is perilous striving with princes. And therefore I would wish you somewhat to incline to the King's pleasure. For, by God's body, Master More, *Indignatio principis mors est."*[195]

"Is that all, my lord?" quoth he. "Then in good faith is there no more difference between your grace and me, but that I shall die today and you tomorrow."

191. disdain.   192. reckoned.   193. agree.
194. "what is put aside is not put off."
195. "The indignation of the prince is death."

So fell it out, within a month or thereabouts after the making of the statute for the Oath of the Supremacy and matrimony, that all the priests of London and Westminster—and no temporal[196] men but he—were sent for to appear at Lambeth before the Bishop of Canterbury, the Lord Chancellor, and Secretary Cromwell, commissioners appointed there to tender the oath unto them.

Then Sir Thomas More, as his accustomed manner was always, ere he entered into any matter of importance, as when he was first chosen of the King's privy council, when he was sent ambassador, appointed Speaker of the Parliament, made Lord Chancellor, or when he took any like weighty matter upon him, to go to church and be confessed, to hear Mass, and be houseled,[197] so did he likewise in the morning early the selfsame day that he was summoned to appear before the Lords at Lambeth.

And whereas he evermore used before at his departure from his wife and children, whom he tenderly loved, to have them bring him to his boat, and there to kiss them all and bid them farewell; then would he suffer none of them forth of the gate to follow him, but pulled the wicket after him and shut them all from him. And with an heavy heart, as by his countenance it appeared, with me and our four servants there took he his boat towards Lambeth. Wherein sitting still sadly a while, at the last he suddenly rounded[198] me in the ear and said: "Son Roper, I thank our Lord the field is won." What he meant thereby I then wist[199] not, yet loath to seem ignorant, I answered: "Sir, I am thereof very glad." But as I conjectured afterwards, it was for that the love he had to God wrought in him so effectually that it conquered all his carnal affections[200] utterly.

Now at his coming to Lambeth, how wisely he behaved himself before the commissioners, at the ministration of the oath unto him, may be found in certain letters of his sent to my wife remain-

196. secular.   197. receive the Eucharist.   198. whispered.
199. knew.   200. *all ... affections:* all his worldly feelings and emotions.

ing in a great book of his works.[201] Where by the space of four days he was betaken to the custody of the Abbot of Westminster, during which time the King consulted with his council what order were meet to be taken with him. And albeit in the beginning they were resolved that with an oath not to be acknowen[202] whether he had to the Supremacy been sworn (or what he thought thereof) he should be discharged, yet did Queen Anne by her importunate clamor so sore exasperate the King against him that, contrary to his former resolution, he caused the said Oath of the Supremacy to be ministered unto him. Who, albeit he made a discreet qualified answer, nevertheless was forthwith committed to the Tower.

Whom, as he was going thitherward, wearing as he commonly did a chain of gold about his neck, Sir Richard Cromwell[203] that had the charge of his conveyance thither, advised him to send home his chain to his wife or to some of his children. "Nay, sir," quoth he, "that I will not. For if I were taken in the field by my enemies, I would they should somewhat fare the better by me."

At whose landing, Master Lieutenant at the Tower-gate was ready to receive him, where the porter demanded of him his upper garment. "Master Porter," quoth he, "here it is." And took off his cap and delivered it him, saying: "I am very sorry it is no better for you." "No, sir," quoth the porter, "I must have your gown."

And so was he by Master Lieutenant conveyed to his lodging where he called unto him one John a Wood, his own servant, there appointed to attend upon him (who could neither write nor read); and sware him before the Lieutenant that if he should hear or see him at any time speak or write any manner of thing against the King, the council, or the state of the realm, he should open it

---

201. More's *English Works* were printed in 1557. Roper may have had an advance copy or he may have been referring to a manuscript collection of More's writing. The latter hypothesis seems to be the more likely one.   202. confessed. 203. The son of Sir Thomas Cromwell's sister. On entering his uncle's service, he assumed the surname of Cromwell.

to the Lieutenant, that the Lieutenant might incontinent[204] reveal it to the council.

Now when he had remained in the Tower a little more than a month, my wife, longing to see her father, by her earnest suit at length got leave to go to him. At whose coming, after the Seven Psalms and Litany said—which, whensoever she came to him, ere he fell in talk of any worldly matters, he used accustomably[205] to say with her—among other communication he said unto her: "I believe, Meg, that they that have put me here ween[206] they have done me a high displeasure. But I assure thee, on my faith, my own good daughter, if it had not been for my wife and you that be my children, whom I accompt the chief part of my charge, I would not have failed long ere this to have closed myself in as strait a room—and straiter, too. But since I am come hither without mine own desert, I trust that God of His goodness will discharge me of my care, and with His gracious help supply my lack among you. I find no cause, I thank God, Meg, to reckon myself in worse case here than in my own house. For me thinketh God maketh me a wanton,[207] and setteth me on His lap and dandleth me."

Thus by his gracious demeanor[208] in tribulation appeared it that all the troubles that ever chanced unto him, by his patient sufferance thereof, were to him no painful punishments but, of[209] his patience, profitable exercises.

And at another time, when he had first questioned with my wife a while of the order of his wife, children, and state of his own house in his absence, he asked her how Queen Anne did. "In faith, father," quoth she, "never better."

"Never better, Meg!" quoth he. "Alas, Meg, alas! It pitieth me to remember into what misery, poor soul, she shall shortly come."

After this, Master Lieutenant, coming into his chamber to visit him, rehearsed the benefits and friendship that he had many ways

204. immediately.   205. customarily.   206. suppose.
207. pampered pet.   208. bearing.   209. as a consequence of.

received at his hands, and how much bounden he was therefore friendly to entertain him and make him good cheer. Which, since the case standing as it did, he could not do without the King's indignation, he trusted, he said, he would accept his good will and such poor cheer as he had. "Master Lieutenant," quoth he again, "I verily believe, as you may, so you are my good friend indeed and would, as you say, with your best cheer entertain me, for the which I most heartily thank you. And assure yourself, Master Lieutenant, I do not mislike my cheer. But whensoever I so do, then thrust me out of your doors."

Whereas the oath confirming the Supremacy and matrimony was by the first statute in few words comprised, the Lord Chancellor and Master Secretary did of their own heads add more words unto it, to make it appear unto the King's ears more pleasant and plausible. And that oath, so amplified, caused they to be ministered to Sir Thomas More and to all other throughout the realm. Which Sir Thomas More perceiving, said unto my wife: "I may tell thee, Meg, they that have committed me hither for refusing of this oath not agreeable with the statute, are not by their own law able to justify my imprisonment. And, surely, daughter, it is great pity that any Christian prince should by a flexible council ready to follow his affections, and by a weak clergy lacking grace constantly to stand to their learning, with flattery be so shamefully abused." But at length the Lord Chancellor and Master Secretary, espying their own oversight in that behalf, were fain afterwards to find the means that another statute should be made, for the confirmation of the oath so amplified with their additions.

After Sir Thomas More had given over his office and all other worldly doings therewith, to the intent he might from thenceforth the more quietly settle himself to the service of God, then made he a conveyance[210] for the disposition of all his lands,

---

210. the transference of property, generally real estate, from one person to another.

reserving to himself an estate thereof only for term of his own life. And after his decease assuring some part of the same to his wife, some to his son's wife, for a jointure,[211] in consideration that she was an inheritress in possession of more than an hundred pounds land by the year, and some to me and my wife in recompense of our marriage money—with divers remainders over. All which conveyance and assurance was perfectly finished long before that matter whereupon he was attained[212] was made an offense, and yet after by statute clearly avoided.[213] And so were all his lands that he had to his wife and children by the said conveyance in such sort assured, contrary to the order of law, taken away from them and brought into the King's hands—saving that portion which he had appointed to my wife and me.

Which, although he had in the foresaid conveyance reserved, as he did the rest, for term of life to himself, nevertheless, upon further consideration two days after by another conveyance, he gave the same immediately to my wife and me in possession. And so because the statute had undone only the first conveyance, giving no more to the King but so much as passed by that, the second conveyance—whereby it was given to my wife and me—being dated two days after, was without the compass of the statute, and so was our portion to us by that means clearly reserved.[214]

As Sir Thomas More in the Tower chanced on a time, looking out of his window, to behold one Master Reynolds, a religious, learned, and virtuous father of Sion and three monks of the Charterhouse, for the matters of the matrimony and Supremacy, going out of the Tower to execution—he, as one longing in that journey to have accompanied them, said unto my wife, then standing

---

211. the holding of property to the joint use of husband and wife for life. 212. accused.   213. made void.

214. After the attainder, the King seized upon those lands which by means of More's "conveyance" were to be distributed following his death. By a second "conveyance," however, More bestowed upon the Ropers their portion of his estate *before* his death, thus making their inheritance relatively safe from the threat of royal confiscation.

there beside him: "Lo, dost thou not see, Meg, that these blessed
fathers be now as cheerfully going to their deaths as bridegrooms
to their marriage? Wherefore thereby mayst thou see, mine own
good daughter, what a great difference there is between such as
have in effect spent all their days in a strait, hard, penitential, and
painful life religiously, and such as have in the world, like worldly
wretches, as thy poor father hath done, consumed all their time in
pleasure and ease licentiously. For God, considering their long-
continued life in most sore and grievous penance, will no longer
suffer them to remain here in this vale of misery and iniquity, but
speedily hence taketh them to the fruition of his everlasting deity.
Whereas thy silly[215] father, Meg, that like a most wicked caitiff,[216]
hath passed forth the whole course of his miserable life most sin-
fully, God thinking him not worthy so soon to come to that eternal felicity, leaveth him here yet still in the world, further to be
plunged and turmoiled with misery."

Within a while after, Master Secretary, coming to him into the
Tower from the King, pretended much friendship towards him,
and for his comfort told him that the King's highness was his
good and gracious lord, and minded not with any matter wherein
he should have any cause of scruple from henceforth to trouble
his conscience. As soon as Master Secretary was gone, to express
what comfort he conceived of his words, he wrote with a coal—
for ink then had he none—these verses following:

> Aye, flattering Fortune, look thou never so fair,
> Nor never so pleasantly begin to smile,
> As though thou wouldst my ruin all repair,
> During my life thou shalt not me beguile!
> Trust I shall God to enter in a while
> His haven of Heaven, sure and uniform:
> Ever after thy calm, look I for a storm.

215. foolish.   216. wretch.

When Sir Thomas More had continued a good while in the Tower, my lady his wife obtained license to see him; who at her first coming, like a simple, ignorant woman and somewhat worldly too, with this manner of salutation bluntly saluted him:

"What the good-year,[217] Master More," quoth she, "I marvel that you that have been always hitherto taken for so wise a man will now so play the fool to lie here in this close, filthy prison and be content thus to be shut up among mice and rats when you might be abroad at your liberty and with the favor and good will both of the King and his council, if you would but do as all the bishops and best learned of this realm have done. And seeing you have at Chelsea a right fair house, your library, your books, your gallery, your garden, your orchard, and all other necessaries so handsome about you, where you might in the company of me your wife, your children, and household, be merry, I muse what, a God's name, you mean here still thus fondly[218] to tarry."

After he had a while quietly heard her, with a cheerful countenance he said unto her:

"I pray thee, good Mistress Alice, tell me one thing."

"What is that?" quoth she.

"Is not this house," quoth he, "as nigh heaven as my own?"

To whom she, after her accustomed homely fashion, not liking such talk, answered: "Tilly-valle, tilly-valle!"[219]

"How say you, Mistress Alice," quoth he, "is it not so?"

"*Bone deus, bone deus,* man, will this gear[220] never be left?" quoth she.

"Well, then, Mistress Alice, if it be so," quoth he, "it is very well. For I see no great cause why I should much joy either of my gay house or of anything belonging there unto, when, if I should but seven years lie buried under the ground and then arise and come thither again, I should not fail to find some therein that

217. an exclamation connoting impatience.   218. foolishly.
219. a colloquialism suggesting impatience.   220. rubbish.

would bid me get me out of doors and tell me it were none of mine. What cause have I then to like such an house as would so soon forget his master?"

So her persuasions moved him but a little.

Not long after came there to him the Lord Chancellor, the Dukes of Norfolk and Suffolk, with Master Secretary, and certain other of the privy council—at two several times—by all policies possible procuring[221] him either precisely[222] to confess the Supremacy or precisely to deny it. Whereunto as appeareth by his examinations in the said great book,[223] they could never bring him.

Shortly hereupon, Master Rich (afterwards Lord Rich), then newly-made the King's Solicitor, Sir Richard Southwell, and one Master Palmer, servant to the Secretary, were sent to Sir Thomas More into the Tower to fetch away his books from him. And while Sir Richard Southwell and Master Palmer were busy in the trussing-up of his books, Master Rich, pretending friendly talk with him, among other things, of a set course as it seemed, said thus unto him:

"Forasmuch as it is well known, Master More, that you are a man both wise and well-learned, as well in the laws of the realm as otherwise, I pray you therefore, sir, let me be so bold as of good will to put unto you this case. Admit there were, sir," quoth he, "an act of Parliament that all the realm should take me for King. Would not you, Master More, take me for King?"

"Yes, sir," quoth Sir Thomas More, "that would I."

"I put case further," quoth Master Rich, "that there were an act of Parliament that all the realm should take me for Pope. Would not you, then, Master More, take me for Pope?"

"For answer, sir," quoth Sir Thomas More, "to your first case. The Parliament may well, Master Rich, meddle with the state of temporal princes. But to make answer to your other case, I will

221. inducing.   222. specifically.   223. See above, p. 225, n. 201.

put you this case: Suppose the Parliament would make a law that God should not be God. Would you, then, Master Rich, say that God were not God?"

"No, sir," quoth he, "that would I not, since no Parliament may make any such law."

"No more," said Sir Thomas More, as Master Rich reported of him, "could the Parliament make the King supreme head of the Church."

Upon whose only[224] report was Sir Thomas More indicted of treason upon the statute whereby it was made treason to deny the King to be supreme head of the Church. Into which indictment were put these heinous words—"Maliciously, traitorously, and diabolically."

When Sir Thomas More was brought from the Tower to Westminster Hall to answer the indictment, and at the King's Bench bar before the judges thereupon arraigned, he openly told them that he would upon that indictment have abidden in law,[225] but that he thereby should have been driven to confess of himself the matter indeed, that was the denial of the King's Supremacy, which he protested was untrue. Wherefore he thereto pleaded not guilty; and so reserved unto himself advantage to be taken of the body of the matter, after verdict, to avoid that indictment. And, moreover, added that if those only[226] odious terms—"Maliciously, traitorously, and diabolically"—were put out of the indictment, he saw therein nothing justly to charge him.

And for proof to the jury that Sir Thomas More was guilty of this treason, Master Rich was called forth to give evidence unto them upon his oath, as he did. Against whom thus sworn, Sir Thomas More began in this wise to say:

"If I were a man, my lords, that did not regard an oath, I needed not, as it is well known, in this place at this time nor in this

---

224. single.   225. *abidden in law:* abided by the law.
226. *those only:* only those.

case, to stand here as an accused person. And if this oath of yours, Master Rich, be true, then pray I that I never see God in the face, which I would not say, were it otherwise, to win the whole world." Then recited he to the court the discourse of all their communication in the Tower according to the truth and said: "In good faith, Master Rich, I am sorrier for your perjury than for my own peril. And you shall understand that neither I, nor no man else to my knowledge, ever took you to be a man of such credit as in any matter of importance I or any other would at any time vouchsafe to communicate with you. And I, as you know, of no small while have been acquainted with you and your conversation,[227] who have known you from your youth hitherto. For we long dwelled both in one parish together where, as yourself can tell (I am sorry you compel me to say) you were esteemed very light of your tongue, a great dicer and of no commendable fame.[228] And so in your house at the Temple,[229] where hath been your chief bringing-up, were you likewise accompted.

"Can it therefore seem likely unto your honorable lordships that I would, in so weighty a cause, so unadvisedly overshoot myself as to trust Master Rich, a man of me always reputed for one of so little truth as your lordships have heard, so far above my sovereign lord the King or any of his noble counsellors, that I would unto him utter the secrets of my conscience touching the King's Supremacy—the special point and only mark at my hands so long sought for? A thing which I never did, nor never would, after the statute thereof made, reveal either to the King's highness himself or to any of his honorable counsellors, as it is not unknown to your honors, at sundry several times sent from his grace's own person unto the Tower unto me for none other purpose. Can this, in your judgments, my lords, seem likely to be true?

227. behavior.   228. reputation.
229. i.e., the Middle Temple, one of the Inns of Court.

"And yet if I had so done indeed, my lords, as Master Rich hath sworn, seeing it was spoken but in familiar secret talk, nothing affirming, and only in putting of cases without other displeasant circumstances, it cannot justly be taken to be spoken 'maliciously.' And where there is no malice, there can be no offense. And over[230] this I can never think, my lords, that so many worthy bishops, so many honorable personages, and so many other worshipful, virtuous, wise, and well-learned men as at the making of that law were in the Parliament assembled, ever meant to have any man punished by death in whom there could be found no malice—taking *'malitia'* for *'malevolentia'*; for if *'malitia'* be generally taken for *'sin,'* no man is there then that can thereof excuse himself: *Quia si dixerimus quod peccatum non habemus, nosmet ipsos seducimus, et veritas in nobis non est.*[231] And only this word *'maliciously'* is in the statute material[232]—as this term *'forcible'* is in the statute of forcible entries. By which statute, if a man enter peaceably, and put not his adversary out forcibly, it is no offense. But if he put him out forcibly, then by that statute it is an offense, and so shall he be punished by this term *'forcibly.'*

"Besides this the manifold goodness of the King's highness himself, that hath been so many ways my singular good lord and gracious sovereign, that hath so dearly loved and trusted me, even at my very first coming into his noble service with the dignity of his honorable privy council vouchsafing to admit me, and to offices of great credit and worship most liberally advanced me, and finally with that weighty room[233] of his grace's High Chancellor (the like whereof he never did to temporal[234] man before) next to his own royal person the highest officer in this noble realm, so far above my merits or qualities able and meet therefore, of his incomparable benignity honored and exalted me, by the space of twenty years and more showing his continual favor

230. besides.   231. I John 1 : 8.   232. relevant.   233. office.
234. secular.

towards me. And, until at my own poor suit, it pleased his highness, giving me license with his majesty's favor, to bestow the
residue of my life for the provision of my soul in the service of
God—of his especial goodness thereof to discharge and unbur-
then me—most benignly heaped honors continually more and
more upon me. All this his highness's goodness, I say, so long thus
bountifully extended towards me, were in my mind, my lords,
matter sufficient to convince[235] this slanderous surmise by this
man so wrongfully imagined against me."

Master Rich, seeing himself so disproved and his credit so
foully defaced, caused Sir Richard Southwell and Master Palmer,
that at the time of their communication were in the chamber,[236] to
be sworn what words had passed between them. Whereupon
Master Palmer, upon his deposition, said that he was so busy
about the trussing-up of Sir Thomas More's books in a sack that
he took no heed to their talk. Sir Richard Southwell likewise,
upon his deposition, said that because he was appointed only to
look unto the conveyance of his books, he gave no ear unto them.

After this were there many other reasons, not now in my
remembrance, by Sir Thomas More in his own defense alleged, to
the discredit of Master Rich's aforesaid evidence and proof of the
clearness of his own conscience. All which notwithstanding, the
jury found him guilty.

And incontinent upon[237] their verdict, the Lord Chancellor, for
that matter chief commissioner, beginning to proceed in judgment against him, Sir Thomas More said to him: "My Lord,
when I was toward[238] the law, the manner in such case was to ask
the prisoner before judgment, why judgment should not be given
against him." Whereupon the Lord Chancellor, staying his judgment, wherein he had partly proceeded, demanded of him what

235. refute.   236. i.e., More's quarters in the Tower.
237. *incontinent upon:* immediately after.   238. engaged in the practice of.

he was able to say to the contrary. Who then in this sort most humbly made answer:

"Forasmuch as, my lord," quoth he, "this indictment is grounded upon an act of Parliament directly repugnant to the laws of God and His Holy Church, the supreme government of which, or of any part whereof, may no temporal prince presume by any law to take upon him, as rightfully belonging to the See of Rome, a spiritual pre-eminence by the mouth of Our Savior himself, personally present upon the earth, only to Saint Peter and his successors, Bishops of the same See, by special prerogative granted; it is therefore in law, amongst Christian men, insufficient to charge any Christian man."

And for proof thereof like as (among divers other reasons and authorities) he declared that this realm, being but one member and small part of the Church, might not make a particular law disagreeable with the general law of Christ's universal Catholic Church, no more than the City of London, being but one poor member in respect of the whole realm, might make a law against an act of Parliament to bind the whole realm. So farther showed he that it was contrary both to the laws and statutes of our own land yet unrepealed, as they might evidently perceive in Magna Charta: *Quod ecclesia Anglicana libera sit, et habeat omnia iura sua integra et libertates suas illaesas;*[239] and also contrary to that sacred oath which the King's highness and every Christian prince always with great solemnity received at their coronations. Alleging, moreover, that no more might this realm of England refuse obedience to the See of Rome than might the child refuse obedience to his own natural father.

For, as Saint Paul said of the Corinthians, "I have regenerated you my children in Christ,"[240] so might Saint Gregory, Pope of Rome, of whom by Saint Augustine, his messenger, we first

---

239. "That the English church may be free, and that it may exist with all its laws uncorrupted and its liberties unviolated."   240. I Corinthians 3 : 1.

received the Christian faith, of us Englishmen truly say: "You are my children because I have given to you everlasting salvation, a far higher and better inheritance than any carnal father can leave to his child, and by regeneration made you my spiritual children in Christ."

Then was it by the Lord Chancellor thereunto answered that, seeing all the bishops, universities, and best learned of this realm had to this act agreed, it was much marvelled that he alone against them all would so stiffly stick[241] thereat, and so vehemently argue there against. To that Sir Thomas More replied, saying:

"If the number of bishops and universities be so material as your lordship seemeth to take it, then see I little cause, my lord, why that thing in my conscience should make any change. For I nothing doubt but that, though not in this realm, yet in Christendom about, of these well-learned bishops and virtuous men that are yet alive, they be not the fewer part that be of my mind therein. But if I should speak of those which already be dead, of whom many be now holy saints in heaven, I am very sure it is the far greater part of them that, all the while they lived, thought in this case that way that I think now. And therefore am I not bound, my lord, to conform my conscience to the council of one realm against the general council of Christendom."

Now when Sir Thomas More, for the avoiding of the indictment, had taken as many exceptions as he thought meet, and many more reasons than I can now remember alleged, the Lord Chancellor, loath to have the burthen of that judgment wholly to depend upon himself, there openly asked the advice of the Lord Fitz-James,[242] then Lord Chief Justice of the King's Bench, and joined in commission with him, whether this indictment were sufficient or not. Who, like a wise man, answered: "My lords all,

241. *stiffly stick:* obstinately refuse.
242. Sir John Fitz-James (1470?–1542?) became Chief Justice in 1526.

by Saint Julian" (that was ever his oath), "I must needs confess that if the act of Parliament be not unlawful, then is not the indictment in my conscience insufficient."

Whereupon the Lord Chancellor said to the rest of the Lords: "Lo, my lords, lo, you hear what my Lord Chief Justice saith," and so immediately gave he judgment against him.

After which ended, the commissioners yet further courteously offered him, if he had anything else to allege for his defense, to grant him favorable audience. Who answered: "More have I not to say, my lords, but like as the blessed apostle Saint Paul, as we read in the Acts of the Apostles, was present and consented to the death of Saint Stephen, and kept their clothes that stoned him to death, and yet be they now both twain holy saints in heaven, and shall continue there friends forever, so I verily trust, and shall therefore right heartily pray, that though your lordships have now here in earth been judges to my condemnation, we may yet hereafter in heaven merrily all meet together, to our everlasting salvation."

Thus much touching Sir Thomas More's arraignment, being not thereat present myself, have I by the credible report partly of the right worshipful Sir Anthony Saint Leger, knight, and partly of Richard Heywood and John Webbe, gentlemen, with others of good credit, at the hearing thereof present themselves, as far as my poor wit and memory would serve me, here truly rehearsed unto you.

Now after this arraignment departed he from the bar to the Tower again, led by Sir William Kingston,[243] a tall, strong, and comely knight, Constable of the Tower, and his very dear friend. Who, when he had brought him from Westminster to the Old Swan towards the Tower, there with an heavy heart, the tears running down by his cheeks, bade him farewell. Sir Thomas

---

243. After a distinguished military career, Sir William was made Constable of the Tower in 1524. He died in 1540.

More, seeing him so sorrowful, comforted him with as good words as he could, saying: "Good Master Kingston, trouble not yourself but be of good cheer; for I will pray for you, and my good Lady, your wife, that we may meet in heaven together, where we shall be merry for ever and ever."

Soon after, Sir William Kingston, talking with me of Sir Thomas More, said: "In good faith, Master Roper, I was ashamed of myself that, at my departing from your father, I found my heart so feeble, and his so strong, that he was fain to comfort me which should rather have comforted him."

When Sir Thomas More came from Westminster to the Tower-ward again, his daughter—my wife—desirous to see her father, whom she thought she should never see in this world after, and also to have his final blessing, gave attendance about the Tower Wharf where she knew he should pass by before he could enter into the Tower—there tarrying for his coming home.

As soon as she saw him—after his blessing on her knees reverently received—she hasting towards him and, without consideration or care of herself, pressing in among the midst of the throng and company of the guard, that with halberds and bills[244] went round about him, hastily ran to him and there openly, in the sight of them all, embraced him, took him about the neck, and kissed him. Who, well liking her most natural and dear daughterly affection towards him, gave her his fatherly blessing and many goodly words of comfort besides.

From whom after she was departed she, not satisfied with the former sight of him and like one that had forgotten herself, being all-ravished with the entire love of her dear father, having respect neither to herself nor to the press of the people and multitude that were there about him, suddenly turned back again, ran to him as before, took him about the neck, and divers times together most lovingly kissed him—and at last, with a full heavy heart, was fain

244. *halberds and bills:* battle-axes and swords.

to depart from him. The beholding whereof was to many of them that were present thereat so lamentable that it made them for very sorrow thereof to mourn and weep.

So remained Sir Thomas More in the Tower more than a seven-night after his judgment. From whence, the day before he suffered,[245] he sent his shirt of hair—not willing to have it seen—to my wife, his dearly beloved daughter, and a letter written with a coal, contained in the foresaid book of his works, plainly expressing the fervent desire he had to suffer on the morrow, in these words following:

"I cumber[246] you, good Margaret, much; but I would be sorry if it should be any longer than tomorrow. For tomorrow is Saint Thomas's Even and the Utas of Saint Peter;[247] and therefore tomorrow long I to go to God. It were a day very meet and convenient for me, etc. I never liked your manner towards me better than when you kissed me last. For I like when daughterly love and dear charity hath no leisure to look to worldly courtesy."

And so upon the next morrow, being Tuesday, Saint Thomas's Even and the Utas of Saint Peter, in the year of our Lord one thousand five hundred thirty and five, according as he in his letter the day before had wished, early in the morning came to him Sir Thomas Pope, his singular friend, on message from the King and his council, that he should before nine of the clock the same morning suffer death. And that therefore forthwith he should prepare himself thereunto.

"Master Pope," quoth he, "for your good tidings I most heartily thank you. I have been always much bounden to the King's highness for the benefits and honors that he hath still from time to time most bountifully heaped upon me. And yet more bound am

---

245. i.e., with the implication of martyrdom.   246. trouble.
247. Saint Thomas's Even and the Utas (i.e., octave) of Saint Peter, a festivity of eight days, do indeed fall on July 6, the day of More's execution. But More was sentenced on July 1. Roper must therefore be in error when he states that More was in the Tower "more than a seven-night after his judgment."

I to his grace for putting me into this place, where I have had convenient time and space to have remembrance of my end. And so help me God, most of all, Master Pope, am I bound to his highness that it pleaseth him so shortly to rid me out of the miseries of this wretched world. And therefore will I not fail earnestly to pray for his grace, both here and also in another world."

"The King's pleasure is further," quoth Master Pope, "that at your execution you shall not use many words."

"Master Pope," quoth he, "you do well to give me warning of his grace's pleasure, for otherwise I had purposed at that time somewhat to have spoken, but of no matter wherewith his grace, or any other, should have had cause to be offended. Nevertheless, whatsoever I intended, I am ready obediently to conform myself to his grace's commandments. And I beseech you, good Master Pope, to be a mean unto his highness that my daughter Margaret may be at my burial."

"The King is content already," quoth Master Pope, "that your wife, children, and other your friends shall have liberty to be present thereat."

"Oh, how much beholden then," said Sir Thomas More, "am I to his grace that unto my poor burial vouchsafeth to have so gracious consideration."

Wherewithal Master Pope, taking his leave of him, could not refrain from weeping. Which Sir Thomas More perceiving, comforted him in this wise: "Quiet yourself, good Master Pope, and be not discomforted. For I trust that we shall, once in heaven, see each other full merrily, where we shall be sure to live and love together in joyful bliss eternally."

Upon whose departure, Sir Thomas More, as one that had been invited to some solemn feast, changed himself into his best apparel. Which Master Lieutenant espying, advised him to put it off, saying that he that should have it was but a javel.[248]

248. rogue.

"What, Master Lieutenant," quoth he, "shall I accompt him a javel that shall do me this day so singular a benefit? Nay, I assure you, were it cloth-of-gold, I would accompt it well bestowed on him, as Saint Cyprian did, who gave his executioner thirty pieces of gold." And albeit at length, through Master Lieutenant's importunate persuasion, he altered his apparel, yet after the example of that holy martyr, Saint Cyprian, did he of that little money that was left him send one angel of gold to his executioner.

And so was he by Master Lieutenant brought out of the Tower and from thence led towards the place of execution. Where, going up the scaffold, which was so weak that it was ready to fall, he said merrily to Master Lieutenant: "I pray you, Master Lieutenant, see me safe up and, for my coming down, let me shift for myself."

Then desired he all the people thereabout to pray for him, and to bear witness with him that he should now there suffer death in and for the faith of the Holy Catholic Church. Which done, he kneeled down and after his prayers said, turned to the executioner and with a cheerful countenance spake thus to him:

"Pluck up thy spirits, man, and be not afraid to do thine office. My neck is very short. Take heed therefore thou strike not awry, for saving of thine honesty."

So passed Sir Thomas More out of this world to God upon the very same day in which himself had most desired.

Soon after whose death came intelligence thereof to the Emperor Charles. Whereupon he sent for Sir Thomas Elyot, our English ambassador, and said unto him: "My Lord Ambassador, we understand that the King, your master, hath put his faithful servant and grave, wise counsellor, Sir Thomas More, to death." Whereunto Sir Thomas Elyot answered that he understood nothing thereof.

"Well," said the Emperor, "it is too true. And this will we say, that if we had been master of such a servant, of whose doings ourself have had these many years no small experience, we would rather have lost the best city of our dominions than have lost such a worthy counsellor."

Which matter was by the same Sir Thomas Elyot to myself, to my wife, to Master Clement and his wife to Master John Heywood and his wife, and unto divers other his friends accordingly reported.

Finis. Deo gratias.

DESCRIPTION OF THOMAS MORE
BY ERASMUS

The following is taken from a 1519 letter in which Erasmus describes his good friend Thomas More [then forty-one years old]:

"You ask me to paint you a full-length portrait of More as in a picture. Would that I could do it as perfectly as you eagerly desire it. At least I will try to give a sketch of the man, as well as from my long familiarity with him I have either observed or can now recall. To begin, then, with what is least known to you, in stature he is not tall, though not remarkably short. His limbs are formed with such perfect symmetry as to leave nothing to be desired. His complexion is white, his face fair rather than pale, and though by no means ruddy, a faint flush of pink appears beneath the whiteness of his skin. His hair is dark brown, or brownish black. The eyes are grayish blue, with some spots, a kind which betokens singular talent, and among the English is considered attractive, whereas Germans generally prefer black. It is said that none are so free from vice.

"His countenance is in harmony with his character, being always expressive of an amiable joyousness, and even an incipient laughter, and, to speak candidly, it is better framed for gladness than for gravity and dignity, though without any approach to folly or buffoonery. The right shoulder is a little higher than the left, especially when he walks. This is not a defect of birth, but the result of habit, such as we often contract. In the rest of his person there is nothing to offend. His hands are the least refined part of his body.

"He was from his boyhood always most careless about whatever concerned his body. His youthful beauty may be guessed from what still remains, though I knew him when he was not more than three-and-twenty. Even now he is not much over forty.

He has good health, though not robust; able to endure all honorable toil, and subject to very few diseases. He seems to promise a long life, as his father still survives in a wonderfully green old age.

"I never saw anyone so indifferent about food. Until he was a young man he delighted in drinking water, but that was natural to him. Yet not to seem singular or morose, he would hide his temperance from his guests by drinking out of a pewter vessel beer almost as light as water, or often pure water. It is the custom in England to pledge each other in drinking wine. In doing so he will merely touch it with his lips, not to seem to dislike it, or to fall in with the custom. He likes to eat corned beef and coarse bread much leavened, rather than what most people count delicacies. Otherwise he has no aversion to what gives harmless pleasure to the body. He prefers milk diet and fruits, and is especially fond of eggs.

"His voice is neither loud nor very weak, but penetrating; not resounding or soft, but that of a clear speaker. Though he delights in every kind of music he has no vocal talents. He speaks with great clearness and perfect articulation, without rapidity or hesitation. He likes a simple dress, using neither silk nor purple nor gold chain, except when it may not be omitted. It is wonderful how negligent he is as regards all the ceremonious forms in which most men make politeness to consist. He does not require them from others, nor is he anxious to use them himself, at interviews or banquets, though he is not unacquainted with them when necessary. But he thinks it unmanly to spend much time in such trifles. Formerly he was most averse to the frequentation of the court, for he has a great hatred of constraint [*tyrannis*] and loves equality. Not without much trouble he was drawn into the court of Henry VIII, though nothing more gentle and modest than that prince can be desired. By nature More is chary of his liberty and of ease, yet, though he enjoys ease, no one is more alert or patient when duty requires it.

"He seems born and framed for friendship, and is a most

faithful and enduring friend. He is easy of access to all; but if he chances to get familiar with one whose vices admit no correction, he manages to loosen and let go the intimacy rather than to break it off suddenly. When he finds any sincere and according to his heart, he so delights in their society and conversation as to place in it the principal charm of life. He abhors games of tennis, dice, cards, and the like, by which most gentlemen kill time. Though he is rather too negligent of his own interests, no one is more diligent in those of his friends. In a word, if you want a perfect model of friendship, you will find it in no one better than in More. In society he is so polite, so sweet-mannered, that no one is of so melancholy a disposition as not to be cheered by him, and there is no misfortune that he does not alleviate. Since his boyhood he has so delighted in merriment, that it seems to be part of his nature; yet he does not carry it to buffoonery, nor did he ever like biting pleasantries. When a youth he both wrote and acted some small comedies. If a retort is made against himself, even without ground, he likes it from the pleasure he finds in witty repartees. Hence he amused himself with composing epigrams when a young man, and enjoyed Lucian above all writers. Indeed, it was he who pushed me to write the *Praise of Folly,* that is to say, he made a camel frisk.

"In human affairs there is nothing from which he does not extract enjoyment, even from things that are most serious. If he converses with the learned and judicious, he delights in their talent; if with the ignorant and foolish, he enjoys their stupidity. He is not even offended by professional jesters. With a wonderful dexterity he accommodates himself to every disposition. As a rule, in talking with women, even with his own wife, he is full of jokes and banter.

"No one is less led by the opinions of the crowd, yet no one departs less from common sense. One of his great delights is to consider the forms, the habits, and the instincts of different kinds of animals. There is hardly a species of bird that he does not keep in his house, and rare animals such as monkeys, foxes, ferrets, weasels and the like. If he meets with anything foreign, or in any way remarkable, he eagerly buys it, so that his house is full of such things, and at every turn they attract the eye of visitors, and his own pleasure is renewed whenever he sees others pleased."[1]

1. The above is taken from the book *Life and Writings of Blessed Thomas More* by T. E. Bridgett, 1913.

SIR THOMAS MORE'S EPITAPH IN CHELSEA OLD CHURCH[1]

Sir Thomas More being lorde Chaunceller of England, gaue ouer that office (by his great sute & labour) the .xvi. day of may, in the yere of our lord god a.1532. and in the .xxiiii. yere of the raigne of king Henry the eight. And after in that somer, he wrote an epitaphy in latin, and caused it to be written vpon his tombe of stone, which himself (while he was lord Chanceller) had caused to be made in his parishe church of Chelsey (where he dwelled) thre smal Miles from London. The copye of which epitaphy here foloweth . . .

"Thomas More, a Londoner borne, of no noble famely, but of an honest stocke, somewhat brought vp in learning, after that in his yong dayes, he had ben a pleader in the lawes of this hall certaine yeres, being one of the vndershrieues of London, was of noble kinge Henry the eight (which alone of all kinges worthely deserued both with the sweorde and penne, to be called the defender of the faith, a glory afore not herd of) called into the court, & chosen one of the counsel, and made knight: then made first vnder treasorer of englande, after that Chanceller of ye Duchy of Lancaster, and last of all (with great fauour of his Prince) lord Chaunceller of England. But in the meane season, he was chosen speker of the parlement, & besides was diuers times in dyuers places the kinges embassator, and last of all at Cameray (ioined felow and companion with Cuthbert Tonstal chief of that embassy than Bishop of London, and wythin a while after Bishop of Durham, who so excelleth in learning wit and vertue, that the

---

1. The epitaph was written in Latin by More himself, in 1532. The English translation is said to be by William Rastell, his nephew. The text is quoted from *"The King's Good Servant": Sir Thomas More.* J. B. Trapp and Hubertus Schulte Herbruggen. Totowa, N.J.: Rowman and Littlefield, The Boydell Press, 1977, pp. 139–140.

whole world scant hath at this daye any more lerned wiser or better) where he both ioyfully saw & was present ebassator, when the
legues betwene the chief Princes of christendome wer renued
againe and peace so long loked for restored to Christendome.
Which peace oure lord stable and make perpetual.

"When he had thus gone throughe thys course of offices or
honours, that neither that gracious prince could disalow his
doinges, nor was he odious to the nobilite, nor vnplesant to the
people, but yet to theues, murderers and heretikes greuous, at
laste John More hys father knight, and chosen of the Prince to be
one of the iustyces of the kynges benche a ciuil man, plesant,
harmless gentil, pitiful, iust, & vncorrupted, in yeres old, but in
body more than for his yeres lusty, after that he parceiued his
sonne lord Chaunceller of Englande, thinking hymselfe nowe to
haue liued long inough, gladly departed to god, his sonne than,
his father being dead, to whome as long as he liued being compared, was wont both to be called yong, & himself so thought to,
missing now his father departed, and seeing .iiii. children of his
own, & of their offspringes xi. began in his own conceit to waxe
old. And this affect of his was increased, by a certayne sickly dis-
posicion of hys brest, euen by & by folowing, as a signe or token of
age creping vpon him. He therfore irke and wery of worldly business, giuing vp his promocions, obtained at last by ye incomparable benefite of his most gentil prince (if it please god to fauour his
enterprise) that thing which from a childe in a manner always he
wished & desyred, that he might haue some yeres of his life fre, in
which he litle and litle withdrawing himself from the business of
this life, might continually remembre the immortalite of the lyfe
to come. And he hath caused this tombe to be made for himselfe
(his firste wiues bones brought hither to) that might euerye day
put him in memory of death that neuer ceaseth to crepe on hym.
And that this tombe made for him in his life time be not in vaine,
nor that he fere death comming vpon him, but that he may willingly for the desire of Christ, die, & find death not vtterly death to

him, but ye gate of a welthyer life, helpe hym (I besech you good reader) nowe with your praiers while he liueth, & when he is dead also."

Under this epitaphy in prose, he caused to be written on his tombe, this latten epitaphy in versis following, which himself had made .xx. yeres before, for Jane Colt:

"Here lieth Ione ye welbeloued wife of me Thomas More, who haue apointed this tombe for Alis my wife and me also, the one being coupled with me in matrimony, in my youthe brought me forth thre daughters & one sone, ye other hath ben so good to my children (which is a rare praise in mothers in law) [ie stopmothers] as scant any could be better to her own. The one so liued with me, & the other nowe so lyueth, that it is doubtfull whether thys or the other were derer vnto me. Oh howe well could we thre haue liued ioined together in matrimony, if fortune and religion wolde haue suffred it. But I beseche our lord that his tombe and heauen may ioine vs togither. So deathe shall give vs, that thyng that life could not."

SUGGESTIONS FOR FURTHER
READING

WORKS OF THOMAS MORE
(arranged by date of publication)

Life of Pico della Mirandola. London: printed by John Rastell, n.d.

The works of Sir Thomas More, Knyght, sometyme Lord Chancellor of England, wrytten by him in the Englysh tonge. Ed. William Rastell. London, 1557.

The English Works of Sir Thomas More. Ed. W. E. Campbell. London, 1931.

The Tower Works: Devotional Writiings. Ed. Garry E. Haupt. New Haven and London: Yale University Press, 1980.

The Yale Edition of the Complete Works of Sir Thomas More. New Haven and London: Yale University Press. Vols. 1–15, 1963–1986.

Utopia. Trans. and ed. Robert M. Adams. New York: W. W. Norton and Co., 1992.

The Last Letters of Thomas More. Ed. Alvaro de Silva. Grand Rapids, Mich.: William B. Eerdmans Publishing Co., 2000.

SECONDARY WORKS

ACKROYD, PETER. *The Life of Thomas More.* New York: Doubleday, 1998.

BARZUN, JACQUES. *From Dawn to Decadence: 1500 to the Present.* New York: HarperCollins, 2000.

BOLT, ROBERT. *A Man for All Seasons: A Play in Two Acts.* New York: Vintage International, 1990; first published 1960.

BRIGDEN, SUSAN. *London and the Reformation.* Oxford: Clarendon Press, 1991.

CAVENDISH, GEORGE, and WILLIAM ROPER. *Two Early Tudor Lives: The Life and Death of Cardinal Wolsey, by George Cavendish; The Life of Sir Thomas More, by William Roper.* Ed. Richard S. Sylvester and Davis P. Harding. New Haven and London: Yale University Press, 1962.

CHAMBERS, R. W. *Thomas More.* Ann Arbor, Mich.: University of Michigan Press, 1958.

DICKENS, A. G. *The English Reformation,* 2nd ed. College Park, Pa.: State University of Pennsylvania Press, 1991.

DICKENS, A. G., and WHITNEY R. D. JONES. *Erasmus the Reformer.* London: Methuen, 2000; first published 1994.

———. *Thomas Cromwell and the English Reformation.* New York: Macmillan, 1959.

DUFFY, EAMON. *The Stripping of the Altars: Traditional Religion in England, c. 1400–c. 1580.* New Haven: Yale University Press, 1992.

ERASMUS, DESIDERIUS. *Enchiridion militis Christiani.* Ed. Anne M. O'Donnell. Oxford: Oxford University Press, 1981.

FARROW, JOHN. *The Story of Thomas More.* New York: Image Books/ Doubleday and Co., 1968.

GUY, JOHN. *The Public Career of Thomas More.* New Haven: Yale University Press, 1980.

HILTON, WALTER. *The Scale of Perfection.* Trans. John Clark and Rosemary Doward. The Classics of Western Spirituality. New York: Paulist Press, 1991.

IVES, E. W. *Anne Boleyn.* Oxford: Basil Blackwell, 1986.

KEMPIS, THOMAS À. *The Imitation of Christ.* Ed. and trans. Joseph Tylenda, S.J. New York: Vintage Spiritual Classics, 1998.

KNOWLES, DOM DAVID. *The English Mystical Tradition.* New York: Harper, 1961.

LUPTON, J. H. *A Life of John Colet, D.D.* London: George Bell and Sons, 1909.

LUTHER, MARTIN. *An Invitation to the Writings of Martin Luther.* Ed. John F. Thornton and Susan B. Varenne. New York: Vintage Spiritual Classics, 2002.

MARIUS, RICHARD. *Thomas More: A Biography.* New York: Vintage Books, 1985; first published 1984.

MARTZ, LOUIS L. *Thomas More: The Search for the Inner Man.* New Haven: Yale University Press, 1990.

MATTINGLY, GARRETT. *Catherine of Aragon.* Boston: Little, Brown and Co., 1941.

NEAME, ALAN. *The Holy Maid of Kent: The Life of Elizabeth Barton, 1506–1534.* London: Hodder and Stoughton, 1971.

OLIN, JOHN. *Catholic Reform: From Cardinal Ximenes to the Council of Trent: 1495–1563.* New York: Fordham University Press, 1990.

———. *The Catholic Reformation: Savonarola to Ignatius Loyola.* New York: Fordham University Press, 1992.

PIUS XI, POPE. "The Two New Saints" (Homily at Canonization of Saints Thomas More and John Fisher, May 19, 1935). *Tablet,* June 1, 1935, 694–95.

POTTER, G. R. *Zwingli.* Cambridge: Cambridge University Press, 1976.

REX, RICHARD. *Henry VIII and the English Reformation*. New York: St. Martin's Press, 1993.

———. *The Theology of John Fisher*. Cambridge: Cambridge University Press, 1991.

REYNOLDS, E. E. *The Field Is Won: The Life and Death of Saint Thomas More*. Milwaukee: Bruce Publishing Co., 1968.

———. *Margaret Roper: Eldest Daughter of St. Thomas More*. New York: P. J. Kennedy and Sons, 1960.

———. *Saint John Fisher*. New York: P. J. Kennedy and Sons, 1955.

———. *Saint Thomas More*. New York: P. J. Kennedy and Sons, 1953.

———. *Thomas More and Erasmus*. London: Burns and Oates, 1965.

SHAKESPEARE, WILLIAM. *The Famous History of the Life of King Henry the Eighth*. Ed. S. Schoenbaum. New York: Signet Classics/New American Library, 1967.

STAPLETON, THOMAS. *The Life and Illustrious Martyrdom of Sir Thomas More* (1588). Trans. Philip E. Hallett. London: Burns and Oates, 1928. This was later revised by E. E. Reynolds (London: Burns and Oates, 1966).

SWANSON, R. N. *Catholic England: Faith, Religion and Observance Before the Reformation*. Manchester, England: Manchester University Press, 1993.

TYNDALE, WILLIAM. *The Work of William Tyndale*. Ed. G. E. Duffield. Philadelphia: Fortress Press, 1965.

———, trans. *Tyndale's New Testament* (1534 edition). Ed. David Daniell. New Haven: Yale University Press, 1995.

WARNICKE, RETHA. *The Rise and Fall of Anne Boleyn: Family Politics at the Court of Henry VIII*. Cambridge: Cambridge University Press, 1989.

JOSEPH W. KOTERSKI, S.J., is Professor of Philosophy at Fordham University and the editor-in-chief of *International Philosophical Quarterly*. He has lectured widely on aspects of Thomas More, as well as on Thomas Aquinas, Dante, and Augustine. He holds a Ph.D. in Philosophy from St. Louis University. His current research interests focus on the influence of philosophy and theology on religion and general culture.

JOHN F. THORNTON is a literary agent, former book editor, and the coeditor, with Katharine Washburn, of *Dumbing Down* (1996) and *Tongues of Angels, Tongues of Men: A Book of Sermons* (1999). He lives in New York City.

SUSAN B. VARENNE is a New York City high-school teacher with a strong avocational interest in and wide experience of spiritual literature (M.A., The University of Chicago Divinity School; Ph.D., Columbia University).

Printed in the United States
by Baker & Taylor Publisher Services